Psyche and Spirit

(Revised Edition)

John J. Heaney,

editor

Paulist Press ◆ *New York* ◆ *Ramsey*

Acknowledgements

The Publisher gratefully acknowledges the use of the following materials: Excerpts from *The Future of an Illusion* by Sigmund Freud, translated and edited by James Strachey, copyright © 1961 by James Strachey are reprinted by permission of W.W. Norton & Company, Inc.; excerpts from *Civilization and Its Discontents* by Sigmund Freud, translated and edited by James Strachey, copyright © 1961 by James Strachey are reprinted by permission of W.W. Norton & Company, Inc.; excerpts from *Does God Exist?* by Hans Küng, copyright © 1978, 1979, 1980 by Doubleday & Company, Inc., are reprinted by permission of the publisher; excerpts from *Psychotherapy and Existentialism* by Viktor E. Frankl, copyright © 1967 by Viktor E. Frankl are reprinted by permission of Pocket Books, a Simon & Schuster division of Gulf & Western Corporation; excerpts from *The Philosophical Approach to God: A Neo-Thomist Perspective* by W. Norris Clarke, edited by William E. Rays, with an introduction by E.M. Adams, are reprinted by permission of Wake Forest University Press, Winston-Salem, N.C.; excerpts from *Man for Himself* by Erich Fromm, copyright 1947, © 1975 by Erich Fromm are reprinted by permission of Holt, Reinhart and Winston, Publishers; excerpts from *Psychology as Religion: The Cult of Self-Worship* by Paul C. Vitz, © 1977 are reprinted by permission of William B. Eerdmans Publishing Company; excerpts from *C.G. Jung and Religion* by Regina Bechtle, S.C. from *The Collected Works of C.G. Jung*, edited by G. Adler, M. Fordham, and H. Read, translated by R.F.C. Hull, Bollingen Series XX, volume 12, *Psychology and Alchemy* (copyright 1953 and 1968 by Bollingen Foundation), are reprinted by permission of Princeton University Press and Routledge & Kegan Paul Ltd; excerpts from C.G. Jung, *Aion. Researches into the Phenomenology of the Self*, second edition, 1959, translated by R.F.C. Hull, are reprinted by permission of Princeton University Press; excerpts from *Psychology and Religion* by C.G. Jung, © 1938 are reprinted by permission of Yale University Press, New Haven; *Peak-Experiences and Religion* by Abraham Maslow, from *Religions, Values, and Peak-Experiences* by Abraham Maslow, The Kappa Delta Pi Lecture Series, copyright 1964 by Kappa Delta Pi, is reprinted by permission of Kappa Delta Pi, an Honor Society in Education; excerpts from David R. Crownfield, "Religion in the Cartography of the Unconscious: A Discussion of Stanley Grof's *Realms of the Human Unconscious*," JAAR 44/2 (1976): 309–315 are reprinted by permission of the Journal of the American Academy of Religion; excerpts from Thomas C. Hennessy, S.J., ed., *Values and Moral Development*, N.Y.: Paulist Press, 1976, are reprinted by permission of Paulist Press; excerpts from "Contemporary Spirituality: The Journey of the Human Community," *Cross Currents*, Vol. XXIV, summer/fall 1974, are reprinted with the permission of Thomas Berry, C.P., of the Riverdale Center For Religious Research.

Contents

iii

Preface

This collection of readings is designed for courses in religion in which the center of interest is contemporary insight into the psychology of religion. The religious viewpoint is that of Christian theology, although many readings are germane to those of other religious beliefs. The selections have been chosen to facilitate a dialogue between psychology and theology. The ordering of the readings has been made according to the following pattern:

Ego Psychology	Self Psychology	Theology
A) The original, undiffer- entiated self	B) ego develop- ment	C) trans- personal states	D) God, the Abso- lute

Chapters I to X concern the move from A to B, from a naive, primitive level of psyche and spirit to the development of a mature ego state of thinking, willing and deciding. Chapters XI to XVI involve the move to transpersonal, symbolical and "mystical" states in which the ego is taken up into higher states of consciousness. Interspersed in these readings are selections from D in order to set up a continuing dialogue between psychology and theology.

The goals of these readings are: (1) to understand the psychological approach to religion as compared with the theological; (2) to gain insight for one's personal development. Psychology studies religion only as a *phenomenon*. It makes no judgment about the existence of a God beyond the phenomena. Theology, however, says there is no final meaning in the phenomena apart from some Divine Ground. We will see that

1

psychology at times brings theology up short as it insists on the human requirements for health and growth, while theology may show that the psychology of religion lacks full sense without a Transcendent Base. Psyche, that is, the psychology of self-transcendence and growth, becomes fully intelligible in view of spirit, that is, a person's openness to the Divine Ground of energy, the Spirit. Self-transcendence is made intelligible through the existence of a Divine Consciousness, and this Divine Consciousness is understood through human growth.

I.
Story and Intelligent Subjectivity

John J. Heaney

Everyone has some faith. Ideally, we have many faiths —faith in oneself, faith in others, faith in some cause. There is religious faith in God or trust in some view of the universe. There is also atheistic faith or belief in the absence of an intelligent power animating the universe.

Religious writers today often speak of "story" as a synonym for faith or for the content of faith. Faith and story can be seen as mutually explanatory. A story is a narrative with symbols that links the sequences of our lives (Novak, 49). Everyone has a story. We all hope or believe that there is some unified meaning to our lives. Our very actions which spin out the threads of our story imply some belief in its meaning. Our stories involve assumptions or presuppositions about life which we often accept unconsciously. These assumptions are fed by symbols or world views, for example, the goodness of humans or their malice, the need to achieve or to climb (the ladder), the need to relate (the web), the need to be number one (narcissism), the need to give (altruism).

But stories are not merely personal. There are also family stories (the tragic family, the happy family), economic stories (capitalism, Marxism), national stories (the flag, democracy, dictatorship), and transcendent stories (Buddhism, Judaism, Christianity). "The Catholic way is not identical with the Methodist, Lutheran or Presbyterian way. The Jewish sensibility and imagination project a unique way of life. The Buddhist does not imagine the basic story of the noble man in the same terms—or in the same context—as the Christian. The American

3

style differs from the Italian style. In a word, *cultural* stories as
well as *personal* stories are in question." (Novak, 49)

From the earliest stages of our lives we share in our stories
with a kind of unthinking participation ("the tribal story"). Our
faith-stories are so close to us that they provide us with our
identities. That is why it is most difficult to alter one's story.
Our commitment to our story is deeper than what is primarily
theoretical. As Ann Ulanov says, even metaphysical systems at
times divide up according to the basic unconscious story at
their base (Ulanov, 45).

Counter-stories emerge which threaten our story, that is,
our identity. That is why people even kill in order that their
story may prevail. But as we grow in intelligence our stories
must change. This causes excitement, but also great distress,
anxiety and fear.

Our story provides us with our *subjectivity*. By subjectivity I
mean our interior life of feeling and value. But as we grow in
intelligence and cultural sense, we are called to a stage of
growth which has been called *intelligent subjectivity* (Novak, 98).
Critical intelligence makes us aware of our presuppositions,
our biases, our selfishness, our limited awareness and our
distortions. Bernard Lonergan, S.J. in his book *Method in Theology* says that one aim of the discipline of theology is the
attainment of *authentic or intelligent subjectivity* (Lonergan, 265,
292). Subjectivity is involved because we cannot live without an
interiority, a point of view, a story. Authenticity and critical
intelligence are involved because we must make judgments
about the authenticity of our story and about counter-stories.

"We change our sense of reality and/or story a) when they
are out of harmony with the dynamics of our unconscious,
which becomes more and more insistent; b) when they are out
of harmony with our efforts to change the world, to get along
with others, or to be at peace with ourselves; c) when they are
superseded by new ones that offer more illumination or satisfactions; d) when they are unable to account for contradictions
introduced by new experience, or tensions in their own structure; e) when they give rise to repeated failures in predicting
consequences or interpreting the behavior of others" (Novak,
72).

While story itself involves struggle, a change of story involves something even more unsettling—a transformation of consciousness. Our story is seen from a standpoint or a specific position. As our experience enlarges, our standpoints change. So does our consciousness. This is called a change of horizon. Lonergan calls a horizon the maximum field of vision from a specific standpoint (Lonergan, 235). Standpoint and horizon are correlative terms. Horizons enlarge under the impact of experience. A transformation of horizons in a religious context is called *conversion.* Conversion may be intellectual, moral, psychic and religious (Lonergan, 237). Intellectual conversion occurs when we change our horizons about what knowing is. It is not merely seeing with the eye of the camera. It means experiencing, understanding, judging and deciding. Moral conversion means changing one's horizons from self-satisfaction to values. Psychic conversion means including in one's horizon a growing conscious knowledge of one's unconscious movements (Doran). Religious conversion means being grasped by ultimate concern. It is total and permanent self-surrender without conditions, qualifications, reservations. It is unrestricted falling in love with God.

In the religious realm, story or faith is sometimes called "myth." Myth here is not used in the old sense of something fictitious or false. Rather it means the presentation of the transcendent in finite terms. Paul Ricoeur, the French religious philosopher, speaks of three stages in the human approach to myth or symbol: a stage of primitive naiveté in which humans are immersed in an unthinking way in their myths; a second stage of critical distancing, of truth at a distance, in which critical questioning supplants commitment; a third stage, called the second naiveté, in which man returns to the immediacy of his symbols but without discarding the critical mode which becomes now, not reductive, but restorative. The last stage, which is a revivification of symbol and myth, is reached only after critical distance is achieved in intelligent demythologization (Ricoeur, 351).

The movement from one stage to the next is usually characterized by great upheaval, a sense of adventure, turmoil and fear. This is true of individuals as they advance through the stages of life and develop their stories. It is also true of cultures as one way of looking at the world is enveloped by another view.

Many people today believe we are witnessing the turmoil of a great change in human consciousness. Some believe we are moving from Ricoeur's first stage to the second. Others think we are moving from his second to his third stage. I believe the movement depends on where each person and each culture stands in relation to their story.

In this book we will be studying the insights gained by human consciousness, the wider horizons reached, and the tentative conversions begun because of the dialogue between religion and psychology. My standpoint is that of a Catholic theologian in dialogue with psychology, principally humanistic psychology. While my horizon is that of the Christian story, I believe that many of the insights presented by various authors will be of value to people with differing religious stories.

Our point of departure is that of the Christian story. Our goal is the attainment of intelligent subjectivity. Our first step will be into Ricoeur's second stage, that of critical distancing, and we can do no better than to begin with Sigmund Freud.

Readings

Ian Barbour, *Myths, Models and Paradigms* (N.Y.: Harper & Row, 1974).

James Barr, "Story and History in Biblical Theology," *Journal of Religion*, Jan. 1976, 1–17.

T. Patrick Burke, "The Theologian as Storyteller," *Horizons,* Fall 1977, 207–215. Problems with story as a theological category.

Louis Cameli, *Stories of Paradise. The Study of Spiritual Autobiography and the Frontiers of Today's Faith* (Paramus, N.J.: Paulist, 1978).

Chicago Studies. The Spring 1978 issue is devoted to religion and story.

Walter Conn, *Conversion. Perspectives on Personal and Social Transformation.* (N.Y.: Alba House, 1978). Section on Lonergan.

Stephen Crites, "The Narrative Quality of Experience," *Journal of the American Academy of Religion,* Vol. XXXIX, 1971.

John Dominic Crossan, *The Dark Interval. Towards a Theology of Story* (Niles, Ill.: Argus, 1975).

Robert M. Doran, *Psychic Conversion and Theological Foundations* (Chico, Calif.: Scholars Press, 1981).

Julian N. Hartt, *Theological Method and Imagination* (N.Y.: Seabury, 1977), esp. 16, 242ff.

John F. Haught, *Religion and Self-Acceptance* (N.Y.: Paulist, 1976), 143ff.

Bernard Lonergan, *Method in Theology* (N.Y.: Herder & Herder, 1972).

James W. McClendon, Jr., *Biography as Theology* (N.Y.: Abingdon, 1974).

John Navone and Thomas Cooper, *Tellers of the Word* (N.Y.: Human Development, 1981). One of the best treatments.

Michael Novak, *Ascent of the Mountain, Flight of the Dove* (N.Y.: Harper and Row, 1971).

Mason Olds, *Story: The Language of Faith* (Washington, D.C.: University Press of America, 1977). Camus, Eliot, etc.

Paul Ricoeur, *The Symbolism of Evil* (Boston: Beacon, 1969).

Roger Schmidt, *Exploring Religion* (Belmont, Cal.: Wadsworth, 1980), 123ff.

John Shea, "Theology and Autobiography," *Commonweal*, June 16, 1978, 358–362. Also *Stories of Faith*, and *Stories of God* (Chicago: Thomas More, 1978 and 1980).

George W. Stroup III, "A Bibliographical Critique," *Theology Today*, July 1975, 133–143.

Stanley Sutphin, *Options in Contemporary Theology* (Washington, D.C.: University Press of America, 1977). Section on story.

Ann and Barry Ulanov, *Religion and the Unconscious* (Philadelphia: Westminster, 1975).

II.
The Phenomenon of Religion

Sigmund Freud

(First excerpt from: Sigmund Freud, *The Future of an Illusion.* Revised and newly edited by James Strachey. Doubleday & Company, Inc., 1961, pages 21, 47, 88.)

(Second excerpt from Sigmund Freud, *Civilization and Its Discontents.* Translated and edited by James Strachey. W.W. Norton & Company, Inc., 1962, pages 13–15, 19.)

Editor's Note

Sigmund Freud (1856–1939) has been aptly called a "natural atheist," and yet throughout his productive life he was obsessed with the phenomenon of religion. Freud held that psychoanalysis should not think it could find a *single* cause of religion. But whatever the cause, he had to find it as natural and within history, not in trans-history or in the eternal. He kept returning to religion as to a problem whose solution he had not fully found, and he tried to be an honest man. There was a strange paradox in Freud. He found meaning in every small detail of life, e.g., jokes and slips of tongue. Everything had a meaning but the whole thing. One might call him a secular mystic, if we think of a mystic as seeing hidden meanings in reality.

To understand Freud's religious thought one must have some general understanding of his psychological theory. Here we can do no more than briefly sketch a few basic notions for further study. The Oedipus Complex is a foundational notion for Freud. Oedipus, in a play by Sophocles, unwittingly killed his father and married his mother. A complex is a cluster of ideas or impulses which is repressed and in strong conflict with other parts of the personality (Chaplin, 103; Spinks, 58). The male infant sees his father as a hated rival and longs to kill him in order to possess the mother. (The role of the female was less studied by Freud; this was later called the Electra Complex.) The

8

male child also can admire the father, and it is this combination of hatred, fear and admiration which brings about the healing result—identification with the father. He "becomes" his father and in this way symbolically possesses the mother. Freud frequently thought that religion began after the male members of the primal horde killed and ate the father. Remembrance of this deed was repressed but the guilt that ensued was the occasion for the arising of religion. This guilt was recalled and assuaged by the tribal totem ceremony. (See *Totem and Taboo* and *Moses and Monotheism.*) The father is the prototype of God and yearning for God is a yearning for the primal father. This brief and inadequate sketch is included here because Freud always thought there was something in it as an explanation for religion. It is often called the "ethnological" explanation as opposed to the psychological explanation which gained a wider following. (The psychological explanations are found in the excerpts which follow.)

Psychic energy was called libido. Libido is not exclusively sex energy for Freud, although Jung and Adler separated from Freud partly because of what they believed was an excessive sexual emphasis. Libido in Freud's mature thought is probably any pleasurable sensation relating to bodily functions (Brown, 20).

In 1922 Freud began using what is called a "topographical model" of the psyche. This model consists of the famous triad, id, ego and superego. As Bruno Bettelheim notes, in the German the three terms are the it, the I and the over-I or upper-I (Bettelheim, 56). The newborn child is a mass of impulses lacking in any guiding consciousness. Because of its impersonal nature, this primitive mass is described as "id" or "it." It resembles the pleasure principle. But since the child must come to terms with external reality, a part of this conglomeration becomes separated off and differentiated as the "ego" or "I." The function of the ego is to test reality so that the child's responses may be in terms of reality and not just movements to immediate satisfactions. (Later, Freud saw the ego as more primordial.) Subsequently, the superego arises out of the need to face society's moral prohibitions (Brown, 28). Freud equated superego with conscience but theology disagrees (see Chapter IV). Through the superego, the child unconsciously identifies with the dictates of authority figures and internalizes them.

For Freud life is a clash between the pleasure principle and the reality principle. We should notice that psychoanalysis here appropriates to itself the judgment as to what reality is. For Freud reality is an experience of life without God and one in which death is the end. Psychoanalysis' goal, as Freud saw it, was to help one accept the reality principle. "Where there was id, let there be ego," or, in Bettelheim's terms, "where there was it, let there be I." Notice, however, that Freud does not say that in choosing the reality principle we abandon the intention of ultimately obtaining pleasure. Pleasure is still the goal, but the road is longer and more indirect. Is pleasure always opposed to reality for Freud? Probably he had a tendency in this direction. But his meaning might be better conveyed by the distinction between the fantasy principle (immediate satisfaction) and the delaying principle.

The reality principle frequently will not allow us to have the object desired. Then energy is displaced onto socially acceptable objects. This is sublimation. Religion as well as art can be the result of acts of sublimation. The mystic, unconsciously desiring sexual relations, turns to God and pursues him with the same energy. Freud believed that this was a fact shown by the frequent use of sexual imagery in mystical writings.

By 1920 in *Beyond the Pleasure Principle* Freud made a distinction between the life instinct and the death instinct. The death instinct represents an innate destructiveness directed primarily against the self. The life instinct is creative and is called Eros. The death instinct, later called Thanatos, is a force which constantly works toward death, that is, toward the original inorganic state of complete freedom from tension and striving (return to the womb), death. Bettelheim points out that Freud did not use the word "instinct" in the original German. This is an important point. An instinct is an unlearned, innate, biological tendency. Freud spoke rather of "impulse" or "drive." An impulse, while coming from the unconscious, is to some degree controllable in contrast to an innate instinct.

Freud saw religion as an obsessional neurosis (1907), an adolescent neurotic phenomenon (1913), a guilt reaction to an historical father-killing (1913), wishful thinking and a father projection (1910, 1927, 1939). He saw mysticism as a return to an infantile "oceanic experience" (1930). In a beguiling treatment in *Totem and Taboo* (1913), he saw both the individual and culture as evolving through three stages. He used the term "ontogenic" for the individual and "phylogenic" for the culture. Following Haeckel, he believed that the ontogenic recapitulated the phylogenic. In the first stage, which he called "narcissism," both the infant and the primitive lived on the same stage, that of *magic*. The characteristic of this stage was the belief in fantasy over reality. In the second stage, the "anaclitic," the outward related dependent stage in which one depends on an external object, in the individual's life there is adolescent dependence. In the life of the race there is monotheism or dependence on God. This is the stage of *religion*. Its characteristic is the prevalence of a general neurosis over private neuroses. The third stage, the "genital" stage or the stage of "object love" and true personal relations, is the stage of adult maturity in the individual and of post-religious autonomy for the race. This stage is called that of *science* or *reason*. Its characteristic is health.

This schema is still presented in recent publications. However, there is an evident a priori thrust in the evolving picture. It has been pointed out that in each stage of culture, all three elements, magic, religion and science or reason, have always been present and still are present.

There is an unresolved tension in Freud's psychological theory. Theoretically, he accepted biological determinism. Yet, at the same time, he had a developmental view of life in which his key words are maturation, fixation, regression and sublimation. And in dying he left his legacy as *lieben und arbeiten* (love and work). Genuine love demands freedom and is incompatible with biological determinism.

Freud believed that religion was not a healthy sublimation because it tinkered too much with reality under the impetus of fancy. Also, it is too demanding and self-seeking in the gratification of its wishes. He felt that it violated his principle: "where there is id, let there be ego." In the following two excerpts, Freud sees religion as the result of wishful thinking and of a father projection, and as a return to an infantile oceanic experience. However, as one reads these excerpts, it should be recalled that Freud said that in *The Future of an Illusion,* the first excerpt, he was much less concerned with the deepest sources of religious feeling than with what the common man understands by his religion (1930, 21).

*　　*　　*

I

We know already how the individual reacts to the injuries which civilization and other men inflict on him: he develops a corresponding degree of resistance to the regulations of civilization and of hostility to it. But how does he defend himself against the superior powers of nature, of Fate, which threaten him as they threaten all the rest?

Civilization relieves him of this task: it performs it in the same way for all alike; and it is noteworthy that in this almost all civilizations act alike. Civilization does not call a halt in the task of defending man against nature, it merely pursues it by other means. The task is a manifold one. Man's self-regard, seriously menaced, calls for consolation; life and the universe must be robbed of their terrors; moreover his curiosity, moved, it is true, by the strongest practical interest, demands an answer.

A great deal is already gained with the first step: the humanization of nature. Impersonal forces and destinies cannot be approached; they remain eternally remote. But if the elements have passions that rage as they do in our own souls, if death itself is not something spontaneous but the violent act of an evil Will, if everywhere in nature there are Beings around us of a kind that we know in our own society, then we can breathe freely, can feel at home in the uncanny and can deal by psychical means with our senseless anxiety. We are still defenseless, perhaps, but we are no longer helplessly paralysed; we can at least react. Perhaps, indeed, we are not even defenceless. We can apply the same methods against these violent supermen outside that we employ in our own society; we can try to adjure them, to appease them, to bribe them, and, so influencing them, we may rob them of a part of their power. A replacement like this of natural science by psychology not only provides immediate relief, but also points the way to a further mastering of the situation.

For this situation is nothing new. It has an infantile prototype, of which it is in fact only the continuation. For once before one has found oneself in a similar state of helplessness: as a small child, in relation to one's parents. One had reason to fear them, and especially one's father; and yet one was sure of his protection against the dangers one knew. Thus it was natural to assimilate the two situations. . . . A man makes the forces of nature not simply into persons with whom he can associate as he would with his equals—that would not do justice to the overpowering impression which those forces make on him—but he gives them the character of a father. He turns them into gods, following in this, as I have tried to show,[1] not only an infantile prototype but a phylogenetic one.

In the course of time the first observations were made of regularity and conformity to law in natural phenomena, and with this the forces of nature lost their human traits. But man's helplessness remains and along with it his longing for his father, and the gods. The gods retain their threefold task: they must exorcize the terrors of nature, they must reconcile men to the cruelty of Fate, particularly as it is shown in death, and they must compensate them for the sufferings and privations which a civilized life in common has imposed on them. . . .

And thus a store of ideas is created, born from man's need to make his helplessness tolerable and built up from the material of memories of the helplessness of his own childhood and the childhood of the human race. It can clearly be seen that the possession of these ideas protects him in two directions—against the dangers of nature and Fate, and against the injuries that threaten him from human society itself. Here is the gist of the matter. Life in this world serves a higher purpose; no doubt it is not easy to guess what that purpose is, but it certainly signifies a perfecting of man's nature. It is probably the spiritual part of man, the soul, which in the course of time has so slowly and unwillingly detached itself from the body, that is the object of this elevation and exaltation. Everything that happens in this world is an expression of the intentions of an intelligence superior to us, which in the end, though its ways and byways are difficult to follow, orders everything for the best—that is, to make it enjoyable for us. Over each one of us there watches a benevolent Providence which is only seemingly stern and which will not suffer us to become a plaything of the over-mighty and pitiless forces of nature. Death itself is not extinction, is not a return to inorganic lifelessness, but the beginning of a new kind of existence which lies on the path of development to something higher. And, looking in the other direction, this view announces that the same moral laws which our civilizations have set up govern the whole universe as well, except that they are maintained by a supreme court of justice with incomparably more power and consistency. In the end all good is rewarded and all evil punished, if not actually in this form of life then in the later existences that begin after death. In this way all the terrors, the sufferings and the hardships of life are destined to be obliterated. Life after death, which continues life on earth just as the invisible part of the spectrum joins on to the visible part, brings us all the perfection that we may perhaps have missed here. And the superior wisdom which directs this course of things, the infinite goodness that expresses itself in it, the justice that achieves its aim in it—these are the attributes of the divine beings who also created us and the world as a whole, or rather, of the one divine being into which, in our civilization, all the gods of antiquity have been condensed. The people which first succeeded in thus concentrating the divine attributes was not a little proud of the advance. It had laid open to view the father who had all along been hidden behind every divine figure as its nucleus. . . .

Thus the benevolent rule of a divine Providence allays our fear of the dangers of life; the establishment of a moral world-order ensures the fulfilment of the demands of justice, which have so often remained unfulfilled in human civilization; and the prolongation of earthly existence in a future life provides the local and temporal framework in which these wish-fulfilments shall take place. Answers to the riddles that tempt the curiosity of man, such as how the universe began or what the relation is between body and mind, are developed in conformity with the underlying assumptions of this system. It is an enormous relief to the individual psyche if the conflicts of its childhood arising from the father-complex—conflicts which it has never wholly overcome—are removed from it and brought to a solution which is universally accepted.

When I say that these things are all illusions, I must define the meaning of the word. An illusion is not the same thing as an error; nor is it necessarily an error. Aristotle's belief that vermin are developed out of dung (a belief to which ignorant people still cling) was an error; so was the belief of a former generation of doctors that *tabes dorsalis* is the result of sexual excess. It would be incorrect to call these errors illusions. On the other hand, it was an illusion of Columbus's that he had discovered a new sea-route to the Indies. The part played by his wish in this error is very clear. One may describe as an illusion the assertion made by certain nationalists that the Indo-Germanic race is the only one capable of civilization; or the belief, which was only destroyed by psychoanalysis, that children are creatures without sexuality. What is characteristic of illusions is that they are derived from human wishes. In this respect they come near to psychiatric delusions. But they differ from them, too, apart from the more complicated structure of delusions. In the case of delusions, we emphasize as essential their being in contradiction with reality. Illusions need not necessarily be false—that is to say, unrealizable or in contradiction to reality. . . .

Thus we call a belief an illusion when a wish-fulfilment is a prominent factor in its motivation, and in doing so we disregard its relations to reality, just as the illusion itself sets no store by verification.

Having thus taken our bearings, let us return once more to the question of religious doctrines. We can now repeat that all of them are illusions and insusceptible of proof. No one can be compelled to think them true, to believe in them. Some of them are so improbable, so incompatible with everything we have laboriously discovered about the reality of the world, that we may compare them—if we pay proper regard to the psychological differences—to delusions. Of the reality value of most of them we cannot judge; just as they cannot be proved, so they cannot be refuted. We still know too little to make a critical approach to them. . . .

The primacy of the intellect lies, it is true, in a distant, distant future, but probably not in an *infinitely* distant one. It will presumably set itself the same aims as those whose realization you expect from your God (of course within human limits—so far as external reality, 'Ανάγκη, allows it), namely the love of man and the decrease of suffering. This being so, we may tell ourselves that our antagonism is only a temporary one and not irreconcilable. We desire the same things, but you are more impatient, more exacting, and—why should I not say it?—more self-seeking than I and those on my side. You would have the state of bliss begin directly after death; you expect the impossible from it and you will not surrender the claims of the individual. Our God, Λόγος,[2] will fulfil whichever of these wishes nature outside us allows, but he will do it very gradually, only in the unforeseeable future, and for a new generation of

men. He promises no compensation for us, who suffer griev-
ously from life. On the way to this distant goal your religious
doctrines will have to be discarded, no matter whether the first
attempts fail, or whether the first substitutes prove to be unten-
able. You know why: in the long run nothing can withstand
reason and experience, and the contradiction which religion
offers to both is all too palpable. Even purified religious ideas
cannot escape this fate, so long as they try to preserve anything
of the consolation of religion. No doubt if they confine themselves to a belief in a higher spiritual being, whose qualities are
indefinable and whose purposes cannot be discerned, they will
be proof against the challenge of science; but then they will
also lose their hold on human interest.

Editor's note: after the publication of *The Future of An Illusion,*
Romain Rolland (1866–1914), a French dramatist, novelist and biog-
rapher, wrote to Freud to complain that he had omitted from his book
any consideration of the true source of religious sentiments, "the
oceanic feeling." This was a sensation of eternity, a feeling as of
something limitless, unbounded, as it were, "oceanic." One may call
oneself religious, he said, on the ground of this feeling alone, even if
one rejects every belief and every illusion.

II

An infant at the breast does not as yet distinguish his ego
from the external world as the source of the sensations flowing
in upon him. He gradually learns to do so, in response to
various promptings.[3] He must be very strongly impressed by
the fact that some sources of excitation, which he will later
recognize as his own bodily organs, can provide him with
sensations at any moment, whereas other sources evade him
from time to time—among them what he desires most of all, his
mother's breast—and only reappear as a result of his screaming
for help. In this way there is for the first time set over against
the ego an 'object', in the form of something which exists
'outside' and which is only forced to appear by a special action.[4] A further incentive to a disengagement of the ego from

the general mass of sensations—that is, to the recognition of an 'outside', an external world—is provided by the frequent, manifold and unavoidable sensations of pain and unpleasure the removal and avoidance of which is enjoined by the pleasure principle, in the exercise of its unrestricted domination. A tendency arises to separate from the ego everything that can become a source of such unpleasure, to throw it outside and to create a pure pleasure-ego which is confronted by a strange and threatening 'outside'. The boundaries of this primitive pleasure-ego cannot escape rectification through experience. Some of the things that one is unwilling to give up, because they give pleasure, are nevertheless not ego but object; and some sufferings that one seeks to expel turn out to be inseparable from the ego in virtue of their internal origin. One comes to learn a procedure by which, through a deliberate direction of one's sensory activities and through suitable muscular action, one can differentiate between what is internal—what belongs to the ego—and what is external—what emanates from the outer world. In this way one makes the first step towards the introduction of the reality principle which is to dominate future development.[5] This differentiation, of course, serves the practical purpose of enabling one to defend oneself against sensations of unpleasure which one actually feels or with which one is threatened. In order to fend off certain unpleasurable excitations arising from within, the ego can use no other methods than those which it uses against unpleasure coming from without, and this is the starting-point of important pathological disturbances.

In this way, then, the ego detaches itself from the external world. Or, to put it more correctly, originally the ego includes everything, later it separates off an external world from itself. Our present ego-feeling is, therefore, only a shrunken residue of a much more inclusive—indeed, an all-embracing—feeling which corresponded to a more intimate bond between the ego and the world about it. If we may assume that there are many people in whose mental life this primary ego-feeling has persisted to a greater or less degree, it would exist in them side by side with the narrower and more sharply demarcated ego-feeling of maturity, like a kind of counterpart to it. In that case, the ideational contents appropriate to it would be precisely those of limitlessness and of a bond with the universe—the same ideas with which my friend elucidated the 'oceanic' feeling. . . .

Thus we are perfectly willing to acknowledge that the 'oceanic' feeling exists in many people, and we are inclined to trace it back to an early phase of ego-feeling. The further question then arises, what claim this feeling has to be regarded as the source of religious needs.

To me the claim does not seem compelling. After all, a feeling can only be a source of energy if it is itself the expression of a strong need. The derivation of religious needs from the infant's helplessness and the longing for the father aroused by it seems to me incontrovertible, especially since the feeling is not simply prolonged from childhood days, but is permanently sustained by fear of the superior power of Fate. I cannot think of any need in childhood as strong as the need for a father's protection. Thus the part played by the oceanic feeling, which might seek something like the restoration of limitless narcissism, is ousted from a place in the foreground. The origin of the religious attitude can be traced back in clear outlines as far as the feeling of infantile helplessness. There may be something further behind that, but for the present it is wrapped in obscurity.

Notes

1. See Section 6 of the fourth essay in *Totem and Taboo* (1912–13), *Standard Ed.*, 13, 146ff.

2. The twin gods Λόγος (*Logos:* Reason) and 'Ανάγκη (*Ananke: Necessity*) of the Dutch writer Multatuli. (Cf. an Editor's footnote to 'The Economic Problem of Masochism' (1924*c*), *Standard Ed.*, 19, 168.)

3. In this paragraph Freud was going over familiar ground. He had discussed the matter not long before, in his paper on 'Negation' (1925*h*), *Standard Ed.*, 19, 236–8. But he had dealt with it on several earlier occasions. See, for instance, 'Instincts and their Vicissitudes' (1915*c*), ibid., 14, 119 and 134–6, and *The Interpretation of Dreams*

(1900*a*), ibid., 5, 565–6. Its essence, indeed, is already to be found in the 'Project' of 1895, Sections 1, 2, 11 and 16 of Part I (Freud, 1950*a*).
4. The 'specific action' of the 'Project'.
5. Cf. 'Formulations on the Two Principles of Mental Functioning' (1911*b*), *Standard Ed.*, 12, 222–3.

Freud on Religion

"Obsessive Actions and Religious Practices" (1907), *Standard Edition* (London: Hogarth, 1959), 117–127; readily accessible in *Personality and Religion*, William Sadler, Jr., ed. (N.Y.: Harper & Row, 1970).
Totem and Taboo (1913). N.Y.: Random House, 1939.
The Future of an Illusion (1927). N.Y.: Norton, 1975.
Civilization and Its Discontents (1930). N.Y.: Norton, 1962.
Moses and Monotheism (1939). N.Y.: Random House, 1955.
New Introductory Lectures on Psychoanalysis (1932). N.Y.: Norton, 1965.

Books on Freud

Bruno Bettelheim, *Freud and Man's Soul.* N.Y.: Knopf, 1983.
James A.C. Brown, *Freud and the Post-Freudians.* Baltimore: Penguin, 1964.
J.P. Chaplin, *Dictionary of Psychology.* N.Y.: Dell, 1975.
Ronald W. Clark, *Freud: The Man and the Cause.* N.Y.: Random House, 1980.
Andrew Reid Fuller, *Psychology and Religion. Eight Points of View.* Washington, D.C.: University Press of America, 1977. A fine synthesis.
Calvin S. Hall, *A Primer of Freudian Psychology.* N.Y.: New American Library, 1964.
Calvin S. Hall and Gardner Lindzey, *Theories of Personality.* N.Y.: Wiley, 1978 ed.
Hans Küng, *Freud and the Problem of God.* New Haven: Yale U. Press, 1979.
H.L. Philp, *Freud and Religious Belief.* N.Y.: Pitman, 1956.
Paul Ricoeur, *Freud and Philosophy. An Essay on Interpretation.* New Haven: Yale U. Press, 1970. A philosophical reading.

G. Stephen Spinks, *Psychology and Religion.* Boston: Beacon, 1963.
Mark Sulloway, *Freud, Biologist of the Mind.* N.Y.: Basic Books, 1979.
   Psychoanalysis as crypto-biology.
Gregory Zilbourg, *Freud and Religion.* Westminster, Md.: Newman, 1964.

(See Chapter III for further readings.)

III.
Reaction to Freud

Hans Küng

(Excerpt from Hans Küng, *Does God Exist? An Answer for Today*. Translated by Edward Quinn, Garden City, N.Y.: Doubleday & Company, 1980, pages 299–301, 304–305, 322–323.)

Editor's Note

Freud's analysis of religion is incomplete, despite his obvious contributions about infantilism and immaturity in religion. He concluded his analysis in *Civilization and Its Discontents* by admitting that there may be more to it than he has said, "but for the present it is wrapped in obscurity" (p. 19).

Freud presented an image of the human being as determined by intrapsychic forces beyond his or her control. But is our ordinary sense of moral responsibility illusory? (Wallwork, 276; Kaufmann, 159). Freud issued a call for psychic responsibility and to some extent for a growth in love. His image of man manifests two conflicting thrusts and it is inconsistent.

A second objection concerns God as a projection of the father. "According to Freud, all religious beliefs deify the attributes of the earthly father. The question arises, therefore, whether this uncritical assumption does justice either to the non-paternal religious beliefs found in many cultures or to the sophisticated doctrines of theologians like Augustine and Aquinas. For the latter, Freud had nothing but contempt. Their elaborate intellectual superstructures, he contends, are nothing but attempts to rationalize essentially infantile convictions. Is such a position sufficient, however, to explain the complicated beliefs of Bultmann, Teilhard, Reinhold Niebuhr, Bonhoeffer and Tillich? Interpreted in their own terms, these theologians

21

scarcely appear to reflect the primitive fantasies described by Freud"
(Wallwork, 276).

With regard to illusions and wishes, Oskar Pfister, the Lutheran
theologian with whom Freud carried on a friendly dialogue, pointed
out that Freud himself had wishes for the future of science. In fact, he
entitled his article, which was a response to *The Future of an Illusion,*
"The Illusion of a Future" (H. Meng, 9). I think some distinction
must be made between wishing and hoping. Wishes are superficial
desires. Hopes are primordial aspirations (Lynch, 109). One may
make the illusionary judgment that, despite ominous dark clouds, it
will not rain, because one wishes to hold a picnic. Such an illusion is
quite different from the deepest hopes of mankind about the meaning
of life. Such hopes are not innocent of critical intelligence. (For
positive evidence from the perspective of a philosophical theology
and of a cosmological view of the universe, see Chapters VI and VII.)

In the following excerpt, Hans Küng, the controversial Catholic
theologian from the University of Tübingen in Germany, discusses
Freud's notions of illusion and wishing. The excerpt is taken from
Küng's book, *Does God Exist? An Answer for Today,* in which he displays
a good deal of sympathy for Freud's insights about immaturity in
religion.

*   *   *

RELIGION—MERELY WISHFUL THINKING?

Historically and biographically, there can be no doubt that
Freud was an atheist from his student years. He was an atheist
long before he became a psychoanalyst. Consequently his atheism was not based on his psychoanalysis but preceded it. This,
too, is what Freud constantly maintained, *that psychoanalysis does
not necessarily lead to atheism.* It is a method of investigation and
healing and can be practiced by both atheists and theists. And
for that very reason, Freud the atheist defends himself against
the charge of extrapolating an atheistic "Weltanschauung"
from a "neutral working tool." Methodological "atheism" must
not be turned into ideological atheism; psychoanalysis cannot
be made into a total explanation of reality.

Freud *took over from Feuerbach and his successors* the essential *arguments for his personal atheism.* As he says, both modestly and correctly, "All I have done—and this is the only thing that is new in my exposition—is to add some psychological foundation to the criticisms of my great predecessors."[1] Feuerbach, as we saw, had already produced a psychological substantiation of atheism: wishes, fantasies, or the power of imagination are responsible for the projection of the idea of God and of the whole religious pseudo or dream world. Like Marx's opium theory, Freud's illusion theory is also based on Feuerbach's projection theory. What is essentially new is merely Freud's psychoanalytical reinforcement of Feuerbach's theory.

But this means also that the arguments against Feuerbach's (and Marx's) atheism, particularly against the evidence drawn from psychology and philosophy of religion, are valid also against Freud's atheism. And in so far as Feuerbach's (and Marx's) atheism turned out in the last resort to be a hypothesis that had not been conclusively proved, so, too, must *Freud's atheism* now be regarded in the last resort as a *hypothesis that has not been conclusively proved.*

Of course, Freud had asked about the background of Feuerbach's psychological projection theory and applied the tests of depth psychology to its unconscious assumptions. Hence he was able to reinforce this hypothesis in the light of the history of religion and of the psychology of religion. But he did not thereby produce—any more than Marx did—an independent argument for the projection theory. For Freud *had taken for granted* the projection theory (apparently irrefutably substantiated by his "great predecessors") and then asked and tried to show how it could be explained in the light of the history and the psychology of religion. And it is precisely this assumption that turns out in the last resort to be unproved.

It is to Freud's immense credit that he worked out how much the unconscious determines the individual human being and the history of mankind, how fundamental even the earliest childhood years, the first parent-child relationships, the approach to sexuality, are also for a person's religious attitudes and ideas. But we saw very clearly in connection with *Feuerbach* (and Marx) that from the indisputable influence of *psychological* (or economic and social) factors on religion and the idea of God no conclusions can be drawn about the existence or non-existence of God. Hence there is really no need of further explanation if we now say much the same about *Freud:* from the indisputable influence of *depth-psychological, unconscious* factors on religion and the idea of God, no *conclusions can be drawn for the existence or nonexistence of God.*

We may put this more concretely in summary form with reference to Freud's main statement on the critique of religion: "Religious ideas are fulfillments of the oldest, strongest and most urgent wishes of mankind." This is quite true, and the believer in God can say the same. At the same time, he will also admit:

Religion, as Marx shows, can certainly be opium, a means of social assuagement and consolation (repression). But it need not be.

Religion, as Freud shows, can certainly be an illusion, the expression of a neurosis and psychological immaturity (regression). But it need not be.

All human believing, hoping, loving—related to a person, a thing, or God—certainly contains an element of projection. But its object need not, for that reason, be a mere projection.

Belief in God can certainly be very greatly influenced by the child's attitude to its father. But this does not mean that God cannot exist.

Consequently the problem does not lie in the fact that belief in God can be psychologically explained. It is not a question of a choice between psychology and not psychology. From the psychological standpoint, belief in God always exhibits the structure and content of a projection and can be suspected as a mere projection. It is the same with lovers: every lover necessarily projects his own image of her onto the beloved. But does this mean that his beloved does not exist or at any rate does not exist substantially as he sees her and thinks of her? With the aid of his projections, may he not even understand her more profoundly than someone who tries as a neutral observer to judge her from outside? The mere fact of projection therefore does not decide the existence or nonexistence of the object to which it refers.

It is at this point that the Freudian conclusion from the abnormal to the normal, from the neurotic to the religious —however well justified—finds its essential limitations. Is religion human *wishful thinking?* And must God for that reason be merely a human wishful construction, an infantile illusion or even purely a neurotic delusion? As we argued against Feuerbach, a real God may certainly correspond to the wish for God. This possibility—to be discussed more closely at a later stage —is one that even Freud did not exclude. And why should wishful thinking be absolutely universally discredited? Is not wishing wholly and entirely human, wishing in small matters or in great, wishing in regard to the good of this world, in regard to our fellow men, to the world and perhaps also in regard to God?

Of course, religious belief would be in a bad way if there were no genuine grounds for it or if no grounds remained after a psychoanalytic treatment of the subject: however devout its appearance, such a faith would be immature, infantile, perhaps even neurotic. But is a faith bad and its truth dubious simply because—like psychoanalysis itself—it also involves all possible instinctual motivations, lustful inclinations, psychodynamic mechanisms, conscious and unconscious wishes? Why in fact should I not be permitted to wish? Why should I not be allowed to wish that the sweat, blood and tears, all the sufferings of millennia, may not have been in vain, that definitive happiness may finally be possible for all human beings—especially the despised and downtrodden? And why should I not, on the other hand, feel an aversion to being required to be satisfied with rare moments of happiness and—for the rest—to come to terms with "normal unhappiness"? May I not feel an aversion also in regard to the idea that the life of the individual and of mankind is governed only by the pitiless laws of nature, by the play of chance and by the survival of the fittest, and that all dying is a dying into nothingness?[2]

It does not follow—as some theologians have mistakenly concluded—from man's profound desire for God and eternal life, that God exists and eternal life and happiness are real. But some atheists, too, are mistaken in thinking that what follows is the nonexistence of God and the unreality of eternal life. It is true that the wish alone does not contain its own fulfillment. It *may* be that nothing corresponds to the oldest, strongest and most urgent wishes of mankind and that mankind has actually been cherishing illusions for millennia. Just like a child that, in its solitude, forsakenness, distress, need for happiness, wishes wholeheartedly, longs, imagines, and fantasizes that it might have a father in some distant Russian camp, cherishes illusions, gives way to self-deception, pursues wish images, unless, unless . . . ? Unless the father, long assumed to be dead, whom the child knows only from hearsay, had by some chance remained alive and—although no one believed it any longer—was still existing. Then—then indeed—the child would actually be right against the many who did not believe in the father's existence. Then there would in fact be a reality corresponding to the child's wishful thinking and one day perhaps might be seen face to face. . . .

It would not be entirely irrelevant to raise the question: Are we perhaps faced here with a repression phenomenon that naturally has its own, and not least historical, roots? The unnecessary controversies, already mentioned, between Church and science explain at least up to a point why scientists today prefer to be silent, rather than to speak of God. We have observed that sexuality can be repressed. Hence it is possible to ask if perhaps the future, fear and hope, the question of the meaning of life, even religious feeling, can also be repressed. One should not appeal too hastily to objective science, to impartial reason. Even scientific reason can be corrupted: by all kinds of wishes, instincts, inclinations, childhood fixations, prejudices. And this occurs particularly at the point where it is not a question of "exact" (mathematical, scientific, technological, "pure") conclusions, but of their assumptions and applications, especially where the problems of one's own life are involved. Atheists accuse religion of being wishful thinking. But we for our part may ask whether *atheism*, too, might not be *wishful thinking, projection.* Raising the question, of course, is not the same thing as answering it.

REPRESSED RELIGIOUS FEELING?

For Freud personally, so far as this is of interest here, the problem became acute. Was there perhaps a repression problem involved in the atheism he maintained to the end? This closing question of the present critique, which we raise with the utmost caution, is not meant in the last resort to interpret Freud's criticism of religion in terms of individual psychology and so neutralize it. Nevertheless there is food for thought in the fact—as we have seen—that Freud was not brought up without religion. He has testified in his *Autobiographical Study* to the fact that he was quite familiar with the Bible, but, oddly enough, in a sentence that was added only in 1935.[3] He also admits that in his early years he had a strong bent toward speculation on the riddle of the world and of man, but again, oddly enough, he resisted this inclination: "As a young man I felt a strong attraction towards speculation and ruthlessly checked it."[4] Thus he "secretly nursed the hope" of arriving by a detour through physiology at his "original objective, philosophy": "for that was my original ambition, before I knew what I was intended to do in the world."[5] At the age of forty he wrote about his *yearning for knowledge* to his friend Fliess: "As a young man my only longing was for philosophical knowledge, and now that I am changing over from medicine to psychology I am in the process of fulfilling this wish. I became a therapist against my will."[6]

Evidently the young Freud was preoccupied with questions that can be called philosophical, ideological or religious. And evidently Freud in his old age—as he has told us himself, everything in the meantime had been merely a "detour"—returned to the questions of his youth and became intensely occupied until his death mainly with problems of religion. In this respect, from his youth onward and from his first biblical studies, nothing fascinated him more than the "founder" of that religion—the Jewish—from which he came. As early as 1913, for three lonely September weeks, he stood every day contemplating the statue of Moses by Michelangelo in San Pietro in Vincoli, in Rome, in order to write his early (anonymously published) work on this figure. And he wrote the last great work of his life also on the history and significance of this same Moses. What was the source of this fascination? . . . .

Freud, the atheist, undoubtedly rejected Christianity in principle. But was he so remote from it in practice? "As you admit, I have done a great deal for love": this is what he wrote as early as 1910 to Pastor Oskar Pfister, the only theologian with whom he remained in intellectual contact throughout his life.[7] In Freud's system at that time, however, there was no place for any concept except that of sexually defined love, the all-embracing libido. It was only at the end of his life that Freud acknowledged nonsexual love.[8] At that point, man became for him more than the mechanistically understood system driven by the ego instinct and libido, *homme machine,* basically isolated and egoistic, which he had constructed under the influence of Brücke and the earlier physiologists. He now saw man as a being essentially related to others, driven by vital instincts demanding union with others. Life and love belong together and are more deeply rooted than all sexuality.

As late as 1930, in his *Civilisation and Its Discontents,* Freud had described the Christian commandment of love of neighbor as "not reasonable," as "unpsychological" and "impossible to fulfil."[9] Three years later, in view of the darkening world situation with Hitler's seizure of power, in an open letter (not published in Germany) to Albert Einstein, Freud called for love "without a sexual aim" as an indirect way of opposing war: "There is no need for psycho-analysis to be ashamed to speak of love in this connection, for religion itself uses the same words: 'Thou shalt love thy neighbour as thyself.' "[10]

What Freud admitted here in theory—love of neighbor—he had practiced for a long time, admittedly without knowing why. As early as 1915, he wrote to James Putnam, the Harvard neurologist: "When I ask myself why I have always behaved honourably, ready to spare others and to be kind wherever possible, and why I did not give up being so when I observed that in that way one harms oneself and becomes an anvil because other people are brutal and untrustworthy, then, it is true, I have no answer."[11]

Is there really no answer?

Editor's note: At this point, in *Freud and the Problem of God,* Küng adds to the same material: "As a believer in God and particularly as a Christian, I have an answer to this question. But this would be the theme of another lecture series" (p. 122).

Notes

1. *The Future of an Illusion, Standard Edition,* XXI, p. 35.
2. Cf. A. Görres, "Alles spricht dafür, nichts Haltbares dage-gen. Kritische Reflexionen eines Analytikers über den christlichen Glauben," in H. Zahrnt (ed.) *Jesus und Freud. Ein Symposion von Psychoanalytikern und Theologen,* Munich, 1972, pp. 36–52.
3. "An Autobiographical Study," *Standard Edition,* XX, p. 8.
4. Cf. Ernest Jones, *Sigmund Freud. Life and Work* (London: Hogarth Press, 3 vols., 1953–1957). Vol. I, pp. 32–33, 38, 67, 324, 327, 382, 421; Vol. II, p. 394.
5. Freud, letter to W. Fliess, Jan. 1, 1869. *The Origins of Psychoanalysis.* London: Imago Publishing Company, 1954, p. 141.
6. Freud, letter to W. Fliess, Apr. 2, 1896. *Letters of Sigmund Freud 1873–1939,* ed. Ernest L. Freud. London: Hogarth Press, 1961, p. 241.
7. S. Freud and O. Pfister, *Briefe 1909–1939,* Frankfurt, 1963, p. 33.
8. Cf. Fromm, *The Anatomy of Human Destructiveness,* N.Y., 1973. Appendix, "Freud's Theory of Aggressiveness and Destructiveness," pp. 439–478.
9. H. Albert, *Traktat über kritische Vernunft,* Tübingen, 1968, p. 119.
10. *Ibid.*
11. H. Albert, *Theologische Holzwege. Gerhard Ebeling und der rechte Gebrauch der Vernunft,* Tübingen, 1973, p. 86.

Readings

Peter L. Benson, Bernard P. Spilka, "God-Image as Function of Self-Esteem and Locus of Control," *Current Perspectives in the Psychology of Religion,* ed. by H. Newton Malony (Grand Rapids, Mich.: Eerdmans, 1977), 209–223.

Anthony J. De Luca, *Freud and Future Religious Experience*. N.Y.: Philosophical Library, 1976.

David Elkind, "The Origins of Religion in the Child," *Current Perspectives in the Psychology of Religion*, 269–278.

Erich Fromm, *Greatness and Limitations of Freud's Thought*. N.Y.: Harper and Row, 1980.

Erich Fromm, *The Anatomy of Human Destructiveness*. N.Y.: Fawcett, 1978.

Hans Küng, *Freud and the Problem of God*. New Haven: Yale U. Press, 1979.

Hans Küng, *Does God Exist? An Answer for Today*. Garden City, N.Y.: Doubleday, 1980.

Walter Kaufmann, *Discovering the Mind*. Volume Three. *Freud Versus Jung and Adler*. N.Y.: McGraw-Hill, 1980.

William F. Lynch, S.J., *Images of Hope*. N.Y.: New American Library, 1965.

Heinrich Meng and Ernest Freud, eds., *Psychoanalysis and Faith. The Letters of Sigmund Freud and Oskar Pfister*. N.Y.: Basic Books, 1963.

H.L. Philp, *Freud and Religious Belief*. Westport, Conn.: Greenwood Press, 1974. A book by book critique.

Paul Ricoeur, *Freud and Philosophy. An Essay on Interpretation*. New Haven: Yale U. Press, 1970. A profound philosophical reading.

Ana-Maria Rizzuto, M.D., *The Birth of the Living God*. Chicago: U. of Chicago, 1979. A non-reductionist Freudian approach.

Antoine Vergote and Alvaro Tamayo, *The Parental Figures and the Representation of God*. Hawthorne, N.Y.: Walter De Gruyter, Inc., 1982.

Antoine Vergote, *The Religious Man*. Dayton: Pflaum, 1969.

Ernest Wallwork, "Sigmund Freud: The Psychoanalytic Diagnosis —Infantile Illusion," *Critical Issues in Modern Religion* (Englewood Cliffs, N.J.: Prentice-Hall, 1973), Roger A. Johnson, Ernest Wallwork, eds., 251–283.

IV.
Conscience and Superego

John W. Glaser

(Excerpt from "Conscience and Superego: A Key Distinction," by John W. Glaser, S.J., published in *Theological Studies* Volume 32, Number 1, March 1971, pages 36–49.)

Editor's Note

In 1914 Freud introduced the term "ego ideal." Later this was called the superego. Finally the ego ideal was seen as the part of the superego which craved perfection while the negative part of the superego represented restriction of wishes (Wolman, 61). The superego is the result of internalized cultural values. It is partly irrational, imposing rigid restrictions not related to present situations.

Freud identified the superego and conscience. However, theologically conscience is not a synonym for the Freudian superego. To say that conscience arises only from society does not explain its original genesis in the race. Futhermore, one can react against general social values. For example, some reacted against society and family norms about anti-Semitism in Nazi Germany. Paradoxically, this might have resulted in guilt feelings. Feelings of guilt or goodness cannot always be the criterion of true conscience. One may feel no guilt while doing what is objectively evil. Adolph Eichmann, who was responsible for the execution of thousands of Jews during World War II, was asked by a psychiatrist on the TV program "60 Minutes" (Feb. 6, 1983) if he ever felt guilty. Eichmann said, "Yes, when I skipped school as a youngster." On the other hand, one may feel guilt when there is no moral or religious responsibility. Due to the superego, one may see the present through the distorting lens of the psychic past. Because the superego has its origin in childhood, and because it does have a valuable function in conserving tradition, there is danger that it will continue to impose an infantile structure on the operation of

31

the ego, unless a person becomes fully aware that it is not necessarily identical with conscience. It is not unknown for a religious writer or preacher to yield to rhetorical exaggeration and make a universal identification of guilt feelings with "theological guilt." God is not always what one feels good after nor evil always what one feels guilty about.

Conscience, in Freudian terms, should be situated more in the ego. St. Thomas considered conscience not as an inner power distinct from other powers but as a habit belonging to reason—to practical reason as it makes decisions about action as opposed to theoretical reason. It was not a simple act of the will nor a mystical light (D'Arcy, 44; Bier, 10). However, conscience cannot be limited to reason. It also arises from feeling and from the whole personality (Conn, 205). It also grows as one's sense of social responsibility grows. "Conscience is the question mark branded irradicably on man. It asks man about himself, but gives no speeches. Silence is the mode of its speech" (Mount, 61). Conscience is a fragile bud which needs to be actively developed. There is an erroneous conscience for whose deficiencies we are responsible, just as there is an erroneous conscience which is totally inculpable.

From a theological point of view, conscience has its ultimate grounding in God. The lure to good cannot have no relationship to the Ultimate Good (Conn, 133). This lure operates whether one believes or does not believe in God. Its roots are deeper than discursive or logical reasoning and more primordial than contemporary social values. Conscience is at the center of the self where person and God touch.

The author of the following excerpt, John W. Glaser, has taught theology at Detroit University and has published extensively in the area of moral and pastoral theology.

*　　*　　*

I
THE SUPEREGO

The superego deals not in the currency of extroverted love but in the introversion of *being lovable*. The dynamic of the superego springs from a frantic compulsion to experience oneself as lovable, not from the call to commit oneself in abiding love.

To understand the superego, we have to begin there where every human being begins—as a child. The child is faced with a problem: he is a bundle of needs, desires, and impulses. They cannot all find satisfaction; very often the fulfilment of one excludes the satisfaction of another (e.g., if a child's desire to grab everything within reach is satisfied, he finds himself confronted with the displeasure and disapproval of his parents, i.e., with the frustration of another of his desires). These desires, needs, and impulses manifest a decided hierarchy of importance and power. Eicke indicates that opinions vary on *the* primary drive, but says that most psychologists seem to see the need to be loved, to enjoy approval and affection, as the strongest, most fundamental of these drives.[1] He goes on to say that the child experiences disapproval, temporary withdrawal of love, as a kind of annihilation. Therefore this fear of punishment is not so much an aversion to physical pain as it is panic at the withdrawal of love. Freud has remarked that being loved is equivalent to life itself for the ego.[2] In these terms the child experiences the disapproval of his parents as a mitigated withdrawal of life itself. In such a situation the child needs a means of so organizing and ordering his various desires that his main need, to be loved, does not get run over by the others. Since there is not yet enough mature psychic equipment at the child's disposal to handle this conflict, the problem is handled by a more primitive (i.e., less personal) mechanism. An instance of censorship forms on this prepersonal level; its function is to so regulate the conduct of the child that he does not lose the primary object of his desires: love, affection, and approval.[3]

One point should be made clear beyond all misunderstanding: the commands and prohibitions of the superego do not arise from any kind of perception of the intrinsic goodness or objectionableness of the action contemplated. *The* source of such commands and prohibitions can be described positively as the desire to be approved and loved or negatively as the fear of loss of such love and approval.[4]

Even this prepersonal instance of censorship manifests

stages of development. It has been observed that during the first few years of a child's life the commands and prohibitions of parents are so identified with the parents themselves that the commands, as it were, leave the room with the parents. These norms are only really effective when the mother or father is actually present.[5]

But even during this time a process of internalization is taking place by which the orders of authority are assimilated in the child and eventually arise from within the child himself. This process involves the psychological mechanisms of introjection and identification.[6] Eicke sums this up thus:

> Through identification a value emerges, a value which I am for myself; but this is also a value according to which I must conduct myself. If I fail to act according to this norm, I experience fears and feelings of guilt; more exactly, fear of not being loved, of being abandoned or persecuted; feelings of not having done the right thing, of not having made myself lovable. As Freud says: "Consciousness of guilt was originally fear of punishment by parents; more exactly, fear of losing their love."[7]

Several things characterize this process of introjection. It is a spontaneous mechanism whose commands speak with a remarkable power (which we will discuss shortly). It is also striking how graphically (almost "photographically" at times) the authority figure takes up a place within the child himself, so that not only the content but also the very voice and formulation of this external person arises from within the child. Zulliger recounts the comment of the nineteenth-century Swiss author Rodolphe Toepffer: "For a long time I was unable to distinguish the inner voice of my conscience from *that of my teacher*. When my conscience spoke to me, I thought I saw it before me in a black cape, with a teacher's frown and glasses sitting on its nose."[8]

Allport brings a delightful and illuminating example which illustrates this process of introjection and the controlling influence it exercises:

I am indebted for this example to my colleague, Henry A. Murray. A three-year-old boy awoke at six in the morning and started his noisy play. The father, sleepy-eyed, went to the boy's room and sternly commanded him, "Get back into bed and don't you dare get up until seven o'clock." The boy obeyed. For a few minutes all was quiet, but soon there were strange sounds that led the father again to look into the room. The boy was in bed as ordered; but putting an arm over the edge, he jerked it back in saying, "Get back in there." Next a leg protruded, only to be roughly retracted with the warning, "You heard what I told you." Finally the boy rolled to the very edge of the bed and then roughly rolled back, sternly warning himself, "Not until seven o'clock!" We could not wish for a clearer instance of interiorizing the father's role as a means to self-control and socialized becoming.[9]

The only exceptional thing about such an instance is that it happened to be observed by an adult, and by one who saw the psychological significance of the event. Zulliger offers numerous examples of the same phenomenon.[10]

The superego as discussed up to now could be characterized as having functions similar to those of what is traditionally known as *conscientia antecedens:* it commands and prohibits certain concrete possibilities in a given situation. The superego, however, also functions in a way similar to *conscientia consequens:* it accuses the offender, it condemns him when he fails to obey. The fury of the violated superego is described by Bergler: "The extent of the power yielded by the Frankenstein which is the superego is still largely unrealized. . . . Man's inhumanity to man is equaled only by man's inhumanity to himself."[11]

The reason for this violent reaction has already been touched upon. The superego must, on the psychological, subconscious level, provide for a person's being loved; it is the guardian of the individual's sense of value. We have already referred to Freud's statement that, for the ego, being loved is equivalent to life itself. Hence the violence of the offended superego arises from the panic of having lost one's right to be loved; on a primitive, psychological level he has "lost his life."[12] The fact that this plays itself out on a nonconceptual level of consciousness in terms of panic, fear, and guilt feelings makes it all the more difficult to cope with, if one is armed only with the weapons of reason and conceptual reflections.

Zulliger spells out the guilt feelings produced by the superego in terms of isolation. "When a child does something wrong, disobeys a command, etc., he experiences a feeling of isolation."[13] He feels that he is "bad" and isolated from those who are "good." Describing such guilt in terms of an experienced isolation helps us find a plausible and consistent explanation of several other phenomena closely connected with such guilt. There is no need here to recount the many examples offered by Zulliger, but by means of these examples several things are made clear: there is a powerful subconscious drive to re-create one's sense of belonging and being accepted by his community, of re-establishing the harmony and solidarity he has forfeited by his fault.

This drive to rejoin the "good" and thus regain one's sense of value, this drive to break out of the panic of isolation, can express itself in a variety of ways. Besides the direct approach of confessing to some authority figure and accepting punishment, there are various indirect ways of attempting to escape the tyranny of an offended superego. Zulliger enumerates three main indirect solutions. First, there is the unconscious betrayal of guilt. This drive to be found out (which is ultimately a drive to be reconciled), though conflicting with the conscious effort to escape detection, finds ways of exposing one's fault and in this way of indirectly confessing and ultimately being reconciled. Another substitute compensation takes the form of seeking punishment.[14] The original misdeed against the norms of the superego is not itself confessed and punished. Rather, the individual provokes punishment through further misdeeds and through this punishment for further and distinct failures attempts to quiet his need for punishment for the original unpunished misdeed. Through a further and distinct misdeed (whose real goal is the reconciliation to follow) he attempts to break out of the isolation created by the original misdeed. His subconscious goal is to have the second misdeed result in punishment-reconciliation and also take care of the original alienation. Finally, there is the indirect escape from isolation which takes the form of creating a new community where the individual will be accepted. This implies provoking others to deeds similar to his own. Instead of re-establishing harmony with the "good," he tends to create a group which will accept him with his misdeeds and even esteem him precisely on their account.[15]

Zulliger's description of the power of the superego in terms of flight from a feeling of acute alienation—an alienation from that group represented by the authority figures in his life, who have communicated what is expected of him if he wants to "belong"—helps us see how much the formal structure of the superego differs from conscience. Conscience is precisely the call of genuine value which can well call one to an extremely isolated position. Motivating an individual's activity on the basis of "acceptance" serves well the socialization and normalization of individuals to prevailing norms; but as a basis of Christian morality (in the mature sense of this word), which should be characterized by a creative thrust into the future, i.e., into the not-yet-ready-to-be-thought, its dynamics are strikingly inadequate. The superego performs well in the process of socialization—training one to function well within a given set of limits; it works well and adequately in toilet-training an infant or housebreaking a pup (both useful results, without which life would be far less pleasant), but its legitimate function deals with the more primitive levels of psychic life. Görres points out that the relationship between superego and id is not so much that of spirit to instinct or rider to horse; rather, it concerns the relationship between instinct and training. "The superego, in Freud's sense, is primarily a function of organization of the primitive levels of psychic life. This is supported by the fact that higher animals are said to have a superego when they have been trained."[16]

The superego is basically a principle of prepersonal censorship and control. This does not mean that it has no meaningful function for man. On the contrary, the role of the superego in the life of an infant is quite meaningful and neces-

sary. It is a primitive stage on the way to the development of
genuine conscience and value perception.[17] Even in the life of a
mature adult the superego is not superfluous. In certain sectors
of life it provides for a conservation of psychic energy and ease
of operation. Görres remarks: "When the superego is integrated into a mature conscience . . . it relieves an individual from
having constantly to decide in all those situations which are
already legitimately decided by custom, taste, and convention
'what one should do' and 'what one should not do.' "[18]

Psychologists are in agreement, however, that this organic
development from the primitive and prepersonal censor of the
infant to a mature and personal value perception does not
automatically and infallibly take place. This means that the
activity of superego in the average adult is not limited to the
healthy and integrated function described above by Görres. In
fact, Görres himself maintains that it is the task, not only of
psychiatry but of education and pastoral practice as well, to
reduce the influence of this childish censor more and more and
thereby allow genuine value perception to grow.[19]

While it is true that the workings of the superego are
generally discussed in the context of the child or the neurotic,
Görres reminds us that the differences here between the neurotic and the "healthy" person are those of degree and not of
kind.[20] According to Odier and Tournier, there are two moral
worlds existing in the normal person: a genuine moral world
and a world of false or pseudo morality and religiosity.[21] Both
of these authors have written extensively on this subject precisely to call attention to the existence and influence of this all
too often overlooked world of childish morality in the life of
the average adult.[22] Felicitas Betz points out that the struggle
to grow up in this regard does not cease at the end of childhood or adolescence but confronts us with a lifelong battle.
"The maturing of one's conscience is a task that takes a life-
time; it is with us far beyond the end of adolescence. For one
who has been the object more of conscience training than
conscience education, this task of arriving at mature conscience
will be particularly difficult, if not impossible."[23]

We might draw up some contrasting characteristics which
exist between the superego and genuine conscience:

SUPEREGO	CONSCIENCE
commands that an act be performed for approval, in order to make oneself lovable, accepted; fear of love-withdrawal is the basis	invites to action, to love, and in this very act of other-directed commitment to cocreate self-value
introverted: the thematic center is a sense of one's own value	extroverted: the thematic center is the value which invites; self-value is concomitant and secondary to this
static: does not grow, does not learn; cannot function creatively in a new situation; merely repeats a basic command	dynamic: an awareness and sensitivity to value which develops and grows; a mind-set which can precisely function in a new situation
authority-figure-oriented: not a question of perceiving and responding to a value but of "obeying" authority's command "blindly"	value-oriented: the value or disvalue is perceived and responded to, regardless of whether authority has commanded or not
"atomized" units of activity are its object	individual acts are seen in their importance as a part of a larger process or pattern
past-oriented: primarily concerned with cleaning up the record with regard to past acts	future-oriented: creative; sees the past as having a future and helping to structure this future as a better future
urge to be punished and thereby earn reconciliation	sees the need to repair by structuring the future orientation toward the value in question (which includes making good past harms)
rapid transition from severe isolation, guilt feelings, etc., to a sense of self-value accomplished by confessing to an authority figure	a sense of the gradual process of growth which characterizes all dimensions of genuine personal development
possible great disproportion between guilt experienced and the value in question; extent of guilt depends more on weight of authority figure and "volume" with which he speaks rather than density of the value in question	experience of guilt proportionate to the importance of the value in question, even though authority may never have addressed this specific value

In light of this less than exhaustive list of contrasts, it should be clear that failing to distinguish these two realities will cause considerable confusion. This confusion is multiplied if one has taken superego data and allowed it to be the weightier element in understanding man as *free*, precisely because it arises from the prepersonal, prefree dimension of an individual. The pastoral and ascetic practice which flows from such a superego-weighted interpretation of guilt, etc., will be to a great extent in radical conflict with man's genuine freedom.

In the following section I want to reflect on some areas where it seems to me we have been mistaken in drawing theological conclusions or in projecting conduct (pastoral, ascetic, sacramental) from data of the superego. These remarks vary in their importance and are less systematically developed than might be desirable; they must stand as the fragmentary reflections that are prompted by my present situation. Hopefully they will stimulate further reflection and application, which will be, among other things, corrective of the following remarks.

II
PROBLEM AREAS WHERE
SUPEREGO IS PART OF PROBLEM

All the following reflections could be subsumed under one rubric: too much theory and practice in the Church arises from data whose source is the superego. Many problem areas which have emerged in the recent past can be traced to a failure to recognize the nature, presence, and power of the superego. This is not an accusation.[24] But given today's vantage point, this is a situation which can be overcome and should not be further tolerated.

Notion of God
Precisely because the voice of the superego is somehow cosmic, vast, and mysterious, arising as it does from the subconscious, it can easily be mistakenly called God's voice. This is true especially if our religious education trains us from childhood on to call this voice of the subconscious God's voice. This

I see as the major danger of failing to distinguish conscience from superego. To associate the mystery of invitation, the absolute yes to man's future, the radical call to eternally abiding love—God—with the hot and cold, arbitrary tyrant of the superego is a matter of grave distortion. It reaches into the totality of a person's explicitly religious life and poisons every fresh spring of the Good News. Such a God deserves to die.

Gregory Baum's comments are much to the point on this question:

> A second reason why the image of the God the punisher has flourished in the Christian and even post-Christian imagination is drawn from personal pathology. The idea of God as judge on a throne, meting out punishment, corresponds to a self-destructive trend of the human psyche. On a previous page we have mentioned man's primitive conscience or, as Freud called it, his superego. The person who is dominated by his superego—and no one is able to escape it altogether—has the accuser, judge, and tormentor all wrapt in one, built into his own psychic makeup. When such a person hears the Christian message with the accent on God the judge, he can project his superego on the divinity and then use religion as an instrument to subject himself to this court and, unknown to himself, to promote his own unconscious self-hatred. As we mentioned more than once in these pages, Jesus has come to save men from their superego. God is not punisher; God saves.[25]

Age of Reason and Transition between Grace and Sin

The theological literature on the fundamental option has drastically revised the common Catholic ideas concerning the "age of reason" and the frequency with which the transition between grace-sin-grace-sin can occur.[26] The speculation of theologians like Rahner, Schüller, Metz, and Mondin has so radically changed the atmosphere in which speculation on core freedom takes place that one is puzzled how thoughts on the "age of reason" (emergence of core freedom) and the frequency of core decisions—which were common fare in moral theology until the recent past—were ever possible. How could we have really thought that ten-year-olds could sin seriously? Or what ever possessed us to think that we could move through serious sin and grace with the frequency that we change shirts?

One major reason why such thoughts were thinkable is surely because theology failed to recognize various kinds of guilt experience and release from this guilt. Theology simply accepted all guilt experience and its release as theological data, as data arising from man's freedom. The nature of superego guilt and its radical difference from genuine moral guilt went unrecognized.

A striking example of this appears in Maritain's *Range of Reason*.[27] Maritain used an excellent analysis of preconceptual knowledge of God to make a far from excellent explanation of why a child can engage his core freedom. At one point in his discussion of this question Maritain seems to reveal, at least in part, the source of his conviction that children can make core-freedom decisions. In what he seems to consider a phenomenological justification for his position he says:

> Yet in some rare cases, the first act of freedom will never be forgotten, especially if the choice—however insignificant its object—through which the soul was introduced into moral life occurred rather late. In other cases there is a remembrance of some childish remorse, whose occasion was unimportant but whose intensity, out of proportion with its object, upset the soul and awakened its moral sense.[28]

To one aware of the dimensions of an act of core freedom on the one hand, and familiar with the nature of the superego on the other, the data described by Maritain is clearly relegated to the area of the superego, not genuine freedom. This acceptance of all guilt data as genuine theological data—which Maritain reveals in the quoted passage—remained for moral theology a silent but functioning presupposition in its consideration of the "age of reason." This error, coupled with an exaggerated conceptualistic model of conscience, helps explain in large part the now incredible conviction with which most of us grew up: children can commit serious sin.

The idea that an individual could sin seriously, repent only to sin seriously again, repent again—and this within a matter of days—also finds at least a partial explanation in the fact that superego guilt and its remission by an authority figure was mistaken for genuine moral guilt and its remission. A very common phenomenon, familiar to anyone who has done pastoral work with Catholic adolescents, certainly *seems* to support the theory that the transition between grace and serious sin can occur relatively frequently. We might describe this datum as the "storm and sunshine phenomenon." It occurs especially in questions of sexual morality. The individual experiences severe guilt feelings after a failing against the sixth commandment: the storm phase. Upon confessing, he experiences a wonderful release from his guilt: the sunshine phase. Such a moving between storm and sunshine might well occur on a weekly basis. The guilt feelings involved represent very often the most severe experience of guilt the individual has ever known; the freeing from this guilt through confession is often the most intense experience of liberation.

Such an undeniable phenomenon seems to offer more than enough concrete evidence that an individual can fluctuate frequently between grace and serious sin. It can do this, however, only if we are ignorant of the nature of the superego; only if we overlook the fact that the area of sexuality is notoriously susceptible to the tyranny of the superego; and only if we fail to realize the vast dimensions of the transition between sin and grace. Because these very facts were not operative in reflection on core freedom (mortal sin), it is easy to understand why traditional moral theology and confessional practice took their theoretical and pastoral-practical categories from the superego-dominated data and found in such data unquestioned support for the conviction that the transition between grace and sin could occur with almost assembly-line frequency.

Diminishing Confessions

From the foregoing it is clear that at least some essential dimensions of confessional practice are based on the nature

and laws of the superego and not of genuine freedom. It seems
to me that these are not merely two exceptional, isolated instances, but two areas which are better seen as examples where
confession's debt to the superego is more blatantly obvious.
They are pocket-sized editions of what is true of confessional
practice as a whole: it is, as traditionally realized, predominant-
ly, though not exclusively, a service of the superego needs of
individuals.

In traditional confession practice therefore, we have an
institution based on heavily-weighted nonfree (superego) data
which purports to be an institutionalization but actually is a
contradiction of genuine freedom. Now this genuine freedom
and its categories of being, growing, etc., are not simply non-
conscious, beyond all awareness; they are somehow present to
man's awareness because of the essential relationship between
freedom and knowledge. Hence we have an awareness, a consciousness "divided" against itself, contradicting itself on
various levels. On the preconceptual level we have an awareness of the true nature and structure of freedom—its laws of
growth, the "units" of core freedom, their duration and possible frequency, etc. On the conceptual level we have categories
which attempt to represent this freedom but are actually derived to a great extent from the superego.

Since the categories drawn from the superego are far
shallower, a much "thinner brew" (see the characteristics mentioned earlier), the person in question experiences present
confessional practice as a trivialization of his genuine freedom.
He experiences himself as dealing with the reality of his freedom—experienced preconceptually in its real depth, richness,
laws of growth and engagement, etc.—in institutionalized categories derived from a far cheaper reality; hence the institutionalized categories are too cheap and too trivial for the reality to
which they supposedly correspond and from which they supposedly derive.

The experience of this "misfit" is recognized, not necessarily in a reflexively formulated way, but in the depth of
consciousness. It is, then, no wonder that a person reacts in a
corresponding way; a person simply finds himself, in an un-

planned and unarticulated way, distancing himself from the practice of confession.

This means that the phenomenon of diminishing confessions is, at least in part, a healthy recognition of the misfit existing between genuine freedom and a system of categories —institutionalized in the traditional practice of confession —derived to a great extent from the superego. Therefore this phenomenon, far from being regrettable, is a sign of health and insight. It cannot be reversed by mere rhetoric; the very nature of genuine freedom does not prompt us to attempt to reverse it. The more nuanced understanding of man's freedom does, however, prompt us to find more adequate forms for the sacrament of penance. Finding these new forms—be they communal and/or "private"—does demand that we recognize the reality of the superego for what it is and thereby avoid merely creating forms of serving the infantile needs of the superego in a new way.

Superego Can Blind to Genuine Value

In discussing some of the pastoral implication of the foregoing pages, I have often heard the comment: "Maybe an individual needs the dynamics of the superego to help himself avoid doing what he really wants to avoid, but cannot—e.g., masturbation. If we take this away, we may be robbing him of a real help."

Several observations on such a comment. First, there is the question of what such "support" is doing to his whole conception of God and his life of partnership with God. Second, the superego is far more infallible as a tormentor of failure than as a source of effective motivation. Hence the question: What is such support doing to his own self-concept? More often than not the superego will be ineffective in overcoming the urge to masturbate; but it will, with inexorable certainty, provide a self-devouring gloom following such an act. The disproportionate guilt will set up the very situation which immerses the individual in even deeper depressions, sense of failure and frustration, fixation on this matter, etc.; in short, the very situation which is most conducive to further masturbation.

Finally, the superego orientation can quite effectively block off the ultimate values at stake. The superego handles individual acts; it demands that these past actions be "confessed" to an authority figure and thereby erased. Such a frame of reference keeps the individual from seeing the larger and more important *process,* which is always the nature of genuine human growth. Instead of experiencing the individual acts precisely as part of a future-oriented growth process, concerned with values that of their inherent power call to growth, the center of attention is focused on righting past wrongs, seen as atomized units.

A counselor told me of a case in which a happily married man with several children had been plagued by masturbation for fifteen years. During these fifteen years he had dutifully gone the route of weekly confession, Communion, etc. The counselor told him to stop thinking of this in terms of serious sin, to go to Communion every Sunday and to confession every six weeks. He tried to help him see his introversion in terms of his own sexual maturity, in terms of his relationship to his wife and children. Within several months this fifteen-year-old "plague" simply vanished from his life. By refusing to follow a pattern of pastoral practice based on the dynamics of the superego, this counselor was able to unlock a logjam of fifteen years; by refusing to deal with the superego as if it were conscience, he freed the genuine values at stake; he allowed them to speak and call the person beyond his present lesser stage of sexual integration. We can pay rent to the superego but the house never becomes our own possession.

The same is true especially in questions of premarital sex. Fostering the mortal sin-grace horizon and plugging it into the confession-Communion-sin network can keep the person from doing the most important thing of all: honestly looking at the delicate, nuanced, process-structured values which are involved; and it is only by becoming increasingly sensitive to these values that one can be helped, through good and bad experience, to continue to grow. Allowing the superego to dominate this pattern of conduct, to atomize the acts, to deal with their guilt and its release in terms of past serious offenses against God which are set right by some authority figure can be the very manner of dealing with the problem which keeps the operative values from ever emerging and calling creatively to further growth.

Notes

1. Dieter Eicke, "Das Gewissen und das Über-Ich," in *Das Gewissen dis Problem* (Darmstadt, 1966) p. 72; cf. also Albert Görres, *Methode und Erfahrung der Psychoanalyse* (Munich, 1965) pp. 166–72.

2. S. Freud, *Gesammelte Werke* 13 (London, 1940ff.) 288.

3. Eicke, *op. cit.*, pp. 97ff.; cf. also Görres, *op. cit.*

4. Hans Zulliger, *Umgang mit dem kindlichen Gewissen* (Stuttgart, 1955) p. 30: "The primitive conscience is built on the basis of fear of punishment and a desire to earn love." Eicke, *op. cit.*, p. 79: "The superego has its source in the naked fear of retribution or withdrawal of love; its organizing function serves to protect the ego from the outside world." Melanie Klein, *Das Seelenleben des Kleinkindes und andere Beiträge zur Psychoanalyse* (Stuttgart, 1962) p. 140: "Experience of guilt is inextricably bound up with fear (more exactly, with a specific form of fear, namely, depressive fear); it drives one to reconciliation and reparation; it emerges in the first few months of an infant's life together with the early stages of the superego." Cf. also Görres, *op. cit.*, p. 170.

5. Felicitas Betz, "Entwicklungsstufen des kindlichen Gewissens," in *Beichte im Zwielicht* (Munich, 1966) p. 33.

6. Cf. Görres, *op. cit.*, p. 166; Eicke, *op. cit.*, pp. 77–80; Zulliger, *op. cit.* pp. 63ff.; Bertha Sommer, "Über neurotische Angst und Schuldgefühle," in Wilhelm Bitter, ed., *Angst und Schuld* (Stuttgart, 1959) p. 44.

7. Eicke, *op. cit.*, p. 80.

8. Zulliger, *op. cit.*, p. 38.

9. Gordon W. Allport, *Becoming* (New Haven, 1966) p. 70.

10. Zulliger, *op. cit.*, pp. 11–45; Betz, *op. cit.*, pp. 29–39.

11. Edmund Bergler, *The Superego* (New York, 1952) p. x. A few pages earlier he says: "To get an approximate idea of the 'benevolence' of inner conscience, one has only to imagine the terms of the relationship between a dictator—any dictator—and an inmate of one of his concentration and extermination camps" (p. viii). Bergler is not given to understatement; but perhaps exaggeration in this question can serve as a needed corrective to emphasize something we have too long overlooked.

12. Klein, *op. cit.*, p. 135.

13. Zulliger, *op. cit.*, pp. 103f., 108f.

14. Besides numerous examples offered by Zulliger, cf. also T. Reik, *Geständniszwang und Strafbedürfnis* (Vienna, 1925); P. Tournier, *Echtes und falsches Schuldgefühl* (Freiburg, 1967).

15. Zulliger, *op. cit.*, pp. 108–24.

16. Görres, *op. cit.*, p. 170.

17. Cf. Tournier, *op. cit.*, p. 57.

18. Görres, *op. cit.*, p. 169. Odier also points out, besides the functions mentioned by Görres, that the superego acts as a censor in dreams, thereby preventing every dream from becoming a nightmare. This is no small service. Cf. Charles Odier, *Les deux sources consciente et inconsciente de la vie morale* (Neuchâtel, 1943) p. 28.

19. A. Görres, "Über-Ich," *Lexikon für Theologie und Kirche* 10 (2nd ed.; Freiburg, 1966) 437.

20. Görres, *Methode und Erfahrung*, p. 171.

21. The very titles of their books indicate and emphasize this conviction; cf. notes 16 and 20 above.

22. Melanie Klein, speaking of guilt as naked fear of rejection, says: "With a small child this is always the case; but even with many adults the only factor that changes is that the larger human society takes the place of the father or both parents" (*op. cit.*, p. 135, n. 22). Cf. also Eicke, *op. cit.*, p. 89.

23. Betz, "Entwicklungsstufen," p. 39. Cf. also Marc Oraison, *Was is Sünde?* (Frankfurt/M., 1968) pp. 28, 63f.; Odier, *op. cit.*, p. 60; Tournier, *op. cit.*, p. 56.

24. I am *not* interested in assigning blame or assessing negligence; I *am* interested in the lesson we should learn from this: theology should be the first discipline to have its mind blown by new discoveries in other fields; it dare not be a slow-learning and suspicious discipline, threatened by whatever findings other sciences discover because this new data reshuffles the traditional deck.

25. Gregory Baum, *Man Becoming* (New York, 1970) pp. 223f.

26. Cf. the two articles mentioned in n. 2: "Transition" and "Man's Existence."

27. J. Maritain, *Range of Reason* (New York, 1952) pp. 66ff. For two other recent authors who share this basic viewpoint and for similar reasons, see Joseph Sikora, "Faith and the First Moral Choice," *Sciences ecclésiastiques*, May-September, 1965, pp. 327–37; Herman Reiners, *Grundintention und sittliches Tun* (Freiburg, 1966) esp. p. 26.

28. Maritain, *op. cit.*, p. 68.

Readings

William C. Bier, S.J., ed., *Conscience. Its Freedom and Limitations.* N.Y.: Fordham U. Press, 1971. Especially articles by Dolan, Campbell, Meissner, Clarke, Cousins.

Christiane Brusselmans, convenor, *Toward Moral and Religious Maturity.* Morristown, N.J.: Silver Burdett Co., 1980. Especially articles by Kohlberg, Fowler, Vergote, Rizzuto, Gilligan and Kegan.

Walter E. Conn, *Conscience: Development and Self-Transcendence.* Birmingham, Alabama: Religious Education Press, 1981. Also, "Ontogenetic Ground of Value," *Theological Studies,* June 1978, 313–335.

Eric D'Arcy, *Conscience and Its Right to Freedom.* N.Y: Sheed and Ward, 1961.

Erich Fromm, *Man for Himself.* Greenwich, Conn.: Fawcett, 1947, 145–175. Also *Sigmund Freud's Mission.* N.Y.: Harper and Row, 1972. Psychoanalysis as a religion and superego as the Mosaic law.

Rudolf Hofmann, "Conscience," *Encyclopedia of Theology.* N.Y.: Seabury, 1975.

Rollo May, *Man's Search for Himself.* N.Y.: New American Library, 1967, 150–190.

Karl Menninger, M.D., *Whatever Became of Sin?* N.Y.: Hawthorn, 1973.

Louis Monden, S.J., *Sin, Liberty and Law.* N.Y.: Sheed & Ward, 1965. Sin related to life option more than to individual acts.

Eric Mount, Jr., *Conscience and Responsibility.* Richmond, Va.: John Knox Press, 1969.

C. Ellis Nelson, ed., *Conscience. Theological and Psychological Perspectives.* N.Y.: Newman Press, 1973. Especially Cousins, Zilboorg, Pattison, McCarthy.

Jeffrey Sobosan, *Guilt and the Christian.* Chicago: Thomas More Press, 1982.

C. Williams, "Conscience," *New Catholic Encyclopedia,* N.Y.: McGraw-Hill, 1967.

Benjamin B. Wolman, *The Unconscious Mind. The Meaning of Freudian Psychology.* Englewood Cliffs, N.J.: Prentice-Hall, 1968.

V.
Man's Search for Meaning

Viktor Frankl

Editor's Note

Viktor Frankl may be considered a member of the "third force" in psychology, that is, he is neither a behaviorist nor an orthodox Freudian. Frankl's existential psychoanalysis originated in Vienna where he was a disciple of Freud. He also studied with Adler. Frankl calls his system "logotherapy." It appeals not chiefly to the unconscious but to values. "A psychology which not only recognizes man's spirit, but actually starts from it, may be termed logotherapy."

In his best known work, *Man's Search for Meaning,* Frankl considered the problem of meaning as it manifested itself in his concentration camp experiences at Auschwitz and Dachau. As a result of that experience a phrase from Nietzsche took on a new light for him, "He who has a *why* to live can bear almost any *how.*" In the concentration camps Frankl became keenly aware that life involves suffering and that if life is meaningful so is suffering.

Frankl could not make prescriptions for the meaning of life for the prisoners in the camp. They had to find their own existential truth of uniqueness, the ability to bear a burden in a unique way. In the camp, Frankl wrote *Man's Search for Meaning* but the manuscript was confiscated. In exchange he received the clothes of a Jew who had been gassed. In the coat was a scrap of paper on which was written, "Love the Lord your God with all your heart and soul and mind." All of his family apart from a sister in Australia died in concentration camps.

Frankl himself is a believer in God and he testified to the power of faith in a living God to sustain him. However, he says that belief in God is not essential to logotherapy, or "healing through meaning." Healing through meaning is open to believer and non-believer alike. Frankl was influenced by philosophical phenomenology, especially that of Ludwig Binswanger and Max Scheler. Binswanger's *Daseinanalyse* is concerned with the analysis of being. Logotherapy is interested not in the analysis of being only, but with therapy, with meaning as therapy. Scheler defined man as a being constituted by values. Man "is an intentional act which smells values." Frankl belongs to the school of philosophers which holds that man's nature, at least unconsciously, is always seeking values rather than pleasure. Value means whatever satisfies a person's higher powers. In the most general terms, this is the true, the good and the beautiful. Freud said that humans always seek pleasure, either directly or indirectly. Frankl says that this is true only of the id stage. Once one's higher powers develop (intellect, will, emotion), something new has evolved and a higher quest is inaugurated which must be satisfied at the expense of frustration and neurosis. Whenever a person's higher powers achieve their true goal which is value, pleasure will always follow immediately as a by-product. But when a person make the plan of his whole life into the seeking of pleasure, he will frustrate his higher nature and often neurosis develops.

Frankl saw that neurosis blocks values. He divided neuroses into three kinds. (1) Psychogenic neurosis arises from psychic conflicts, as between the id and the ego, or between the ego and the superego. Here logotherapy operates somewhat like conventional psychotherapy. (2) Somatogenic neurosis arises from vegetative and endocrine disorders. Frankl did not reduce all neuroses to the psyche in origin, and he was one of the first to make use of anti-depressant medication. (3) Noogenic neurosis (from the Greek *nous*, spirit) results from a spiritual vacuum or from unresolved moral conflicts. It is in this area that logotherapy places its chief emphasis. Notice that noogenic neurosis is not the same as "existential frustration." The latter is not an illness, but a conditional of spiritual distress and struggle. "It is something human, even the most human of all there may be in man."

Frankl speaks of "the will to meaning." Some have incorrectly believed that Frankl means that a person can will meaning in a purely subjective fashion by a naked act of the will. But Frankl says that he is opposed to Sartre's idea that we can invent meaning. Frankl says, no, we must find or discover meaning. He uses the word "will" to show that the desire for meaning cannot be passive absorption of meaning from the world, but that we must add something of our own in discovering where meaning is. One cannot wait passively until truth becomes so strong that it takes over. Frankl says that when we ask "Is there meaning to life?" we must see that we are not just asking a question, but we are being questioned, "What meaning do you give to life?" Man should not ask "What is the meaning of life?" as if the question were asked to someone else. He should realize that he himself is being questioned. Therefore human beings must actively contribute to finding meaning, both in its local or daily sense and in its ultimate sense.

Freud had said, "The moment a man questions the meaning and value of life, he is sick." Frankl says, "I think on the contrary that such a man only proves he is already a human being" (1968, 20). I believe that Frankl is right, although Freud may have meant that one especially questions meaning when life is not going well.

When Frankl speaks of "meaning," he is referring not only to ultimate meaning but also to daily meaning such as that found in creative work, hobbies, daily tasks, love and growth through difficulty. Some people have a sense of ultimate meaning but not of daily meaning. "Depression, for example, may be due to an abundance of meaning but a deficiency in techniques of acquiring meaningful ends" (1968, 193). Secondly, meaning is uniquely personal. "When we speak of meaning, this is not intended in a general way but in a personal, concrete way, such as the attainment of vocational fulfillment, innermost values and wishes, a sense of personal mission which cannot be fulfilled by anyone else but only by one's own personality."

Frankl believes that meaning is not found in the will to pleasure, nor even in self-actualization (cf. Maslow). He believes that self-actualization and self-identity are automatic by-products of the achieving of values.

Frankl's word "meaning" has a number of characteristics. (1) Meaning implies or demands self-transcendence. "Existence fails unless it is lived in terms of transcendence toward something beyond itself." (2) Meaning has an eternal quality. "Having completed a task means having become eternal." This is true, "irrespective of whether there is anyone around who may remember or forget." (Whether this would be acceptable to a non-theistic secular audience is a valid question.) (3) Meaning implies values as goals. Values are goals whose grasp fulfills the person's cherished powers. "The meaning which a being has to fulfill is something beyond himself, it is never just himself." It is "something worth longing for and groping for." (4) Meaning is not grasped only intellectually. "What is demanded of man is not, as some existential philosophers teach, to endure the meaninglessness of life; but rather to bear his incapacity to grasp its unconditional meaningfulness in rational terms." One's whole personality, and not just one's intellect, is involved in finding meaning. "Ultimate meaning is accessible only through the mediation of symbol" (1978, 2, 188). Symbols demand the participation of the whole person. (5) Meaning is accessible only by an act of commitment. Ultimate meaning is found in a "basic trust in being." Frankl does not enter into a philosophical or theological discussion of the reasons for this trust in being. (For a discussion on this point, see Chapters VI and VII in this volume.) However, from his book, *The Unconscious God,* it is clear that Frankl believes this trust is based on an unconscious relation to God (1976, 63). The spiritual basis of human existence, he says, is ultimately unconscious, but this aspect of the unconscious is specifically human and spiritual and not just instinctual. Yet, in most of his work, Frankl leaves the ground for the basic trust in being undetermined and thus offers logotherapy as healing-through-meaning to both the believer and the unbeliever alike.

Frankl suggests that meaning can be found especially in three experiences, responsibleness to values, love and suffering. In the following excerpt, after discussing his famous therapeutic method of "paradoxical intention" which aims at self-transcendence through humor, he begins with an analysis of the will to meaning.

*   *   *

THE WILL TO MEANING

For didactic reasons the will to meaning has been counterposed by way of a heuristic oversimplification both to the pleasure principle, which is so pervasive in psychoanalytic motivational theories, and to the will to power, the concept which plays such a decisive role in Adlerian psychology. I do not weary of contending that the will to pleasure is really a self-defeating principle inasmuch as the more a man would actually set out to strive for pleasure the less he would gain it. This is due to the fundamental fact that pleasure is a by-product, or side effect, of the fulfillment of our strivings, but is destroyed and spoiled to the extent to which it is made a goal or target. The more a man aims at pleasure by way of a direct intention, the more he misses his aim. And this, I venture to say, is a mechanism etiologically underlying most cases of sexual neurosis. Accordingly, a logotherapeutic technique based on this theory of the self-thwarting quality of pleasure intention yields remarkable short-term results, and this technique has been used effectively even by psychodynamically oriented therapists on my staff. One of them, to whom I have assigned the responsibility for treatment of all sexually neurotic patients, has used this technique exclusively—in terms of a short-term procedure which has been the only one indicated in the given setting.

In the last analysis, it turns out that both the will to pleasure and the will to power are derivatives of the original will to meaning. Pleasure, as we have said above, is an effect of meaning fulfillment; power is a means to an end. A certain amount of power, such as economic or financial power, is generally a prerequisite for meaning fulfillment. Thus we could say that while the will to pleasure mistakes the effect for the end, the will to power mistakes the means to an end for the end itself.

We are not really justified, however, in speaking of a *will* to pleasure or power in connection with psychodynamically oriented schools of thought; they assume that man aims for the goals of his behavior unwillingly and unwittingly and that his conscious motivations are not his actual motivations. Erich Fromm, for instance, only recently spoke of "the motivating forces which make man act in certain ways, the drives which propel him to strive in certain directions."[1] As for myself, however, it is not conceivable that man be really driven to strivings; I would say either that he is striving or that he is driven. *Tertium non datur.* Ignoring this difference or, rather, sacrificing one phenomenon to another, is a procedure unworthy of a scientist. To do so is to allow one's adherence to hypotheses to blind one to facts. One such distortion is the assumption that man "is lived by" his instincts. Since the man quoted here is Sigmund Freud, for the sake of justice, another of Freud's statements which is not so well known must be added. In a book review he wrote for the *Wiener Medizinische*

Wochenschrift in 1889, he says: "Reverence before the greatness of a genius is certainly a great thing. But our reverence before facts should exceed it."

Freud, and consequently his epigones, have taught us always to see something behind, or beneath, human volitions: unconscious motivations, underlying dynamics. Freud never took a human phenomenon at its face value; or, to adopt the formulation used by Gordon W. Allport, "Freud was a specialist in precisely those motives that cannot be taken at their face value."[2] Does this, however, imply that there are no motives at all which should be taken at their face value? Such an assumption is comparable to the attitude of the man who, when he was shown a stork, said, "Oh, I thought the stork didn't exist!" Does the fact that the stork has been used to hide the facts of life from children in any way deny that bird's reality?

The reality principle is, according to Freud's own words, a mere extension of the pleasure principle; one which serves the pleasure principle's purpose. One could just as well say that the pleasure principle itself is a mere extension working in the service of a wider concept called the homeostasis principle and serves *its* purposes. Ultimately, the psychodynamic concept of man presents him as a being basically concerned with maintaining or restoring his inner equilibrium, and in order to do so, he is trying to gratify his drives and satisfy his instincts. Even in the perspective in which man has been portrayed by Jungian psychology, human motivation is interpreted along this line. Just think of archetypes. They, too, are mythical beings (as Freud called the instincts). Again man is seen as bent on getting rid of tensions, be they aroused by drives and instincts claiming their gratification and satisfaction, or by archetypes urging their materialization. In either case, reality, the world of beings and meanings, is debased and degraded to a pool of more or less workable instruments to be used to get rid of various stimuli such as irritating superegos or archetypes. What has been sacrificed, however, and hence totally eliminated in this view of man, is the fundamental fact which lends itself to a phenomenological analysis—namely, that man is a being encountering other beings and reaching out for meanings to fulfill.

And this is precisely the reason why I speak of a will to meaning rather than a need for meaning or a drive to meaning. If man were really driven to meaning he would embark on meaning fulfillment solely for the sake of getting rid of this drive, in order to restore homeostasis within himself. At the same time, however, he would no longer be really concerned with meaning itself but rather with his own equilibrium and thus, in the final analysis, with himself.

It may now have become clear that a concept such as self-actualization, or self-realization, is not a sufficient ground for a motivational theory. This is mainly due to the fact that self-actualization, like power and pleasure, also belongs to the class of phenomena which can only be obtained as a side effect and are thwarted precisely to the degree to which they are made a matter of direct intention. Self-actualization is a good thing; however, I maintain that man can only actualize himself to the extent to which he fulfills meaning. Then self-actualization occurs spontaneously; it is contravened when it is made an end in itself.

When I was lecturing at Melbourne University some years ago, I was given as a souvenir an Australian boomerang. While contemplating this unusual gift, it occurred to me that in a sense it was a symbol of human existence. Generally, one assumes that a boomerang returns to the hunter; but actually, I have been told in Australia, a boomerang only comes back to the hunter when it has missed its target, the prey. Well, man also only returns to himself, to being concerned with his self, after he has missed his mission, has failed to find a meaning in his life.

Ernest Keen, one of my assistants during a teaching period at the Harvard Summer Session, devoted his doctoral dissertation to demonstrating that the shortcomings of Freudian psychoanalysis have been compensated for by Heinz Hartmann's ego psychology, and the deficiencies of ego psychology, in turn, by Erikson's identity concept. However, Keen contends, a last link was still missing, and this link is logotherapy. In fact, it is my conviction that man should not, indeed cannot, struggle for identity in a direct way; he rather finds identity to the extent to which he commits himself to something beyond himself, to a cause greater than himself. No one has put it as cogently as Karl Jaspers did when he said: "What man is, he ultimately becomes through the cause which he has made his own.". . .

The otherness of the other being should not be blurred in existential thinking, as Erwin Straus has so rightly stressed; and this also holds true for meaning. The meaning which a being has to fulfill is something beyond himself, it is never just himself. Only if this otherness is retained by meaning, can meaning exert upon a being that demand quality which yields itself to a phenomenological analysis of our experience of existence. Only a meaning which is not just an expression of the being itself represents a true challenge. You remember the story in the Bible: When the Israelites wandered through the desert God's glory went before in the form of a cloud; only in this way was it possible for the Israelites to be guided by God. Imagine, on the other hand, what would have happened if God's presence, the cloud, had dwelled in the midst of Israelites; rather than leading them the right way, this cloud would have clouded everything, and the Israelites would have gone astray.

In other words, meaning must not coincide with being; meaning must be ahead of being. Meaning sets the pace for being. Existence falters unless it is lived in terms of transcendence toward something beyond itself. Viewed from this angle, we might distinguish between people who are pacemakers and those who are peacemakers: the former confront us with meanings and values, thus supporting our meaning orientation; the latter alleviate the burden of meaning confrontation. In this sense Moses was a pacemaker; he did not soothe man's conscience but rather stirred it up. Moses confronted his people with the Ten Commandments and did not spare them confrontation with ideals and values. Peacemakers, on the other hand, appease people; they try to reconcile them with themselves. "Let's face facts," they say. "Why worry about your shortcomings? Only a minority live up to ideals. So let's forget them; let's care for peace of mind, or soul, rather than those existential meanings which just arouse tensions in human beings."

What the peacemakers overlook is the wisdom laid down in Goethe's warning: "If we take man as he is, we make him worse; if we take him as he ought to be, we help him become it."

Once meaning orientation turns into meaning confrontation, that stage of maturation and development is reached in which freedom—that concept so much emphasized by existentialist philosophy—becomes responsibleness. Man is responsible for the fulfillment of the specific meaning of his personal life. But he is also responsible *before* something, or *to* something, be it society, or humanity, or mankind, or his own conscience. However, there is a significant number of people who interpret their own existence not just in terms of being responsible to something but rather to someone, namely to God.[3]

Logotherapy, as a secular theory and medical practice, must restrict itself to factual statements, leaving to the patient the decision as to how to understand his own being-responsible: whether along the lines of religious beliefs or agnostic convictions. Logotherapy must remain available for everyone; I would be obliged to adhere to this by my Hippocratic oath, if for no other reason. Logotherapy is applicable in cases of atheistic patients and usable in the hands of atheistic doctors. In any case, logotherapy sees in responsibleness the very essence of human existence. Capitalizing on responsibleness to this extent, a logotherapist cannot spare his patient the decision for what, and to what, or to whom, he feels responsible.

A logotherapist is not entitled consciously to influence the patient's decision as to how to interpret his own responsibleness, or as to what to embrace as his personal meaning. Anyone's conscience, as anything human, is subject to error; but this does not release man from his obligation to obey it—existence involves the risk of error. Man must risk committing himself to a cause not worthy of his commitment. Perhaps my commitment to the cause of logotherapy is erroneous. But I prefer to live in a world in which man has the right to make choices, even if they are wrong choices, rather than a world in which no choice at all is left to him. In other words, I prefer a world in which, on the one hand, a phenomenon such as Adolf Hitler can occur, and on the other hand, phenomena such as the many saints who have lived can occur also. I prefer this world to a world of total, or totalitarian, conformism and collectivism in which man is debased and degraded to a mere functionary of a party or the state.

The Meaning of Life

We have now reached the point of the third basic assumption: After discussing freedom of will and will to meaning, meaning itself becomes the topic.

While no logotherapist *prescribes* a meaning he may well *describe* it. By this I mean describing what is going on in a man when he experiences something as meaningful, without applying to such experiences any preconceived pattern of interpretation. In short, our task is to resort to a phenomenological investigation of the immediate data of actual life experience. In a phenomenological way, the logotherapist might widen and broaden the visual field of his patient in terms of meanings and values, making them loom large, as it were. In the course of a growing awareness, it might then finally turn out that life never ceases to hold and retain a meaning up to its very last moment. This is due to the fact that, as a phenomenological analysis can show us, man not only finds his life meaningful through his deeds, his works, his creativity, but also through his experiences, his encounters with what is true, good, and beautiful in the world, and last but not least, his encounter with others, with fellow human beings and their unique qualities. To grasp another person in his uniqueness means to love him. But even in a situation in which man is deprived of both creativity and receptivity, he can still fulfill a meaning in his life. It is precisely when facing such a fate, when being confronted with a hopeless situation, that man is given a last opportunity to fulfill a meaning—to realize even the highest value, to fulfill even the deepest meaning—and that is the meaning of suffering.[4]

Let me summarize. Life can be made meaningful in a threefold way: first, through *what we give* to life (in terms of our creative works); second, by *what we take* from the world (in terms of our experiencing values); and third, through *the stand we take* toward a fate we no longer can change (an incurable disease, an inoperable cancer, or the like). However, even apart from this, man is not spared facing his human condition which includes what I call the tragic triad of human existence; namely, pain, death, and guilt. By pain, I mean suffering; by the two other constituents of the tragic triad, I mean the twofold fact of man's mortality and fallibility.

Stressing these tragic aspects of man's life is not as superfluous as it may seem to be at first sight. In particular, the fear of aging and dying is pervasive in the present culture, and Edith Weisskopf-Joelson, professor of psychology at Duke University, has claimed that logotherapy might help counteract these particularly widespread American anxieties. As a matter of fact, it is my contention, and a tenet of logotherapy, that life's transitoriness does not in the least detract from its meaningfulness. The same holds for man's fallibility. So there is no need to reinforce our patients' escapism in the face of the tragic triad of existence. . . .

It is not the least task of psychotherapy to bring about reconciliation and to bring consolation: Man has to be reconciled to his finiteness, and he also has to be enabled to face the transitoriness of his life. With these efforts psychotherapy indeed touches the realm of religion. There is common ground enough to warrant mutual rapprochement. Bridging, however, does not mean merging. There still remains the essential difference between the respective aims of psychotherapy and religion. The goal of psychotherapy, of psychiatry and, quite generally, of medicine, is health. The goal of religion, however, is something essentially different: salvation. So much for the difference of goals. The results achieved, however, are another matter. Although religion may not aim at mental health it might result in it. Psychotherapy, in turn, often results in an analogous by-product; while the doctor is not, and must not be, concerned with helping the patient to regain his belief in God, time and again this is just what occurs, unintended and unexpected as it is.

How, then, does this occur in the actual situation? Let me return to the logotherapeutic group session, or logodrama, which I mentioned before. During the discussion of the meaning of suffering I asked the whole group whether an ape which is punctured many times in order to develop poliomyelitis serum is able to grasp the meaning of its suffering. Unanimously the group replied, "Of course it would not! For with its limited intelligence it cannot enter the world of man, i.e., that world in which its suffering would be understandable." I then pressed on with the following: "And what about man? Are you sure that the human world is the terminal point in the evolution of the cosmos? Is it not conceivable that there is still another dimension, a world beyond man's world; a world in which the question of an ultimate meaning to man's suffering is answered?"

By its very nature this ultimate meaning exceeds man's limited intellectual capacity. In contrast to those existential writers who declare that man has to stand the ultimate absurdity of being human, it is my contention that man has to stand only his incapacity to grasp the ultimate meaning on intellectual grounds. Man is only called upon to decide between the alternatives of "ultimate absurdity or ultimate meaning" on existential grounds, through the mode of existence which he chooses. In the "How" of existence, I would say, lies the answer to the question for its "Why."

Thus, the ultimate meaning is no longer a matter of intellectual cognition but of existential commitment. One might as well say that a meaning can be understood but that the ultimate meaning must be interpreted. An interpretation, however, involves a decision. . . .

Man cannot avoid decisions. Reality inescapably forces man to decide. Man makes decisions in every moment, even unwittingly and against his will. Through these decisions man decides upon himself. Continually and incessantly he shapes and reshapes himself. Thomas Aquinas' *"agere sequitur esse"* is but half the truth: Man not only behaves according to what he is, he also becomes what he is according to how he behaves. Man is not a thing among others—things determine each other—but man is ultimately self-determining. What he becomes —within the limits of endowment and environment—he has made himself. In the living laboratories of the concentration camps we watched comrades behaving like swine while others behaved like saints. Man has both these potentialities within himself. Which one he actualizes depends on decision, not on conditions. It is time that this decision quality of human existence be included in our definition of man. Our generation has come to know man as he really is: the being that has invented the gas chambers of Auschwitz, and also the being who entered those gas chambers upright, the Lord's Prayer or the *Shema Yisrael* on his lips.

Notes

1. *Beyond the Chains of Illusion* (New York: Simon & Schuster, Inc., 1962), p. 38.

2. *Personality and Social Encounter* (Boston: Beacon Press, 1960), p. 103.

3. I personally doubt whether, within religion, truth can ever be distinguished from untruth by evidence which is universally acceptable to man. It seems to me that the various religious denominations are something like different languages. It is not possible, either, to declare that any one of them is superior to the others. Similarly, no language can justifiably be called "true" or "false," but through each of them truth—the one truth—may be approached as if from different sides, and through each language it is also possible to err, and even to lie.

4. It goes without saying that suffering can be meaningful only if the situation cannot be changed—otherwise we would not be dealing with heroism but rather masochism.

Frankl's Works

Psychotherapy and Existentialism. N.Y.: Simon and Schuster, 1968.

The Will to Meaning. N.Y.: New American Library, 1969.

Man's Search for Meaning. An Introduction to Logotherapy. N.Y.: Simon and Schuster, 1970.

The Doctor and the Soul. From Psychotherapy to Logotherapy. N.Y.: Randon House, 1973.

The Unconscious God. N.Y.: Simon and Schuster, 1976.

The Unheard Cry For Meaning. Psychotherapy and Humanism. N.Y.: Simon and Schuster, 1978.

"Man's Search For Ultimate Meaning," in *The Way to Self-Knowledge,* eds. Jacob Needleman and Dennis Lewis, N.Y.: Knopf, 1978.

On Frankl

Joseph B. Fabry, *The Pursuit of Meaning. Viktor Frankl, Logotherapy and Life.* N.Y.: Harper and Row, 1980.

Andrew Reid Fuller, *Psychology and Religion: Eight Points of View.* Washington, D.C.: University Press of America, 1977, 98–113. Fine summary.

A. Sutich and M. Vich, eds., *Readings in Humanistic Psychology.* N.Y.: Free Press, 1969. Chapters 5 and 6, an exchange between Maslow and Frankl on self-actualization.

VI.
The Dynamism of the Spirit and the Infinite Within

W. Norris Clarke, S.J.

(Excerpt from W. Norris Clarke, S.J., *The Philosophical Approach to God.* Winston Salem, N.C.: Wake Forest University Press, 1981, pages 15–28.)

Editor's Note

We now move from the psychological to a more philosophical-theological approach. Immanuel Kant (1724–1804) had an influence on many of the psychologists treated in this book, such as Freud, Frankl, Fromm and Jung. Kant held that knowing involved two elements, one a priori, the other a posteriori. The a posteriori element is sense data. The a priori element consists of subjective categories which we impose on sense data. Examples of such a priori categories are time, space, substance and causality. To know, therefore, means to combine a posteriori sense data with a priori subjective categories. All our understanding comes through these categories as through grids.

The a posteriori data and the a priori categories are *finite,* and thus all knowledge or understanding is limited to sense experience which is finite. Kant distinguished between *phenomena* and the *noumenon* (plural: *noumena*). Phenomena are what understanding (we might say "science") attains. The noumenon is the thing-in-itself, such as God and the soul. Science or understanding can reach only phenomena and not noumena.

Kant's argument touches both metaphysics and all approaches to God by reason. For example, natural theology is the attempt to show by reason that God exists. But, Kant said, natural theology uses and is based upon the categories, especially that of causality. For example, natural theology says that all finite reality needs a First or Infinite Cause. But Kant said that all deduction from finite effects to an Infinite God is impossible. From the finite one reaches only the finite. Thus, from theoretical reason alone, one reaches only the world of finite experience and not God. (For Kant, intuition or immediate knowledge without the use of logical deduction or inference exists only in *sense* knowledge. There is no such thing as *intellectual* intuition or immediate knowledge of God's existence through the intellect.)

However, Kant was a theist and he said that there was a kind of *practical reason* through which one could *postulate* the existence of God. Practical reason produces judgments under the influence of the unconditional moral commands of the conscience, as well as one's desires and emotional needs in living. God may be postulated by practical reason. That is, one can say God *ought to be* (practical reason) if the moral law is to make sense, but one cannot say that God *is* (theoretical reason). Kant said that a moral being deserves to be happy. But this does not always happen in this life. Therefore, we legitimately postulate the existence of a Being who will bring about the identity between morality and happiness. Our ethical imperatives seem to postulate a God.

The Transcendental Thomists (a current of thinking running from Maurice Blondel at the turn of the century, to Joseph Maréchal, to Karl Rahner and others today) believe that Kant did not push his analysis deeply enough. A basic tenet of this school is that one should consider not only the *content* of the mind, or the *object* of desire, but also and more fundamentally the *dynamic movement* of the mind and will. The model of the self or person used here is that of body-spirit. This includes memory, willing (ranging from superficial wishes to the deep primordial will), feeling (ranging from surface feeling to one's deepest emotions and affectivity), and intellect (ranging from logical, discursive reasoning to intellectual intuition). At the center of the person or self is a dynamic fusion of body, memory, affective will and intuition. This is called by various authors "heart," "spirit," "imagination" or "intuition."

In the following excerpt, W. Norris Clarke, S.J., professor of philosophy at Fordham University, explains the main thrust of Transcendental Thomism. There is a dynamic movement in the spirit which has infinite characteristics. The only sufficient reason for this activity is the presence and attracting power of Infinite Goodness within the person. (This is more primordial than Kant's a priori categories, if they exist.) Fr. Clarke introduces an option into this framework. This option is required in the midst of the contemporary mistrust of metaphysics and where there is a vital awareness of human freedom and its capacity for a radical option that the universe does not make sense.

With regard to Freud, notice that in the following approach God would not be the substitute for the father, but the father (or mother) would be the first substitute for God.

* * *

The essence of the Transcendental Thomist approach to God seems to me to be this: it has brought out of obscurity into full development St. Thomas's own profound doctrine of the dynamism of the human spirit, both as intellect and will, toward the Infinite—a dynamism inscribed in the very nature of man as *a priori* condition of possibility of both his knowing and his willing activities—and then applied this doctrine to ground epistemology, philosophical anthropology, metaphysics, and the flowering of the latter into natural theology. Using this radical dynamism of the human spirit to illuminate the foundations of the whole of Thomistic philosophy—in particular the rational ascent to God—was entirely in harmony with St. Thomas's own deepest thought. Let me now present briefly the essential core of this analysis, insofar as I myself can take philosophical responsibility for it and make it my own.

THE ASCENT THROUGH THE
DYNAMISM OF THE INTELLECT

As we reflect on the activities of our knowing power, we come to recognize it as an inexhaustible dynamism of inquiry, ever searching to lay hold more deeply and widely on the universe of reality. It is impossible to restrict its horizon of inquiry to any limited area of reality, to any goal short of all that there is to know about all that there is. For our experience of knowing reveals to us that each time we come to know some new object or aspect of reality we rest in it at first, savoring and exploring its intelligibility as far as we can. But as soon as we run up against its limits and discover that it is finite, the mind at once rebounds farther, reaching beyond it to wherever else it leads, to whatever else there is to be known beyond it. This process continues indefinitely in ever-expanding and ever-deepening circles. As we reflect on the significance of this inexhaustible and unquenchable drive toward the fullness of all there is to know, we realize that the only adequate goal of our dynamism of knowing is the totality of all being. We live mentally, therefore, as they express it, in "the horizon of being"—or, as St. Thomas himself puts it in his own technical terminology, the only adequate formal object of the human mind is being itself.

This means that the mind must have a dynamic *a priori* orientation, an aptitude or affinity, for all that is, for the totality of being—an aptitude that constitutes it precisely as a knowing nature in the intellectual and not merely the sensible order. Now every dynamism or active potency, St. Thomas holds, has its goal already inscribed in it in some way, in the mode of final cause, as that toward which it naturally tends, as that which naturally attracts or draws it to itself, and therefore as that which is somehow already present to it. In a dynamism which is as self-aware as ours is—aware not only of the contents of its knowledge, but also of its own activity of knowing and radical desire to know—there must accordingly be a dim, obscure, implicit, but nonetheless real awareness of this goal as drawing it.

This means that the mind has, from its first conscious movement from emptiness toward fulfillment, a kind of implicit, pre-conceptual, anticipatory grasp or foretaste of being as the encompassing horizon and goal of all its inquires. As Karl Rahner and the Germans like to put it, this is not a *Begriff* (i.e., an explicit, thematized concept or distinct idea of being); it is rather a *Vorgriff* (i.e, a pre-conceptual, implicit, unthematized, anticipatory awareness of being present to the mind as its goal, as its connatural good drawing it). This is to live mentally within the horizon of being. It is because of this innate *a priori* orientation that all our questions are directed toward being: "*Is* this the case? What *is* this? How *is* it?" All the answers, too, to our determinate inquiries are framed against the background of being. All our judgments reflect, at least implicitly, this insertion of our knowledge into the horizon of being. The "is" of being is the hidden backdrop and frame of all our assertions. We continually say, "This *is*, that *is*, this *is* such and such." and by so doing we insert some limited essence or aspect of the real in its place in the whole of being. Thus we assert implicitly the participation of all finite essences or modes of being in the ultimate, all-pervasive attribute of all things, the very act of presence or existence itself, expressed by the inconspicuous but omnipresent "is" that in some equivalent way is the inner form of all human judgments.

This *a priori* orientation toward being—with its implicit pre-conceptual awareness of being by connatural affinity and desire, as we know a good by being drawn to it—is a genuine *a priori* presence of being to the human mind constitutive of its very nature as a dynamic faculty. It is not, however, a Cartesian innate idea, since it is not present as a clear and distinct conceptual content, and takes a long experience of conscious, reflective knowing before it can emerge into explicit conscious awareness expressible in conceptual form. The entire mental life of man consists in gradually filling in this at first conceptually empty and indeterminate but limitless horizon of being with increasingly determinate conceptual comprehension, as we step by step come to know one part of this totality after another.

Let us further analyze this vague and indeterminate horizon of being which defines ahead of time the whole enterprise of human knowing and is present to it in an implicit, pre-conceptual lived awareness, as a connatural attracting goal, from the first breath of intellectual life.

The first point we notice is that no limits can be set to this field of intentionality, this anticipated horizon of being. Any attempt to do so immediately stimulates the mind to leap beyond these limits in intentional thrust and desire. Thus this horizon or totality of being-to-be-known appears at first as an indefinite, indeterminate, but unlimited and unlimitable field, a field to which no determinate limits can be set.

What is the actual content of this field? There are only two alternatives. If the actual content of being is nothing but an endless or indefinite field of *all finite* entities or intelligible structures, the dynamism of the mind is doomed to endless rebounding from one finite to another, with no final satisfaction or unqualified fulfillment ever attainable, or even possible. Our restless, unquenchable search has no actually existing final goal. It trails off endlessly into ever-receding, always finite horizons, its inexhaustible abyss of longing and capacity ever unfilled and in principle unfillable. Once we postulate that this situation is definitive and cannot be overcome—that there is no proportion between the depths of our capacity, the reach of our mind, and what there is for it actually to grasp—the very possibility arouses a profound metaphysical restlessness and sadness within us; the dynamism of our mind turns out to be a strange existential surd, an anomaly. It is a dynamism ordered precisely toward a non-existent goal; a drive through all finites toward nothing; an innate, inextinguishable summons to frustration: a living absurdity. Sartre would indeed be right.

The other possibility is that somewhere hidden within this unlimited horizon of being there exists an actually infinite Plenitude of Being, in which all other beings participate yet of which they are but imperfect images. This actually Infinite Plenitude St. Thomas describes not as a particular being—with its connotation of determinate limits setting it off from other equally finite beings—but rather as the pure subsistent plenitude of be-ing, of the act of existence itself, *Ipsum Esse Subsistens*, pure subsistent to-be. It now becomes the adequate, totally fulfilling goal of the dynamism of our minds, matching superabundantly the inexhaustible abyss of our own capacity and desire to know: one abyss, a negative one, calling out to another, a positive one. As the German mystical poet Angelus Silesius so beautifully put it, "The abyss in me calls out to the abyss in God. Tell me, which is deeper?" The existence of this Infinite Center of being (obviously it would have to be *actually existent,* for if it were merely possible, nothing else could bring it into existence and it would be in fact impossible) now gives full intelligibility to the horizon of being itself, as its unifying center and source, and also confers full and magnificent intelligibility on the natural dynamism of my mind and the whole intellectual life arising out of it. This implies, of course, that it is in some way possible, if only as a loving gift originating from the Center, for me to achieve actual union with this ultimate fullness, the ultimate *Whereunto* of my whole intellectual life.

At this point the objection naturally arises—and it deserves the most careful consideration and personal reflection to test out its validity concretely in our inner life—why there cannot be a *third* alternative. Why could it not be that the human mind would be adequately fulfilled and entirely content as long as it was assured of an unending series of finites to know and enjoy, assured of inexhaustible novelty? I am well aware that such an alternative may seem plausible at first blush. But working through it carefully in a thought experiment will, I think, show clearly enough that it must finally collapse. Such an alternative must be set in a framework of immortality and eternity of time; otherwise the series would come to an end without fulfillment; fulfillment depends necessarily in this conception on the *unending* sequence. In this perspective, surely a series of endless repetitions of the same *kind* of finite satisfactions, a mere quantitative repetition, would eventually pall on us and leave us open again to a profound and insatiable restlessness. For the human mind—and will—has a remarkable and wonderful capacity to transcend whole series at a time, to sum up their quality if not their quantity; and if the former remains always finite, the mind at once leaps beyond the whole series questing for a qualitatively *more*, a *richer*.

To sum up the whole point I am making, we have not really taken full possession of our own inner dynamism of inquiry until we keep penetrating to its profoundest depths and suddenly become aware in a kind of flash of self-discovery precisely that its very nature *is* to be an inexhaustible abyss that can comprehend and leap beyond any finite or series of finites, unending or not. This involves perhaps more existential self-discovery than logical or abstract reasoning.

The last point I would like to make is that for many people the notion of an Infinite Plenitude and union with it carries with it a certain block, because this is conceived as a static state—finished once and for all with nothing further going on, carrying with it its own hint of boredom. But there is no reason at all to conceive the infinite and total fulfillment through union with it in this way. It is more natural to think of it as a fullness out of which continually and spontaneously overflow free creative *expressions* of ecstatic joy. These are not *necessary steps on the way* to achieve fulfillment, but a natural spontaneous overflow of *expression* because we *have reached* it. There would still be endless novelty, but no longer as fulfilling ever-unsatiated *need*.

Now that we have again reduced our ultimate alternatives to two, the crucial question arises: which of these two is actually the case? Which should I opt for? Which is the more reasonable to opt for? On the one hand is the acceptance of myself, in the profoundest depths of my intellectual nature, as a living frustration, an existential absurdity, ordered ineluctably toward a simply non-existent goal, magnetized, so to speak, by the abyss of nothingness, of what is not and can never be—a dynamism doomed eternally to temporary gratification but permanent unfulfillment. On the other hand lies the acceptance of my nature as drawn, magnetized toward an actually existing, totally fulfilling goal, which confers upon it total and magnificent meaningfulness and opens out before it a destiny filled with inexhaustible light and hope. On the one hand, the darkness of ultimate nothingness of what can never be; on the other, the fullness of ultimate Light, which already awaits our coming.

How is this most radical of all options to be decided? The founder of Transcendental Thomism, Joseph Maréchal—and perhaps most others in this tradition—insist that the structure of human thought as oriented toward Infinite Being is a necessary *a priori* structure or condition of possibility of all our thinking. We cannot help, if we think at all, living in the limitless horizon of being and tending toward the fullness of being as fulfilling goal; we cannot help but make all our judgments by affirming every finite being against the implicit background of the infinite, as stepping-stones toward the infinite. "Man is an embodied affirmation of the Infinite," as Father Donceel likes to put it. We can conceptually and verbally deny the existence of this Infinite as the ultimate *Whereunto* of our whole drive to know. But the very exercise of the mind even in the most ordinary everyday affirmation implicitly reaffirms what we explicitly deny, putting us not in a logical but in a lived contradiction with ourselves. We are committed *a priori*, by

nature, to the affirmation of the reality of the infinite—whether
we call it by the term "being" or some other, or only point to it
in eloquent silence—no matter how much we deny it on the
conscious, explicit level of our knowing.

There is much to be said for this strong position. However,
I myself prefer to dig a little deeper, if possible, and move the
option into the realm of a radical existential decision in the
order of freedom, of free self-assumption of our own nature as
gift. For it does seem that the above argument for the rigorous
necessity of this implicit affirmation of God in all knowing rests
on the tacit assumption that the dynamism of my intelligence
does actually make ultimate sense, is not a radical absurdity,
and hence must have some really existing final goal, since an
existing dynamism without goal would be unintelligible. Yet
modern man—as Sartre, Camus, and others have shown us
—does seem to have an astonishing capacity for self-negation
as well as self-affirmation, irrational as this may be. Man is the
being who can affirm or deny his own rationality.

Hence it seems to me that there is no *logical argument* by
which one can be *forced* to choose one side of the option rather
than the other, light rather than darkness. The issue lies beyond the level of rational or logical argument, because it is at
the root of all rationality. Hence I would like to propose it as a
radical option open to man's freedom, where he is free to
assume his own rational nature as gift and follow its natural call
to total fulfillment, or else to reject this call and refuse to
commit himself, on the level of conscious affirmation and de-
liberately lived belief, to the summons of his nature calling
from the depths of the dynamism of intelligence as such. All
the light lies on one side, and our whole nature positively pulls
us in this direction; only ultimate darkness lies on the other,
and cannot pull us as either rational or good. But we do remain
free, I am willing to allow, to make this radical assumption, to
accept our own nature, or to reject it. This existential choice,
obscure and implicit though it may be (and though it may never
reach the conceptual clarity and explicitness of a choice for
"God" or "no God"), is still the most important choice of our
lives, giving ultimate form and meaning to the whole.

If I accept and listen to this radical innate pull of my nature as intellectual being, if I accept this nature gratefully and humbly as a gift, I will affirm with conviction the existence of the ultimate Fullness and Center of all being, the lodestar that draws my intelligence ever onward, even though this ultimate goal remains for me at present only obscurely discerned, seen through a mirror darkly, pointed to beyond all conceptual grasp as the mystery of inexhaustible Light, a Light that with my present, body-obscured vision I cannot directly penetrate or master with my own powers, but that renders all else intelligible.

THE ASCENT THROUGH THE
DYNAMISM OF THE WILL

The same process of discovery works even more powerfully and effectively—from the point of view of its psychological impact—when applied to the correlative dynamism of the human will, operating within the limitless horizon of being as the good, as the valuable and lovable. Reflecting on the operation of my human will, I come to discover or unveil the nature of this faculty, or active potency in Thomistic terms, as an unrestricted and inexhaustible drive toward the good, as presented by my intelligence. Our entire life of willing, desiring, loving, avoiding, is carried on within the horizon of the good, the formal object of the will as such. But this horizon of being as the good, like that of being as truth for the intellect, reveals itself to be also unlimited, unbounded. The process of discovery is similar. Each time we take possession of some new finite good, we are temporarily satisfied as we explore and enjoy its goodness for us. But again, as soon as we discover its limits, its finitude, our wills at once spontaneously rebound beyond, in prospective desire and longing for further fulfillment. Over and over throughout our lives this process is repeated.

Reflecting now on this process as a whole, we can disengage its meaning in the light of its final cause or goal. Its ultimate goal, through which alone this dynamism—like any dynamism—is rendered intelligible, can be nothing less than the totality of the good, whatever that may turn out to be.

There is, therefore, in the will a dynamic *a priori* orientation toward the good as such—i.e., a natural affinity, connaturality, aptitude for the good, which is written into the very nature of the will as dynamic faculty before any particular experience of an individual good, and defines this nature as such. Everything it desires and loves it loves *as good,* as situated within this all-embracing horizon of the good, as participating in some way in the transcendental character of goodness.

Now this *a priori* orientation and natural affinity for the good implies that the will, in order to recognize and respond to a good when it finds it, must have written within it—analogously to the intellect—a pre-conceptual "background consciousness," an anticipatory grasp—unthematized or implicit, obscure and indistinct—of the good as somehow present in its very depths, magnetizing and attracting it, luring it on to actual fulfillment of its innate potentiality by distinct conscious appropriations of actually existing concrete goods. This is what it means to live volitively in the horizon of the good. The entire life of the will consists in filling in determinately and concretely this unbounded, all-embracing, indeterminate, intentional horizon of the good as anticipated field of all possible fulfillment. As Plato said long ago in the *Meno,* in one of his profoundest insights, in any inquiry or search, unless we somehow dimly and implicitly knew ahead of time what we were looking for, we would never recognize an answer *as* an answer to our search. The passage is not from total non-knowledge or absence of the good to knowledge or presence, but from implicit and indistinct to explicit and distinct awareness. As St. Thomas put it in a striking formula, often highlighted by Transcendental Thomists, "Every knower knows God implicitly in anything it knows." Similarly, every will implicitly loves God in anything it loves.

We must now analyze more precisely what must be the content of this unlimited horizon of the good, ever-present by anticipation as implicit "background consciousness" in the will and drawing it like a lodestar or hidden magnet. This analysis can be set, if one wishes, in the outer form of an Aristotelian demonstration; but in fact its inner soul is the drawing out into explicitness of what is already necessarily contained implicitly in the life of the will, if the latter is not to collapse into unintelligibility. The horizon of the good appears to us first as a vague, indefinite, indeterminate totality. It must be somehow a unity, first because of the analogous similarity of all that draws the will *as good*, second because the unity of any dynamism or active potency is at least partly dependent on the unity of its goal. A totally unrelated multiplicity of final goals would fragment the unity of the dynamism into an unintelligible, unintegrated multiplicity of drives. Now as we analyze the dynamism of the will, as above, we discover that no finite particular good can be its adequate final goal, for it at once rebounds beyond any finite object once its limits have been discovered. And just as no one finite can satisfy adequately this drive, neither can any sum of all finite members, not even an endless series of all finite goods. Once the mind has gathered, in a single synthetic act of comprehension, the meaning of the whole series, and realizes that this is all there ever will be, or can be, it then becomes clear that the will would be doomed to an endless unfulfilledness; it would be an unfillable, insatiable abyss of longing—in a word, an ultimate frustration, an onto-logical surd. It would be an actually existing dynamism, or-dered by an *a priori* orientation constitutive of its very nature—about which, therefore, it can do nothing—ordered precisely toward a non-existent final goal; an active potency ordered toward nothing proportionate to its potentiality; an innate drive toward nothing.

The only other alternative is that within this limitless, indeterminate horizon of the good lies hidden as its center and source an actually existing Infinite Plenitude of Goodness, not this or that particular good, but the Good itself, subsisting in its all its essential unparticipated fullness, from which all finite goods possess their limited goodness by participation. In this case the dynamism of the human will takes on ultimate and magnificent sense, is ordered toward a totally fulfilling final goal which must be at least possible for it to obtain (whether by its own power or by free gift is not yet clear), and the whole of human life takes on the structure of hope rather than of frustra-tion and absurdity.

Again, as in the case of the drive of the intellect toward

being as truth, we are brought up against a radical option. To which alternative shall we—ought we—commit ourselves? Again, some of the Transcendental Thomists say that whether we like it or not we are committed by the dynamism of final causality built into our nature to affirm implicitly the *actual existence* of the Infinite Good, since if it were only possible it would actually be impossible, as we have seen. If we deny it on the conscious conceptual and verbal level, as we are free to do, we put ourselves in a state of lived—not logical—contradiction between the actual use of our power of willing and what we say about it. As St. Thomas would say, all lovers implicitly love God in each thing they love.

But again, as I proposed above in the case of the intellect, this stand, impressive and defensible though it may be, still seems to me to presuppose as already accepted the intelligibility of the life of the will, and modern man has the ability to put the very intelligibility of his own nature radically in question. Hence I prefer again to propose the option as appealing to the radical freedom of each human person to assume or reject, freely, the ultimate meaningfulness of his or her own human nature as power of willing and loving the good. No *logical* argument can force me to choose one alternative over the other. Yet the luminous fullness of meaningfulness draws me with the whole spontaneous pull of my nature toward the real existence of the Infinite Good as a magnet fully adequate to, even far exceeding, the profoundest imaginable reaches of my capacity for love. Full intelligibility lies only this way. On the other side, there is only the prospect of an endless chain of unfinished and unfinishable business, trailing off into the darkness of ultimate frustration—an abyss to whose profoundest longing cry there can be no responsive echo. If I humbly and gratefully accept my nature with its natural pull toward the Infinite as a meaningful gift, I will commit myself to affirm —and to reach out with anticipatory, hope-filled love toward—a Center of Infinite Goodness as actually existing and somehow possible for me to be united with, though veiled from me at present in mystery.

This approach to God through the dynamism of the will toward the good has a far more powerful appeal to most people than the approach through the intellect alone as ordered toward truth. Many people, at least in certain moods and at certain times of their lives, feel that they could do without the fullness of knowledge; at least its drawing power is not overwhelming. But there is nobody, intellectual or not, who is not constantly and wholeheartedly longing for happiness. This is the deepest and most urgent of all drives in man—in fact, the dynamo behind all others. For as St. Thomas points out, unless possessing the truth appeared to us as a good attracting the will, we would not be drawn to seek knowledge at all.

I would like to share with you, as an example, an actual case from my own experience. One day I was being driven in a cab in New York City. The cab driver being very talkative, I decided to turn the conversation to some useful purpose. So I asked him if he was happy. "No, too many problems," he answered. "What would make you happy then?" I asked. "Give me a million dollars and all my problems would be solved. I'd be a happy man and could enjoy life." "All right," I replied, "you have the million dollars. Now what?" Then he said he would pay off all his debts. "All right, they are paid. Now what?" Then he said he would buy a house. Several, in fact. "Done," I replied. "Now what?" Then he got himself a nice wife—in fact several, in different cities. "Done. Now what?" Then he traveled, went through a whole long set of things he wanted to do; and each time I replied the same: "Granted. Now what?" Finally he began to quiet down. Then he suddenly turned all the way around, in the middle of traffic, giving me quite a scare, and said: "Say, there's something funny going on here. I can't seem to get to the bottom of all this. What am I really looking for after all?" He had suddenly totaled up the whole series, past *and to come,* and caught the point. Then I began . . .

DYNAMISM OF THE SPIRIT
AS THE IMAGE OF GOD IN MAN

Before leaving this topic, we should not fail to note that this Thomistic analysis of the dynamism of the spirit also

provides us with a profound metaphysical analysis of the ancient religious-mystical-philosophical doctrine of man as the
image of God, principally through the intellect and will. For
man to be truly the image of God in any strong sense, it would
seem appropriate (necessary?) that there be some mark or
manifestation of the divine infinity itself in man. This obviously
cannot be a positive infinite plenitude; that is proper to God
alone. But there can be an image of the divine infinity in
silhouette—in reverse, so to speak—within man, precisely in
his possession of an *infinite capacity* for God, or, more accurate-
ly, a capacity *for the Infinite,* which can be satisfied by nothing
less. This negative image points unerringly toward the positive
infinity of its original, and is intrinsically constituted by this
relation of tendential capacity. It is as though—as with the
ancient myths—God had broken the coin of His infinity in two,
holding on to the positive side Himself and giving us the
negative side, then launching us into the world of finites with
the mission to search until we have matched our half-coin with
His. By this only we shall know that we have reached the goal of
our lives, our final happiness.

In connection with this notion of the dynamism of the
spirit as a veiled revelation of ourselves as image of God, I
would like to share with you an interesting experiment I have
tried with marked success on many student groups and individual people. It is an attempt to answer the common complaint
one so often hears: why is it that God remains so obscure and
difficult to find? With His omnipotent power, you would think
it would be the easiest thing in the world for Him to reveal
Himself with perfect clarity to almost anybody, without having
to pass through the obscurity of faith or the difficulty of philosophical argument.

My answer is this. All right, suppose you are God, omniscient and omnipotent. Now suppose you wanted to manifest
your true nature to men, as *Infinite Spirit.* You can use any
means—but not faith, or direct mystical experience, because
most people are not prepared for that and could not receive it
or interpret it properly; it takes a long process of purification to
be able to receive it without distortion. You think it would be

such an easy job—if you were God. Go ahead and try. What would you do?

Some come up with sensational physical cures. I laugh, and point out that some higher space-man could do that. Others would produce great natural cataclysms, whirling planets, and so forth. I point out that these things do presuppose a much higher power than ours, but not an *infinite* power, let alone a pure spirit. I keep on knocking down every physical or psychic feat they produce as nowhere near the mark. When they have finally given up, I suggest that maybe it's not such an easy thing to do after all, even for God. Maybe God, too, has His own problems with self-manifestation to man.

Then I suggest that there may perhaps be only one way (one or two bright ones occasionally think of it first) even for God to do this: by leaving some mark of His infinity directly imprinted within us. But the only kind possible is a negative infinity of capacity and longing, which can only be matched by His own self, and hence, even though it gives us no positive clear picture of Him, nevertheless serves us as guide to eliminate all other contenders less than Himself for our final goal. Thus this apparently obscure way of revealing Himself may in fact be the best if not the only one available, given our situation and His. If we explore it all the way to its depths, our dynamism for the infinite turns out to be a remarkably eloquent reverse image and pointer toward God as He is in Himself, beyond all possible finites.

Readings

Henri Bouillard, *Blondel and Christianity*. Washington, D.C.: Corpus Books, 1969. 60–77 on Blondel.

Frederick Copelston, S.J., *History of Philosophy*, Vol. 6, Part II, *Kant*. Garden City, N.Y.: Doubleday, 1964. Especially 224ff.

Joseph Donceel, S.J., *The Searching Mind. An Introduction to a Philosophy of God*. (Notre Dame: U. of Notre Dame Press, 1979. 55ff. on Rahner; 93ff. on Blondel.

Joseph Donceel, S.J., "Can We Still Make a Case in Reason for the Existence of God?" in *God, Knowable and Unknowable*, Robert

Roth, S.J., ed., N.Y.: Fordham University Press, 1973. On the infinite in man, 175ff.

Louis Dupré, *The Other Dimension*. Garden City, N.Y.: Doubleday, 1972. Sees Rahner as showing merely an indefinite and not an infinite dynamism in man: 133ff.

C.S. Evans, *Subjectivity and Religious Belief*. Washington, D.C.: University Press of America, 1983. On Kant, 50ff.

John J. Heaney, "Meaning and Action: The Blondelian Spirit," in *Psyche and Spirit* (N.Y.: Paulist, 1973), 237–252.

William Kelly, S.J., *Karl Rahner. Discoverer in Theology*. Milwaukee: Marquette U. Press, 1980.

Hans Küng, *Does God Exist? An Answer for Today*. Garden City, N.Y.: Doubleday, 1980. 529ff.

Leo O'Donovan, S.J., ed., *A World of Grace*. N.Y.: Seabury, 1980. Esp. Chapters 2 and 3 on Rahner's thought.

Karl Rahner, *Foundations of Christian Faith. An Introduction to the Idea of Christianity*. N.Y.: Seabury, 1978, 51–71.

Nicholas Rescher, *The Primacy of Practice*. Oxford: Blackwell, 1973. The principle of sufficient reason, the basis of theoretical knowledge, is a principle of practical reason.

Karl-Heinz Weger, *Karl Rahner. An Introduction to His Theology*. N.Y.: Seabury, 1980, esp. 46–85.

VII.
The Psyche and the Cosmos: Pierre Teilhard de Chardin

John J. Heaney

There is an Infinite within the human. Maurice Blondel called it "the Beyond Within." But this Infinite cannot be the projection of the finite person. This insight emerges more clearly when we investigate the psyche in relation to the cosmos. There we find a Power which was in action before humans existed, and it cannot be the result of their projection.

A chapter on the psyche and the cosmos belongs in a work devoted to the study of the psyche because psyche and cosmos can no longer be radically separated. The very atoms in our bodies originated in solar furnaces. Carl Jung said, "Since psyche and matter are contained in one and the same world, and moreover are in continuous contact with one another and ultimately rest on irrepresentable, transcendental factors, it is not only possible but fairly probable even that psyche and matter are two different aspects of one and the same thing."[1]

Teilhard de Chardin demonstrated an intimate relationship between evolution, as seen by physics and biology, and psycho-cultural evolution. He wrote, "A natural connection is drawn between the two worlds of physics and psychology, hitherto supposed irreconcilable. Matter and consciousness are bound together; not in the sense that consciousness becomes directly measurable, but in the sense that it becomes organically and physically rooted in the same cosmic process with which physics is concerned."[2] Thus the journey within the psyche is complemented by the journey to the beyond.

Let us look at the journey to "the Beyond Within." We will

center on the ideas of the Jesuit paleontologist, Pierre Teilhard de Chardin (1818–1955). Our chief points of interest will be his notions of the universe as a domain of psychic consciousness, the "within" of the spirit, and the objective reality of God in this psychic universe.

Complexity Consciousness. Teilhard held that evolution has become conscious of itself in human beings, or "centers of consciousness." The human mind has discerned that as evolution progressed, matter became more complex.[3] On the microscopic level, matter moved from particles to atoms, to molecules, to cells, then to pluricellular creatures, and from the most primitive of these up to human centers of consciousness. On the macroscopic level of the heavens, matter moved from energy, to clouds of atoms, to stars. From the stars were formed the humble planets where the necessary requirements for human life existed.

Teilhard did not mean only that matter became organized into larger units, though this is usually involved. He was speaking about the complexity of the organization of matter, as in the human brain. To Teilhard's mind, evolution was in some sense designed for "centers of consciousness." At least, evolution only after "great struggle" gave birth to humankind. To characterize this process Teilhard coined the phrase "complexity consciousness." That is, as matter becomes more complex, it becomes more conscious. This is easily seen with regard to man. But did Teilhard mean that realities inferior to humans and animals are conscious?

The Within. Teilhard believed that nothing suddenly appeared higher up on the ladder of evolution that did not exist in some pre-form in earlier evolution. If "consciousness" appeared with man, something like it must have existed earlier. But it would be so tenuous and minimal that we could not detect it. He called this reality "the within."[4] For him, all non-artificial reality had a "within" as well as a "without." The "without" was what science studied. He did not imply that science does not penetrate deeply within matter, but that it was strictly quantitative. The within could be concluded to by reason as it pondered the results of science. It was reached by what he called a "hyperphysics," a kind of blend of science and philosophy.

This "within" might be defined as the interior organizing principle of an organism. It is the inner bonding power or principle of unification which makes a thing what it is. It is not itself precisely a physical energy but it is what gives energy its pattern. If we think of a cell, for example, the "within" is not the membrane, nor is it the code in the nucleus. The within is what determines the code.

Every thing, therefore, has its signature, as it were. In an atom, it is the rhythm of the field around the nucleus. The within is the organizer of this rhythm. Is the within conscious? Even the lowest fragment of matter has some inwardly organized action. Whatever is centered and acts has a within. In matter on the lowest level, as we know today, there is both organization and action. This action contains an element of unpredictability, loosely akin to freedom on the human level. Therefore, even in the smallest particles, there is a within, a reflection of consciousness which is found higher up on the human level. Teilhard, therefore, stretching the word and using it metaphorically to an extent, says that "psychism" is in all reality and all through the universe.

Teilhard said that science by its nature must analyze, that is, break up into parts.[5] But the within will not be found in the parts. The within is the organizing power of the totality. In reality nothing exists in broken up parts. There is some organizing reality or a within in everything. Science by its own limitations misses the whole of a reality. This becomes most evident when some scientists say that a person is a vial of chemicals worth so many dollars.

The Within in Things Reflects the Great Within or Omega. Teilhard believed that there had to be some deep reason for this apparently purposeful organizing power all through things and all through the universe. Because, as he saw it, the universe was "centering," there had to be some power to account for this organizing phenomenon. Notice that Teilhard did not see a sharp dichotomy between matter and spirit as many have in the past. Matter and spirit are not identical. But they are, as it were, on a continuum. At the lowest end is congealed matter. As matter rises higher and higher in its evolution, it becomes more complex and more perfect in its action. There are *jumps* between stages.[6] Finally there is spirit.

Teilhard believed that this process had to be organized by some power beyond matter. This power he called "Omega" or God.[7] Let us consider his thought on this point. For Teilhard energy is centering. We see it in the steady creative power in the universe which is more fundamental than the counter-evolutionary force of entropy. We see it in "planetization." We see it in the "noosphere" or the appearance of mind in the universe. "The universe is a collector and custodian of consciousness." We see it in "noogenesis" or the growth of mind, or what we might call culture. Teilhard did not separate the evolution of matter from the growth of culture as a process of evolution.

Love. Love is the highest activity which has arisen from evolution. "Considered in its full biological reality, love—that is to say, the affinity of being with being—is not peculiar to man. It is the general propensity of all life. . . . If there were no internal propensity to unite, even at the prodigiously rudimentary level—indeed in the molecule itself—it would be physically impossible for love to appear higher up, with us, in hominised form. . . . Love in all its subtleties is . . . the direct race marked on the heart of the element by the physical convergence of the universe upon itself."[8]

Now, common sense says that to love all and everyone is contradictory. But a universal love is not only psychologically possible. It is the only complete and final way in which we are able to love. But common sense is right in that it is impossible to give oneself to an anonymous number. The only way in which love can be explained and operate is if the universe ahead of us assumes a face and a heart.

This face and heart Teilhard calls "Omega." Omega is personal or hyper-personal. It is not dependent on the reversible law of energy or entropy. Omega initiates the centering of "the world's reflective particles." "But how could it exercise this action were it not in some sort loving and loveable *at this very moment?* Love, I said, dies in contact with the impersonal and the anonymous. With equal infallibility it becomes impoverished with remoteness in space and time. For love to be possible there must be co-existence. . . . A present and real noosphere goes with a present and real center. To be supremely attractive, Omega must be supremely present."[9] Omega alone is capable of uniting living beings in such a way as to complete and fulfill them, for it alone joins them by what is deepest in themselves. Omega is a distinct Center radiating at the core of a system of centers.

Design or Chance? Teilhard saw the universe as being organized or lured by Omega. From this aspect of luring the world forward, Omega is called "the Final Gatherer."[10] Out of evolution, the Final Gatherer has lured love, the highest production yet. The power behind the universe must be both Spirit and Loving, since it is the ground of these qualities. What Teilhard presents, admittedly in a much more scientific framework, sounds very much like the older argument from design. But the modern mind has problems with this approach to God. Teilhard himself was aware of the problem and his answer to it is intimated throughout his writings.

Let us look at the problem. Many thinkers say that what looks like design is really the result of many chance collisions of things, operating according to the laws of natural selection. Whatever is not lucky dies off. The results are really from chance but they look like design. For example, a Siberian tiger seems to be beautifully designed. But suppose that, when the climate of Siberia was warm, there were three types of Siberian tigers. When the climate changed, tiger number one had too short a coat to withstand the cold and died. Tiger number two had not enough speed to survive when other animals became scarce. Thus type number three, the beautiful Siberian tiger that we know, is very well suited to the region, but it is by chance. At least, so the objection runs.

To handle this problem, the approach from the Ultimate Gatherer, or from a designer, is in my opinion not enough. There must be added to it the idea of a Prime Mover. (Teilhard combined both approaches in speaking of "the Prime Mover Ahead."[11]) One must push further and further into the past. At each stage, one will find some organized beings and "chance" happenings, random mutations, climate changes, etc. One is finally forced back to the very beginning, however the world as we know it began. At that point, there already was structure and countless laws (order), laws of gravity, of light, of magnetic attraction, of speed, and of the interaction between orbits of atoms when they began to exist.

In such a world, how can one explain such and so many ordered realities. As Michael Novak, following Lonergan, has put it, "Without an intelligent source, the intelligibility of the real is mere accident and hence unintelligible."[12] Here we are at the central option in the intellectual life. Teilhard believed that the only reality which could account for such structuring was Mind, or Omega. We might say that just as our minds organize reality in thinking and perceive reality only through its being ordered (we could not fathom pure chaos), so there must be "behind" the universe something akin to Mind. No doubt Teilhard's religious faith played a central role in coming to this decision. But what is not often pointed out when this is re-marked upon is the fact that faith is not blind feeling. Faith too involves intelligence.

For Teilhard, then, the whole universe is, as it were, alive. Even matter isn't "dead." Teilhard's approach is often called "panentheism" (all in God). He once said, "The world is God's body." He did not mean this literally as if he were a pantheist. He took it in an extended sense. God's closeness to the world might be loosely compared to the relationship between body and spirit in us. We live in a "Divine Milieu."

Before we leave this point, let me mention that Teilhard held that chance in a certain sense also existed in the universe. There are "chance" happenings together with design.[13] He liked to call this "directed chance." Chance was designed into evolution. He said that evolution had "a constant direction" together with "a billionfold trial and error." The universe "gropes," he said. Groping implies a constant goal but a diversity of short run directions. "Chance" happenings represent something loosely akin to freedom on the human level. Creatures grope toward goals. Sometimes they meet dead ends and die out. But, without groping, there would be no advance in evolution unless God directed it like someone who winds up a toy. One of Teilhard's great principles was, "God makes things make themselves."

Evil. But there are not only the effects of lure and direction in the world. There is also disorder. There is evil. Some philosophers who approach this question say that God is either not omnipotent since he cannot prevent evil, or that he is not good since he allows evil to exist. Teilhard held that God is both good and omnipotent, and yet he cannot prevent evil in the world as he has arranged it. By this he meant that if human beings were to be free, then God cannot in this kind of a world prevent moral evil, which also results in pain and death. Secondly, if God set up a world in which matter was in evolution, there cannot be matter plus change and no friction. In the world God has set up, there cannot be a law of gravity which works only in a helpful way.

For Teilhard, all evil is disunion.[14] Evil is physical when there is deterioration in physical corruption, suffering and death. Evil is moral when disunion affects "the free zones of the soul." In an evolutionary world, God himself cannot prevent evil without counteracting his own purposes. On the physical level, everything that is not yet finished being organized must inevitably suffer in its lack of organization. On the moral level, sin is a statistical necessity in a multitude in a freely evolving world. This does not mean that any individual sins by necessity. The phrase "statistical necessity" is drawn from empirical observation and merely describes what in fact does happen. Evil exists at all levels and is the "ransom of progress."

Original Sin. Teilhard's view of original sin was very disturbing to many Christians when it was first presented. Before humans sinned, evil (physical) was already in the world.[15] Fossil evidence shows that animals died before the human species appeared. For Teilhard, there was, strictly speaking, no single Adam. "Adam" is a universalized symbol for the hidden universal law of perversion and reversion. "Adam" is a symbol of the human tendency against evolution. Just as there is entropy in the physical world, so there is the counterforce of "Adam" in the spiritual world. Christ is called "the second Adam" (2 Cor 1:20) because he reverses Adam's "no." He is the "yes," the "amen" to evolution. Teilhard saw "original sin" not so much a "fall" as a refusal to ascend. The fall is mankind's refusal to join in the evolutionary movement toward union and love. Just to be human means to possess a counter-evolutionary tendency.

Jesus. In order to unite to himself a world, God revealed his word in the person of Jesus, so that the goal could be seen to be not an abstract collectivity, not something, but Someone, for in Christ "the universe ahead of us assumes a face and a heart." The incarnation is the plunging of the divine unity into the ultimate depths of multiplicity.[16] This is the *kenosis* or self-emptying doctrine of St. Paul (Phil 2:6). For Teilhard, Jesus' act of redemption has been presented in a too negative manner.[17] The model used to explain redemption has been a juridical model of the rights of God and the penalties to be paid for offending God. This is an extremely inadequate model. Explaining Teilhard here, we might point out that to redeem means to buy back. The idea of buying back or paying a price implies that payment is made to someone. To whom was the price paid by Jesus? To Satan? He has no rights. To the Father? This is a strange and even barbaric image of God. Teilhard understands Jesus' mission within his picture of evolution as moving to unity. Jesus' purpose was not death precisely. He did not come to die or to choose death. His death came about as a result of the collision of absolute goodness with evil. Jesus' purpose was to lead human beings to oneness with God. As divinely chosen leader, his purpose was to unite, not primarily to suffer. But since the counter-evolutionary pull of evil was present in the world, union with God involved suffering as a necessary by-product. If a price was paid by Jesus, it was to the nature of reality. "Christ is he who structurally in himself and for all of us overcomes the resistance to unification offered by the multiple resistance to the rise of Spirit inherent in matter."

"With this approach . . . the cross would appear as symbolizing . . . the upward and laborious rise of all creation." The cross is not a symbol of sadness, of limitation and repression. It is the symbol of the laborious rise of all creation, of the painful effort of creative unification. It involves the creative pain of a specific effort at unification that goes against a kind of inclination or inertia of existence because of which creatures tend constantly to fall back into multiplicity. But the pain is only the negative side of the true and joyful purpose, at-one-ment with God and all mankind. We share in this through Christ, because, as Teilhard said, the incarnation is not a completed fact on the first Christmas. The fullness of incarnation will not be complete until the substance of all reality "has finally joined itself to the Center of its fulfillment," the Center which holds all together.

Jesus is the visibilization of the Logos, of God's perfect image. Christ-Logos is the Omega or Within which is mirrored in every within. "All things have been created through and unto him . . . and in him all things hold together" (Col 1:17). Teilhard did not separate the Cosmic Christ from the historical Jesus, but he was more drawn to the Cosmic Christ. He wrote, "The God for whom our century is waiting must be: 1. as vast and mysterious as the Cosmos. 2. as immediate and all embracing as Life. 3. as linked (in some way) to our effort as mankind. . . . A God who made the World less mysterious, or smaller, or less important to us, than our heart and our reason show it to be, that God will never more be He to whom the earth kneels." "Now, a Christ who extended to only a part of the universe, a Christ who did not in some way assume the world in Himself, would seem to me a Christ smaller than the Real . . . The God of our faith would seem to me less grand, less dominant, than the Universe of our experience."[18]

Notes

1. Aniela Jaffé, *From the Life and Work of C. G. Jung.* N.Y.: Harper & Row, 1971, 44.

2. *The Vision of the Past.* N.Y.: Harper & Row, 1966, 227.

3. *The Phenomenon of Man.* N.Y.: Harper & Row, 1959, 229ff.

4. *Ibid.,* 71–76; Christopher Mooney, S.J., *Teilhard de Chardin and the Mystery of Christ.* N.Y.: Harper & Row, 1967, 38.

5. *Science and Christ.* N.Y.: Harper & Row, 1968, 25ff.

6. Modern thought calls this "punctuational evolution." See Steven M. Stanley, *The New Evolutionary Time Table.* N.Y.: Basic Books, 1981.

7. *The Phenomenon of Man,* 257ff.

8. *Ibid.,* 264.
9. *Ibid.,* 269.
10. *Science and Christ,* 179.
11. *The Phenomenon of Man,* 271.
12. Michael Novak, *Belief and Unbelief.* N.Y.: Macmillan, 1965, 146–147.
13. *Christianity and Evolution.* N.Y.: Harcourt Brace Jovanovich, 1974, 218; *The Phenomenon of Man,* 307, 301.
14. Mooney, *Teilhard and the Mystery of Christ,* 104ff.; Robert L. Faricy, S.J., *Teilhard de Chardin's Theology of the Christian in the World.* N.Y.: Sheed and Ward, 1967, 139ff.
15. *Christianity and Evolution,* 81.
16. *Science and Christ,* 60.
17. Faricy, *Teilhard de Chardin's Theology,* 139ff.
18. *The Heart of the Matter.* N.Y.: Harcourt Brace Jovanovich, 1980, 201, 212.

Teilhard de Chardin

See the works listed above in the footnotes. Also:
The Divine Milieu. N.Y.: Harper & Row, 1969. A short introduction to his thought.
Hymn of the Universe. N.Y.: Harper & Row, 1961. Spiritual thoughts.
Building the Earth. Wilkes Barre: Dimension Books, 1965. Catches the inspiration of his thought.
The Future of Man. N.Y.: Harper & Row, 1964. The future of evolution.

Books on Teilhard

Robert L. Faricy, S.J., *Teilhard de Chardin's Theology of the Christian in the World.* N.Y.: Sheed and Ward, 1967.
Thomas King, S.J. and James Salmon, S.J., eds., *Teilhard and the Unity of Knowing.* N.Y.: Paulist Press, 1983.
Thomas King, *Teilhard's Mysticism of Knowing.* N.Y.: Seabury, 1981.
Ursula King, *Towards a New Mysticism. Teilhard de Chardin and Eastern Religions.* N.Y.: Seabury, 1981.
Christopher F. Mooney, S.J., *Teilhard de Chardin and the Mystery of Christ.* N.Y.: Harper & Row, 1967. An excellent introduction.

Robert J. O'Connell, S.J., *Teilhard's Vision of the Past.* N.Y.: Fordham University Press, 1982. Teilhard's method and science.

Emile Rideau, *Teilhard de Chardin. A Guide to His Thought.* N.Y.: Harper & Row, 1967.

Approaches Similar to That of Teilhard

Robert E.D. Clark, *The Universe: Plan or Accident?* Grand Rapids: Zondervan, 1972.

Hoimar Ditforth, *The Origins of Life: Evolution as Creation.* N.Y.: Harper & Row, 1981.

John F. Haught, *Nature and Purpose.* Washington, D.C.: University Press of America, 1980.

Stanley Jaki, *The Roads of Science and the Way to God.* Chicago: U. of Chicago Press, 1978.

Arthur R. Peacocke, *Creation and the World of Science.* N.Y.: Oxford, 1981.

A.R. Peacocke, ed., *The Sciences and Theology and the Twentieth Century.* London: Oriel Press, 1981. Especially Bowker, Chapter 5.

VIII.
Humanistic Religion

Erich Fromm

(Excerpts from (1) *Psychoanalysis and Religion*, pages 34–38. Copyright © 1950 by Erich Fromm. (2) *Man for Himself*, pages 133–137. Holt, Rinehart & Winston, Inc., 1947.)

Editor's Note

Erich Fromm was born in 1900 in Frankfurt-on-Mainz. His father Naphtali, the son of a rabbi and the grandson of two rabbis, was an independent businessman, and his mother Rosa was the daughter of a cigar manufacturer. Erich was an only son. His family situation was a tense one. His father was moody and "over-anxious," and his mother was "depression-prone" (Hausdorf, 13).

He studied the Old Testament and the Talmud but he left organized Judaism at about the age of twenty-seven. He married Frieda Fromm (Reichmann) in 1926, was divorced, and married Hennie Gurland (d. 1952). In 1953 he married Annis Freeman. He has given us very little autobiography. One of his fundamental recognitions was about the problem of loneliness and the need of relatedness. Fromm died in 1980.

Fromm was never a medical doctor, and he is less biological in stress and terminology than Freud. His writings have more of an ethical and committed flavor than that of the detached spectator.

Fromm reinterpreted Freud's Oedipus Complex in interpersonal rather than in sexual terms. The "incestuous craving" is not sexual but the much more profound desire to remain a child, to return to the womb. Freud placed great emphasis on biological instinct. He saw the basic conflict as between man's instinct (e.g., id) and society's norms. For Freud, evil (the death instinct) was within the person. While Fromm does not deny the existence of the Freudian instincts, he sees *culture* as the more crucial factor. Culture itself controls early-life

92

training since the parent who trains the child is simply the agent transmitting society's requirements. Thus, when Fromm considers "evil," he centers more on its origin in external society than in the individual. But in his later writings, he insisted that this does not mean that there is not a potential for evil as well as for good in man (1964, 13).

Fromm believed that in our society an economic model of the person held sway. Each person works for himself but needs others as customers. Thus other individuals are always a *means* to an end. For Fromm, the true goal of humanity is not the exploitation of the marketplace but development in interpersonal relations. One grows out of the marketing attitude into the love attitude. Fromm found the marketing, economic model of the person in capitalistic ideals as they are applied to human relationships. It is a major cause of neurosis. (He also attacked communism, though he admired Marx's early humanistic theory.)

Human Basic Needs. Man is a "freak" of the universe. He emerges from the primary unity with the mother ("symbiosis") and he moves into a world which lacks harmonious community life, significant communal values and a frame of reference and devotion. He experiences *loneliness* and *alienation.* "Having lost Paradise, the unity with nature, he has become the eternal wanderer (Odysseus, Oedipus, Abraham, Faust)" (1950, 23). Man is a freak because he is part of nature yet he transcends it. He is self-aware and thus realizes his powerlessness. His mind tells him he will die but he cannot get rid of his mind. What does man *need* to solve his problem?

He has certain basic needs which must be satisfied. (1) *A Sense of Identity:* a need to actively find his place in the world, to be distinctive, unique. (2) *Rootedness:* humans need traditions, customs and ritual in order to find a sense of identity, because they stand for beliefs that are greater than the individual. (3) *Relatedness:* because the person is torn from the animal's primary unity with nature, he or she must have relatedness to be "productive," i.e. healthy. (4) *Transcendence:* man needs to transcend the animal state, but since he can't find this transcendence ready-made, he must create it. He must create his own world and vision. (5) *Frame of Reference:* but to create, man must have a frame of reference to give stability and consistency to his behavior. Thus, there is a need for "humanistic religion." Humanistic religion is "any system of thought and action shared by a group which gives the individual a frame of orientation and an object of devotion" which promotes productive, caring existence.

Humanistic Religion. Thus man, even atheistic man, needs humanistic religion. This is a kind of union with "the All" in relatedness to the world and one's fellows. As Sam Keen once said, Fromm's position might be stated, paraphrasing St. Augustine, as, "Our hearts are restless, O God, and they will not rest until they rest in we." Fromm was not a theistic believer. For him, God was the projection or symbol of our highest ideals. However, he saw himself as a "benign atheist." He saw the great choice to be, not that between belief and unbelief, but between *caring* and *not-caring*. Fromm is much more positive on religion than was Freud. Freud saw religion as a form of universal neurosis, but Fromm sees neurosis as a form of private religion. Man must lose his loneliness and develop the capacity to love and the capacity for creative achievement. The cure will be found in humanistic religion.

Fromm was very severe with "authoritarian religion," in fact with authoritarian society in general. It is not chiefly in the individual but in society that the block to self-realization and freedom is found. Authoritarian imposition leads to a loss of selfhood. Without productive love, the greater the power of the parent, the less the power of the child. Similarly, he saw modern society, both capitalistic and communistic, as built on a master-slave business relationship. They are based on power structures of an impersonal nature. He saw the same situation as existing in authoritarian religion.

One is taught to adjust to authoritarian society or authoritarian religion through the development of a *sadomasochistic* personality. The characteristics of this personality are dependence, passivity, and a willingness to comply. Thus there arises the symbiotic relationship of a slave. Man becomes sadomasochistic to avoid loneliness and isolation, unless he takes the road of creativity and love. He subjects himself to *authoritarian conscience*. He obeys because it relieves inward tension (Glenn, 98). Thus he has no inner freedom or spontaneity.

Paradoxically, the result is hostility which leads to guilt because of dependence on irrational authority. Then these guilt feelings consolidate and increase dependency. (See the following excerpt.)

Fromm believed that "God" has evolved from anthropomorphic conceptions of a despotic tribal chief, to a loving father who counsels truth and justice, to the symbol of the principle of unity behind the manifoldness of phenomena. God's personal characteristics vanish. He becomes abstract, nameless, the Endless One (Hausdorf, 101).

There are two movements within religion as Fromm sees it. (1) He sees the Old Testament as moving from incestuous (meaning passive attachment to mother, home, tribe, religion) to productive orientations. This productive orientation is found in the symbol of "the messianic times." The "fall" of Adam is seen as man's loss of his pre-individualistic harmony with nature and with others (paradise). Man has a non-productive desire to return to what was his home before he achieved reason and self-awareness. He wants to return to the womb. But the messianic times demand the ability for independent love and community. (2) The second trend he sees is a kind of negative theology ("the Nameless One"). This trend started with God's answer to Moses, "I am who am." This really means that, unlike idols, I have no name (1966, 29–51). God is a living process, a becoming. Only a thing that is, that has reached its final form, can have a name. From Moses to Maimonides (1135–1204), Judaism developed a negative theology. The thrust was chiefly against idols. "Mankind for its salvation does not need to worship God. All it needs is not to blaspheme God and not to worship idols." Fromm complained that "those who cannot accept the concept of God find themselves outside the system of concepts which makes up the Jewish religion" even though they might be close to its spirit if they believe in its ethical system and right living. This might be called the ethic of Jewish messianism.

The "X" Experience. Fromm is often called an "ego psychologist." However, some of his thought has a kind of transpersonal, mystical base. This is especially true in what he called "the X Experience." Its characteristics are: (a) to experience life as a problem, as a question that requires an answer: (b) to have a definite hierarchy of values, in which the highest involves the optimal development of one's powers of reason, love, compassion and courage; (c) to see persons as ends and never as means; (d) to aim at letting go of one's ego, one's greed, one's fears, "a giving up the wish to hold onto the ego as if it were an indestructible, separate entity"; (e) to aim at transcendence, transcending the ego, leaving the prison of one's selfishness and separateness. Whether transcendence is toward God is a matter of conceptualization (1966, 58).

Love. With regard to the second excerpt below, it will be helpful to add a few words on Fromm's concept of love. "Love," as a term, tends to become a "buzz" word without content or challenge unless we break it down into its various types and components. There are five forms of love. (1) *Brotherly love:* this is a love between equals involving care, responsibility, respect, knowledge. (2) *Motherly love:* unconditional affirmation of a child's needs and life. It is a love of inequality. It differs from fatherly love, Fromm believes, in that the latter is conditional and earned. (3) *Erotic love:* a craving for complete union with another person. Without brotherly love as a component,

erotic love is mere sexual desire and not true love. By nature it is
exclusive and not universal, but it can love all mankind in the other
person. It is perhaps the most deceptive form of love there is. Fromm
sees a will commitment even in erotic love in its fullest form. He sees
it as "standing in" love rather than a "falling in" love. (4) *Self-love:*
this is not selfishness or narcissism. A love for oneself is connected
with and a pre-requisite for brotherly love ("Love thy neighbor as
thyself"). One is loved only if one can love. Neurotic "love" arises out
of a lack of true self-love and self-acceptance. (5) *Love of God:* this is
the highest value to which man aspires and which he represents by
the concept "God." God is man's highest ideal. This love is an
expression of the need for completeness. Mysticism, even for an
atheist, is the search for completeness.

*   *   *

I

Can we trust religion to be the representative of religious
needs or must we not separate these needs from organized,
traditional religion in order to prevent the collapse of our
moral structure?

In considering an answer to this question we must remember that no intelligent discussion of the problem is possible as
long as we deal with religion in general instead of differentiating between various types of religion and religious experience.
It would far transcend the scope of this chapter to attempt a
review of all types of religion. Even to discuss only those types
which are relevant from the psychological standpoint cannot be
undertaken here. I shall therefore deal with only one distinction, but one which in my opinion is the most important, and
which cuts across nontheistic and theistic religions: that between *authoritarian* and *humanistic* religions.

What is the principle of authoritarian religion? The definition of religion given in the *Oxford Dictionary,* while attempting
to define religion as such, is a rather accurate definition of
authoritarian religion. It reads: "[Religion is] recognition on
the part of man of some higher unseen power as having control

of his destiny, and as being entitled to obedience, reverence, and worship."

Here the emphasis is on the recognition that man is controlled by a higher power outside of himself. But this alone does not constitute authoritarian religion. What makes it so is the idea that this power, because of the control it exercises, is *entitled* to "obedience, reverence and worship." I italicize the word "entitled" because it shows that the reason for worship, obedience, and reverence lies not in the moral qualities of the deity, not in love or justice, but in the fact that it has control, that is, has power over man. Furthermore it shows that the higher power has a right to force man to worship him and that lack of reverence and obedience constitutes sin.

The essential element in authoritarian religion and in the authoritarian religious experience is the surrender to a power transcending man. The main virtue of this type of religion is obedience, its cardinal sin is disobedience. Just as the deity is conceived as omnipotent or omniscient, man is conceived as being powerless and insignificant. Only as he can gain grace or help from the deity by complete surrender can he feel strength. Submission to a powerful authority is one of the avenues by which man escapes from his feeling of aloneness and limitation. In the act of surrender he loses his independence and integrity as an individual but he gains the feeling of being protected by an awe-inspiring power of which, as it were, he becomes a part.

In Calvin's theology we find a vivid picture of authoritarian, theistic thinking. "For I do not call it humility," says Calvin, "if you suppose that we have anything left. . . . We cannot think of ourselves as we ought to think without utterly despising everything that may be supposed an excellence in us. This humility is unfeigned submission of a mind overwhelmed with a weighty sense of its own misery and poverty; for such is the uniform description of it in the word of God."[1]

The experience which Calvin describes here, that of despising everything in oneself, of the submission of the mind overwhelmed by its own poverty, is the very essence of all authoritarian religions whether they are couched in secular or in theological language.[2] In authoritarian religion God is a symbol of power and force, He is supreme because He has supreme power, and man in juxtaposition is utterly powerless.

Authoritarian secular religion follows the same principle. Here the Führer or the beloved "Father of His People" or the State or the Race or the Socialist Fatherland becomes the object of worship; the life of the individual becomes insignificant and man's worth consists in the very denial of his worth and strength. Frequently authoritarian religion postulates an ideal which is so abstract and so distant that it has hardly any connection with the real life of real people. To such ideals as "life after death" or "the future of mankind" the life and happiness of persons living here and now may be sacrificed; the alleged ends justify every means and become symbols in the names of which religious or secular "elites" control the lives of their fellow men.

Humanistic religion, on the contrary, is centered around man and his strength. Man must develop his power of reason in order to understand himself, his relationship to his fellow men and his position in the universe. He must recognize the truth, both with regard to his limitations and his potentialities. He must develop his powers of love for others as well as for himself and experience the solidarity of all living beings. He must have principles and norms to guide him in this aim. Religious experience in this kind of religion is the experience of oneness with the All, based on one's relatedness to the world as it is grasped with thought and with love. Man's aim in humanistic religion is to achieve the greatest strength, not the greatest powerlessness; virtue is self-realization, not obedience. Faith is certainty of conviction based on one's experience of thought and feeling, not assent to propositions on credit of the proposer. The prevailing mood is that of joy, while the prevailing mood in authoritarian religion is that of sorrow and of guilt.

Inasmuch as humanistic religions are theistic, God is a symbol of *man's own powers* which he tries to realize in his life, and is not a symbol of force and domination, having *power over man*.

Illustrations of humanistic religions are early Buddhism, Taoism, the teachings of Isaiah, Jesus, Socrates, Spinoza, certain trends in the Jewish and Christian religions (particularly mysticism), the religion of Reason of the French Revolution. It is evident from these that the distinction between authoritarian and humanistic religion cuts across the distinction between theistic and nontheistic, and between religions in the narrow sense of the word and philosophical systems of religious character. What matters in all such systems is not the thought system as such but the human attitude underlying their doctrines.

Notes

1. Johannes Calvin, *Institutes of the Christian Religion* (Presbyterian Board of Christian Education, 1928), p. 681.
2. See Erich Fromm, *Escape from Freedom* (Farrar & Rinehart, 1941), pp. 141ff. The attitude toward authority is described there in detail.

II

Before we start the discussion of the psychological aspect of selfishness and self-love, the logical fallacy in the notion that love for others and love for oneself are mutually exclusive should be stressed. If it is a virtue to love my neighbor as a human being, it must be a virtue—and not a vice—to love myself since I am a human being too. There is no concept of man in which I myself am not included. A doctrine which proclaims such an exclusion proves itself to be intrinsically contradictory. The idea expressed in the Biblical "Love thy neighbor as thyself!" implies that respect for one's own integrity and uniqueness, love for and understanding of one's own self, can not be separated from respect for and love and understanding of another individual. The love for my own self is inseparably connected with the love for any other self.

We have come now to the basic psychological premises on which the conclusions of our argument are built. Generally, these premises are as follows: not only others, but we ourselves are the "object" of our feelings and attitudes; the attitudes toward others and toward ourselves, far from being contradictory, are basically *conjunctive.* With regard to the problem under discussion this means: Love of others and love of ourselves are not alternatives. On the contrary, an attitude of love toward themselves will be found in all those who are capable of loving others. *Love,* in principle, *is indivisible as far as the connection between "objects" and one's own self is concerned.* Genuine love is an expression of productiveness and implies care, respect, responsibility, and knowledge. It is not an "affect" in the sense of being affected by somebody, but an active striving for the growth and happiness of the loved person, rooted in one's own capacity to love.

To love is an expression of one's power to love, and to love somebody is the actualization and concentration of this power with regard to one person. It is not true, as the idea of romantic love would have it, that there is only *the* one person in the world whom one could love and that it is the great chance of one's life to find that one person. Nor is it true, if that person be found, that love for him (or her) results in a withdrawal of love from others. Love which can only be experienced with regard to one person demonstrates by this very fact that it is not love, but a symbiotic attachment. The basic affirmation contained in love is directed toward the beloved person as an incarnation of essentially human qualities. Love of one person implies love of man as such. The kind of "division of labor," as William James calls it, by which one loves one's family but is without feeling for the "stranger," is a sign of a basic inability to love. Love of man is not, as is frequently supposed, an abstraction coming after the love for a specific person, but it is its premise, although, genetically, it is acquired in loving specific individuals.

From this it follows that my own self, in principle, must be as much an object of my love as another person. *The affirmation of one's own life, happiness, growth, freedom, is rooted in one's capacity to love,* i.e., in care, respect, responsibility, and knowledge. If an individual is able to love productively, he loves himself too; if he can love *only* others, he can not love at all.

Granted that love for oneself and for others in principle is conjunctive, how do we explain selfishness, which obviously excludes any genuine concern for others? The *selfish* person is interested only in himself, wants everything for himself, feels no pleasure in giving, but only in taking. The world outside is looked at only from the standpoint of what he can get out of it; he lacks interest in the needs of others, and respect for their dignity and integrity. He can see nothing but himself; he judges everyone and everything from its usefulness to him; he is basically unable to love. Does not this prove that concern for others and concern for oneself are unavoidable alternatives? This would be so if selfishness and self-love were identical. But that assumption is the very fallacy which has led to so many mistaken conclusions concerning our problem. *Selfishness and self-love, far from being identical, are actually opposites.* The selfish person does not love himself too much but too little; in fact he hates himself. This lack of fondness and care for himself, which is only one expression of his lack of productiveness, leaves him empty and frustrated. He is necessarily unhappy and anxiously concerned to snatch from life the satisfactions which he blocks himself from attaining. He seems to care too much for himself but actually he only makes an unsuccessful attempt to cover up and compensate for his failure to care for his real self. Freud holds that the selfish person is narcissistic, as if he had withdrawn his love from others and turned it toward his own person. *It is true that selfish persons are incapable of loving others, but they are not capable of loving themselves either.*

It is easier to understand selfishness by comparing it with greedy concern for others, as we find it, for instance, in an oversolicitous, dominating mother. While she consciously believes that she is particularly fond of her child, she has actually a deeply repressed hostility toward the object of her concern. She is overconcerned not because she loves the child too much, but because she has to compensate for her lack of capacity to love him at all.

This theory of the nature of selfishness is borne out by psychoanalytic experience with neurotic "unselfishness," a symptom of neurosis observed in not a few people who usually are troubled not by this symptom but by others connected with it, like depression, tiredness, inability to work, failure in love relationships, and so on. Not only is unselfishness not felt as a "symptom"; it is often the one redeeming character trait on which such people pride themselves. The "unselfish" person "does not want anything for himself"; he "lives only for others," is proud that he does not consider himself important. He is puzzled to find that in spite of his unselfishness he is unhappy, and that his relationships to those closest to him are unsatisfactory. He wants to have what he considers are his symptoms removed—but not his unselfishness. Analytic work shows that his unselfishness is not something apart from his other symptoms but one of them; in fact often the most important one; that he is paralyzed in his capacity to love or to enjoy anything; that he is pervaded by hostility against life and that behind the façade of unselfishness a subtle but not less intense self-centeredness is hidden. This person can be cured only if his unselfishness too is interpreted as a symptom along with the others so that his lack of productiveness, which is at the root of both his unselfishness *and* his other troubles, can be corrected.

The nature of unselfishness becomes particularly apparent in its effect on others and most frequently, in our culture, in the effect the "unselfish" mother has on her children. She believes that by her unselfishness her children will experience what it means to be loved and to learn, in turn, what it means to love. The effect of her unselfishness, however, does not at all correspond to her expectations. The children do not show the happiness of persons who are convinced that they are loved; they are anxious, tense, afraid of the mother's disapproval and anxious to live up to her expectations. Usually, they are affected by their mother's hidden hostility against life, which they sense rather than recognize, and eventually become imbued with it themselves. Altogether, the effect of the "unselfish" mother is not too different from that of the selfish one; indeed, it is often worse because the mother's unselfishness prevents the children from criticizing her. They are put under the obligation not to disappoint her; they are taught, under the mask of virtue, dislike for life. If one has a chance to study the effect of a mother with genuine self-love, one can see that there is nothing more conducive to giving a child the experience of what love, joy, and happiness are than being loved by a mother who loves herself.

Works by Fromm

Man for Himself. N.Y.: Fawcett, 1947.
Psychoanalysis and Religion. New Haven: Yale U. Press, 1950.
The Art of Loving. N.Y.: Harper & Row, 1956.
Sigmund Freud's Mission. N.Y.: Harper & Row, 1959.
Zen Buddhism and Psychoanalysis. N.Y.: Harper & Row, 1960.
The Heart of Man. Its Genius for Good and Evil. N.Y.: Harper & Row, 1964.
You Shall Be As Gods. A Radical Interpretation of the Old Testament. N.Y.: Harper & Row, 1966.
To Have or To Be? N.Y.: Harper & Row, 1976.
The Anatomy of Human Destructiveness. N.Y.: Fawcett, 1978.
Greatness and Limitations of Freud's Thought. N.Y.: New American Library, 1981.
On Disobedience and Other Essays. N.Y.: Seabury Press, 1982. Final thoughts.

Works on Fromm

Andrew Reid Fuller, *Psychology and Religion: Eight Points of View.* Washington, D.C.: University Press of America, 1977.
J. Stanley Glenn, *Erich Fromm: A Protestant Critique.* Philadelphia: Westminster Press, 1966. Useful on Fromm's use of Feuerbach and of Calvin's thought.
Guyton Hammond, *Man in Estrangement.* Nashville: Vanderbilt U. Press, 1965. A comparison of Fromm and Tillich.
Don Hausdorf, *Erich Fromm.* N.Y.: Twayne Publishers, 1972. A good synthesis.
John H. Schaar, *Escape from Authority—The Perspectives of Erich Fromm.* N.Y.: Harper & Row, 1961. A criticism of Fromm's approach to authority.

IX.
Humanistic Psychology and Evil

Paul C. Vitz

(Excerpt from Paul C. Vitz, *Psychology as Religion: The Cult of Self-Worship.* Grand Rapids, Michigan: Eerdmans Publishing Company, 1977, pages 91–105.)

Editor's Note

Humanistic psychologists, like Fromm, Abraham Maslow and Carl Rogers, have been accused of being "Pollyannas" about the good in humanity. It has been said that they practice a high romanticism in blithely neglecting the evil in human nature. One of the reasons for the staying power of Freud is his firm hold on the tragic dimension of man in whom Eros and Thanatos wage their endless duel. (Teilhard's evolutionary and counter-evolutionary drives in humanity are very similar to Freud's two adversaries on this point.)

In an investigation of God and growth, which is the theme of this anthology, it would be illusionary to omit a consideration of the question of evil in humanity. Both Fromm and Maslow said that they were closer to the Pelagian view of man than to the Augustinian emphasis on human sinfulness. However, Fromm wrote: "As one whose views have often been misrepresented as underestimating the potential of evil within man, I want to emphasize that such sentimental optimism is not the mood of my thought" (1964, 13). "Man is inclined to good *and* to evil" (1964, 193). But Fromm disliked the doctrine of original sin because, apart from its mythological elements, it might increase the sense of powerlessness that grips people today and allow them to rationalize in a defeatist way the evils in the world (1964, 13).

Carl Rogers also said, "I do not have a Pollyanna view of human nature." For Rogers, man grows alienated from himself and his feelings and he undergoes a kind of "bondage of the will," experiencing a "distortion in awareness" and anxiety. Yet Rogers' popularity is due in part to his emphasis on growth and on becoming a person without lingering on the negative elements in man (Oden, 83).

Abraham Maslow seems to have the most optimistic theory about human nature. Man is basically good. "It is only life's pressures and frustrations that makes him seem, all too often, otherwise" (Lowry, 20). Maslow was strongly opposed to the doctrine of original sin. "Any doctrine of the innate depravity of man or any maligning of his animal nature very easily leads to some extra-human interpretation of goodness, saintliness, virtue.... The worse man is ... the more necessary becomes god" (1964, 36). However, Maslow did not neglect the evil in the world (1971, xvii). But he tended to attribute it to ignorance or to the environment.

Those psychologists who stress environment alone as the cause of evil cannot answer the question as to how the environment, which is composed of people, can bring evil into the world. Also, those who emphasize ignorance as the cause of evil do not sufficiently consider to what degree ignorance can be culpable.

However, there is another side to the question. All growth psychologies imply something which is to be conquered in growing, whether it be false defenses, psychic distortion, or selfishness—that is, evil. These psychologists believe that more is accomplished by stressing the positive goal of growth than the negative "evil" to be overcome. As Teilhard de Chardin put it, "We must replace the negative doctrine of renunciation by abstention with the positive idea of renunciation by devotion to the greater than self" (*Toward the Future*, 32).

However, unless some stress is placed upon the evil possibilities in human beings, a very unreal picture of human nature emerges. One also runs the danger of falling into what Dr. Paul Vitz in *Psychology as Religion* calls the "secular cult of selfism." Vitz, associate professor of psychology at New York University, writes from a radically conservative viewpoint, but the points he makes in the following excerpt deserve our attention.

*   *   *

Selfism as Idolatry

It should be obvious—though it has apparently not been so to many—that the relentless and single-minded search for and glorification of the self is at direct cross-purposes with the Christian injunction to *lose* the self. Certainly Jesus Christ neither lived nor advocated a life that would qualify by today's standards as "self-actualized." For the Christian the self is the problem, not the potential paradise. Understanding this problem involves an awareness of sin, especially of the sin of pride; correcting this condition requires the practice of such un-self-actualized states as contrition and penitence, humility, obedience, and trust in God.

Some comments from Paul Ramsey's *Basic Christian Ethics* are appropriate.

> The first assertion Christian ethics makes about man is that he was created for personal existence within the image of God, and that Jesus Christ most perfectly reveals this image. The second assertion is that man is sinful. So fundamental is this doctrine in Christian thought that it cannot be overlooked. Indeed, many theologians regard it as basic equally with the first for any full understanding of man in the light of God. This has been the view not only of the more "pessimistic" thinkers; it was the view also of John Wesley, whose emphasis upon "going on to perfection" is well known.[1]

The Christian position is clear that sin is not exclusively or primarily something in society. It is something that all humans do, and do as a willed act, not merely as the consequence of outside influences on them. The locus of sin, therefore, is in the will of each of us. This central Christian doctrine has been under relentless attack for many years by almost all advocates of social science from traditional economics and sociology to Socialism and Communism. Ordinary Christians, undefended by their own theologians, have often succumbed to the position that evil lies only or primarily in society. As a consequence a central foundation of their doctrinal system has been undermined. A recent powerful and imaginative attack on the social

science position comes from the Russian Christian Aleksandr
Solzhenitsyn:

> Gradually it was disclosed to me that the line separat-
> ing good and evil passes not through states, nor
> between classes, nor between political parties either
> —but right through every human heart. . . .
>
> Since then I have come to understand the truth of
> all the religions of the world: they struggle with the
> *evil inside a human being* (inside every human being). It
> is impossible to expel evil from the world in its entire-
> ty, but it is possible to constrict it within each person.
>
> And since that time I have come to understand
> the falsehood of all revolutions in history: they destroy
> only *those carriers* of evil contemporary with them (and
> also out of haste, to discriminate the carriers of good
> as well). And they then take to themselves as their
> heritage the actual evil itself, magnified still more.[2]

In spite of the anti-religious prejudice of modern psychology at
least one prominent psychologist appreciates the psychological
necessity of accepting sin. This is O. Hobart Mowrer, who has
written as follows:

> For several decades we psychologists looked upon the
> whole matter of sin and moral accountability as a great
> incubus and acclaimed our liberation from its as ep-
> och-making. But at length we have discovered that to
> be "free" in this sense, i.e., to have the excuse of
> being "sick" rather than sinful, is to court the danger
> of also becoming lost. This danger is, I believe, beto-
> kened by the widespread interest in Existentialism
> which we are presently witnessing. In becoming amor-
> al, ethically neutral, and "free," we have cut the very
> roots of our being; lost our deepest sense of self-hood
> and identity; and with neurotics themselves, find our-
> selves asking: "who *am* I?"[3]

The great benefit of the doctrine of sin is that it reintroduces responsibility for our own behavior, responsibility for changing as well as giving meaning to our condition. Mowrer describes these benefits from the acceptance of sin:

> Recovery (constructive change, redemption) is most assuredly attained, not by helping a person reject and rise above his sins, but by helping him *accept them.* This is the paradox which we have not at all understood and which is the very crux of the problem. Just so long as a person lives under the shadow of real, unacknowledged, and unexpiated guilt, he *cannot* (if he has any character at all) "accept himself"; and all *our* efforts to reassure and accept him will avail nothing. He will continue to hate himself and to suffer the inevitable consequences of self-hatred. But the moment he (with or without "assistance") begins to accept his guilt and sinfulness, the possibility of radical reformation opens up; and with this, the individual may legitimately, though not without pain and effort, pass from deep, pervasive self-rejection and self-torture to a new freedom, of self-respect and peace.[4]

The problems posed by humanistic selfism are not new to Christianity: indeed, they can be traced back to early conflicts with Stoicism and other sophisticated Graeco-Roman philosophical and ethical systems. To worship one's self (in self-realization) or to worship all humanity is, in Christian terms, simple idolatry operating from the usual motive of unconscious egotism. Unconscious or disguised self-love has long been recognized as the source of idolatry. Otto Baab, in his study of Old Testament theology, describes it thus:

> Idolatry is well understood in the Bible as differing from the pure worship of Israel's God in the fact of its personification and objectification of the human will in contrast with the superhuman transcendence of the true God. When an idol is worshipped, man is worshipping himself, his desires, his purposes and his

will. . . . As a consequence of this type of idolatry man
was outrageously guilty of giving himself the status of
God and of exalting his own will as of supreme worth.[5]

Such an analysis makes it clear that in religious terms selfist
humanism is just another example of idolatrous narcissism.

After the establishment of Christianity the worship of the
self continued as a many-faceted heresy. Elements of modern
selfism are found in Gnosticism, in the medieval Brethren of
the Free Spirit, and in many other sects.[6] The present form of
selfism also contains strong Pelagian strands. Pelagius, a
fourth-century theologian from Britain, opposed the doctrine
of original sin and argued that man was capable of living a
perfect and sinless life, thus downgrading the importance of
God's grace.* Evans in a recent scholarly book points out that
Pelagius' position was not as extreme as his critics have often
portrayed it.[7] He remained a Christian theologian and even so
vigorous an opponent of his as St. Augustine acknowledged
him to be a "saintly man." But a strong element in his theology
might, under the traditional and rather extreme interpretation
of it, be viewed as akin to humanist selfism. So it has been
accepted by Fromm, who cites Pelagius as an ally and representative of what he calls "humanistic" religion, in contrast to the

_____

*The humanist aspect of Pelagius' theology is sometimes said to be temperamen-
tally natural to the English and by extension to Americans. There may be some small
grain of truth here but the relative quiescence of Pelagianism in England for more than
a thousand years after his death raises questions for such an interpretation. A more
probable explanation would involve the unusual economic and social factors present in
England in the latter fourth century, the formative time for Pelagius' thinking. The first
was a preceding period of nearly two hundred years of increasing economic prosperi-
ty—roughly from the second to the end of the fourth century. This was the British-
Roman period of country villas and baths. The second condition was the probable
effect of the combined Roman and Christian culture—both powerful and civilizing
imports to a previously pagan and rather primitive Britain. Such a qualitatively new and
superior culture combined with a substantial long-term increase in wealth could easily
have created the belief in Britain and in some other parts of the Roman empire that a
new era had dawned and the old laws of human nature and history no longer operated.
Shortly after the death of Pelagius, about 431, Britain relapsed into wars, social
breakdown, and barbarism—all of which may have provided more effective anti-
Pelagian "arguments" than those of St. Augustine or St. Jerome. There is in this
example an obvious historical similarity to America's two hundred years of greatly
increasing wealth combined with the belief that science has ushered in a new condition
of progress in which the old understanding of human nature and its limits is no longer
relevant.

"authoritarian" religion typified by Augustine.[8] Evans, however, notes that Fromm's categories of "humanistic" and "authoritarian" religion do not fit the theologies of either Pelagius or Augustine. (This is just one example of how Fromm's bias in his writings concerning Christianity leads him to misread Christian theology and faith.)

Furthermore, with respect to the problem of authoritarianism, it should be noted that Christians from the beginning have been aware of the problems of excessive institutionalized authority and the dangers of bad faith which it can create. Over a two-thousand-year period the Christian response has been recurring spiritual revival and renewal. While there is a legitimate dichotomy between frozen, institutionalized or severely formalized religion and living, spiritual faith, authority *per se* operates in both types of religion. Today's bureaucratized, secularized, and highly humanized Protestantism provides an example of an overly intellectualized dead faith. Much of this Christianity has been drained of its vitality by an over-generalized psychology, of which an obvious example is the very humanist selfism Fromm espouses, which has become increasingly authoritative!

Like all popular heresy selfism has some positive and appealing properties. That you should look out for yourself is nice (and useful) to hear; that you should love and care for others is a familiar and great moral position. What is excluded is the spiritual life of prayer, meditation, and worship—the essential vertical dimension of Christianity, the relation to God. Selfism is an example of a horizontal heresy, with its emphasis only on the present, and on self-centered ethics. At its very best (which is not often), it is Christianity without the first commandment.

CHRISTIAN LOVE AND SELFIST LOVE

Christianity and selfism differ not just over the self and self-love but about the very nature of love. To begin reflection on the Christian conception of love, recall that Christ summarized the whole law in two commands to love: "Thou shalt love the Lord thy God with all thy heart, with all thy soul and with

all thy strength" and "Thou shalt love thy neighbor as thyself."
The love of God is first. It is primary, and love of neighbor
stems from it. Love in these two forms is at the very center of
the Christian faith. Note, too, that there is no direct command
to love the self—an adequate degree of self-love being assumed
as natural.

This Christian theory of love has been expressed for nearly
two thousand years in what is now an enormous tradition. It
shines forth in the life and death of Jesus as recorded in the
four gospels; it is disclosed in the writings of St. Paul, St.
Augustine, St. Bernard, Martin Luther, Tolstoy, C. S. Lewis
and many, many more; it is given contemporary application in a
wide variety of personal and institutional practices. Christian
love has been shown in the early Christian communities, in the
age-old and still lively monastic tradition, in the expressions of
medieval and Eastern Orthodox mysticism, in the emotional
caring shown by pietist groups, in Christian hospitals, missions,
and the Salvation Army. The lives of St. Francis in thirteenth-
century Europe and Mother Theresa in twentieth-century Cal-
cutta, of the host of saints and of countless other good quiet
Christians are such remarkable and historically unique examples of the expression of love that it should be obvious that
their faith had something to do with it. It is by turns flabber-
gasting and disturbing that nowhere in the selfist writings
about love is this large body of Christian theory and practice
ever discussed.

Fromm in his well-known book *The Art of Loving* presents
what he describes as "The Theory of Love." In the discussion
of love of God he follows the Feuerbachian approach by assum-
ing that "the understanding of the concept of God must . . .
start with an analysis of the character structure of the person
who worships God."[9] Although he is less blatantly hostile to
Christianity here than in his earlier work *The Dogma of Christ,* he
does conclude, by various social and vaguely historical arguments, that the God professed by Christian theology is an
illusion. His discussion of love does include some citations
from the Christian mystic Meister Eckhart which imply that
man is God. But these quotations are certainly not Christian
and seriously misrepresent Meister Eckhart's theology. Eck-

hart's view of self-love is quite explicit: he calls it "the root and cause of all evil, depriving us of all goodness and perfection. Therefore, if the soul is to know God it must forget and lose itself; so long as it mirrors its own image it does not see or know God."[10] There is no word about keeping the self's integrity, using the self to define what is good, or any other of the familiar selfist themes. Fromm, in addition to misrepresenting Eckhart, completely neglects the major body of Christian writing on love.

Similarly, Maslow, in his major work *Motivation and Personality,* primarily discusses love between the sexes; and he has no Christian references. In some of his later writings, however, he does take seriously the mystic experience.[11] But Maslow's writings contain no treatment of Christian mysticism, much less any discussion of Christian love.

Carl Rogers in his best-known contribution to personality theory and psychotherapy, *On Becoming a Person,* has no treatment of love at all! Nor is love discussed in Rogers' book on encounter groups; and even his *Becoming Partners* has no theory of love—its emphasis is on sexual compatibility, changing roles and relationships, learning to trust the self and others, and the like. Needless to say there is no recognition or acknowledgment of the Christian theory of love.

As was pointed out above, it is essential in discussing Christian love to emphasize love of God—above all to emphasize that the love of God is for a Christian not primarily an intellectual dogma but an empirical fact, an overwhelming experiential reality. It is from this experienced reality that theology begins. In the final analysis all Christian theology is a theory of love, of divine love. Those unfamiliar with or dubious about such a spiritual state can translate "the love of God" into such terms as contemplation, meditation, mystic experience. This translation is *not* adequate for Christian theology, but will suffice for the present analysis.

The Christian theoretical claim is that love of God or Christ not only justifies the love of others, but also greatly facilitates it. St. Bernard's four-stage hierarchical model of the love of God is a famous twelfth-century conceptualization of the Christian's relation to the first commandment and the resulting consequences for the love of others. A brief summary of his position (from his *The Love of God—De Diligendo Deo*) exemplifies the kind of literature the selfists overlook. St. Bernard begins by saying that the reason the wise man loves God is because God *is* God, but for others amplification is needed. The first degree of love is "love of the self for self," which he assumes to be natural and good, unless it runs to excess when at this stage it should be controlled by the command to love one's neighbor as oneself. The second degree is "love of God for what he gives." For the Christian the initial reason for loving God is that God loves him, that God has loved first. This love, expressed in the creation of the world, reaches sublime expression in the New Testament, "For God so loved the world that he gave his only Son, that whoever believes in him should not perish but have eternal life" (John 3:16). Thus, this degree is love of God for his many blessings, including solace found in times of trouble. It is through this love that the Christian first learns his limitations and weaknesses.

The third stage is "love of God for what he is." In this stage God is loved purely for himself, because we "know how gracious the Lord is." In this degree the Christian finds "no difficulty in obeying the command to love our neighbor. The man who loves like this loves truly; and in so doing he loves the things of God. He loves purely and without self-interest."[12] This occurs, in part, "because he freely gives who freely has received." Finally, Bernard describes the fourth degree, which is difficult and rare: "A mountain is this fourth degree of love, God's own 'high hill,' a mountain strong, fertile, and rich. . . . Happy is he, and holy too, to whom it has been given, here in this mortal life rarely or even once, for one brief moment only, to taste this kind of love! . . . it is the bliss of heaven." This bliss can come about if we aim at conforming ourselves perfectly to the Creator and "living according to his will."[13]

The defender of selfism may retort that the highest and purest form of love advocated by such humanists as Fromm has nothing to do with selfishness in any of its expressions. There are, indeed, very positive-sounding descriptions of this kind of love in Fromm's writings. For instance, he states quite explicitly that humanist self-love is the opposite of selfishness and narcissism. He defines humanist self-love as union with the loved one while preserving one's own integrity; this love involves active concern and care for the other.[14] In spite of this admittedly inspiring conception of love the spread of self-theory psychology has resulted in a rapid dilution of the higher aspects of selfism and in more and more of the kinds of abuses we have described previously. The frequent collapse of higher selfist ideals may be attributed directly to many of the other, more fundamental concepts found in the selfist position. Selfish theory emphasizes the isolated conscious self as the sole judge of what the self should value and how it should act. Such an emphasis almost guarantees the breakdown of the higher ideals into a rationalization of selfishness permeated with narcissism. Hostility toward tradition and any other authority tends to have similar effects. It is no wonder that narcissism is the most rapidly increasing clinical syndrome and a lively theoretical issue in psychotherapy today.*

THE NATURE OF SUFFERING

A final profound conflict between Christianity and selfism centers around the meaning of suffering. The Christian acknowledges evil—with its consequent pain and ultimately death—as a fact of life. Through the Christian's losing of his ordinary self in discipleship, in the imitation of Christ, such suffering can serve as the experience out of which a higher spiritual life is attained. This fundamental view is at the very heart of Christianity, as represented by the passion of the cross followed by the joy of Easter. All the great religions accept the

---

*Heinz Kohut and Otto Kernberg are among those who have documented a dramatic increase in narcissistic problems. In part this is an increase in the amount of narcissistic attachment to the self but it also involves an increased instability in people's self-evaluations. For example, today's externally controlled evaluations often lead to intense self-love and self-esteem followed by self-hate and then a general mood of meaninglessness. The collapse of legitimate authority and meaning combined with the disintegration of family relationships contribute much to this problem, since internalized structures of meaning are necessary for stable self-evaluations. Such people are potentially very open to authoritarian social movements like est, the cult of Reverend Sun Myung Moon, and the like.

existence of sin, illusion, and death and then provide a way to transform and transcend it. This Way is always terribly difficult, but when successfully traveled it is described in the highest terms. Most of us fear the sacrifice and challenge which the true religious life presents; as a result all over the world the genuine saint or holy man is a hero.

In contrast selfish philosophy trivializes life by claiming that suffering (and by implication even death) is without intrinsic meaning. Suffering is seen as some sort of absurdity, usually a man-made mistake which could have been avoided by the use of knowledge to gain control of the environment. The selfist position sounds optimistic and plausible particularly when advocated during materially prosperous times. But it is a superficial view, which loses its convincing character with wider experience of a kind that is now becoming common. Millions who enthusiastically endorsed optimistic selfism in the prime of life are now beginning to experience the ancient lessons of physical decline, of loss, of sickness and death—lessons which puncture all superficial optimism about the continued happy growth of the wonderful self. Even institutions have begun to be haunted by the specters of age and death. And materialistic optimism is further undermined by the growing publicity given to such intractable problems as resource exhaustion, nuclear war, worldwide weather shifts, famines, chronic inflation, huge unrepayable debts, the worldwide retreat of democracy.

What does one tell a chronically over-ambitious man who learns at age forty that further advancement is over and that he has a serious, possibly fatal, illness? What does one tell a woman whose early career hopes have ended in a wearisome and dead-end bureaucratic job? What does one say to the older worker who has lost his job, whose skills are not wanted? What does one tell the woman who is desperately alone inside an aging body and with a history of failed relationships? Does one advise such people to become more autonomous and independent? Does one say "go actualize yourself in creative activity"? For people in those circumstances such advice is not just irrelevant, it is an insult. It is exactly such suffering, however, which is at the center of the meaning and hope of the religious life. By starting with an unsentimental realism about existence religion is able to provide an honest and ultimately optimistic understanding of the human condition. Christianity starts with suffering and ends with joy. Selfist humanism starts with optimism but ends in pessimism. And its pessimism is doubly depressing, for in spite of its many religious characteristics, the selfist position is in the final analysis a kind of false or substitute religion based on denying the *meaning* in suffering and death, experiences from which it cannot protect us.

Notes

1. Paul Ramsey, *Basic Christian Ethics* (New York: Scribner's, 1950), p. 284.

2. Alesandr Solzhenitsyn, *The Gulag Archipelago,* III-IV (New York: Harper & Row, 1975), pp. 615–616. See also Leonard Schapiro, "Disturbing, Fanatical, and Heroic," *New York Review of Books,* Nov. 13, 1975, p. 10; and Solzhenitsyn and others, *From Under the Rubble* (Boston: Little Brown, 1975), esp. essay by A. B.

3. O. Hobart Mowrer, "Sin, The Lesser of Two Evils," *American Psychologist,* XV (1960), 301–304.

4. *Ibid.*

5. Otto Baab, *The Theology of the Old Testament* (New York: Abingdon-Cokesbury, 1949), pp. 105, 110; quoted by Ramsey, *op. cit.,* p. 298.

6. See Paul Zweig, *The Heresy of Self-Love* (New York: Harper & Row, 1968).

7. On Pelagius, see Robert F. Evans, *Pelagius: Inquiries and Reappraisals* (New York: Seabury, 1968).

8. Erich Fromm, *Psychoanalysis and Religion,* p. 34.

9. Erich Fromm, *The Art of Loving* (New York: Harper, 1956), p.63.

10. Quoted by Otto Karrer (ed.), *Meister Eckhart Speaks* (London: Blackfriars, 1957), p. 41. See also J.M. Clark, *The Great German Mystics* (Oxford, 1949) and Etienne Gilson, *Christian Philosophy in the Middle Ages* (New York: Random House, 1955).

11. See for example Abraham Maslow, *Religions, Values and Peak Experiences* (New York: Viking, 1970). Some of Maslow's later writings go beyond humanistic selfism into what is now called transpersonal psychology. This vertical emphasis derives from his hierarchical the-

ory of personality which clearly implies a series of higher and higher levels of mental life.

12. Saint Bernard, *On the Love of God (De Diligendo Deo)*, tr. Sister Penelope (London: Mowbrays, 1950), ch. 9

13. *Ibid.*, p. 64.

14. Fromm, *The Art of Loving*, p. 60.

X.
Belief and Growth

James W. Fowler

(Excerpt from Thomas C. Hennessy, S.J., ed., *Values and Moral Development.* Paulist Press, 1976, pages 183–185, 191–203.)

Editor's Note

Religious maturity and human maturity are intimately connected. An immature religious view of life may be the result of not having negotiated the stages of human growth. However, religious structures themselves have at times inhibited human growth.

It is very difficult to find agreement on what is meant by "growth," "maturity" and "health," both in the secular and in the religious sphere. The norms differ, at least to some degre, according to culture. Abraham Maslow described the healthy person as one who has the following characteristics. 1. Clearer, more efficient perception of reality. 2. More openness to experience. 3. Increased integration, wholeness, and unity of the person. 4. Increased spontaneity, expressiveness, full functioning, aliveness. 5. A real self; a firm identity; autonomy, uniqueness. 6. Increased objectivity, detachment, transcendence of self. 7. Recovery of creativeness. 8. Ability to fuse concreteness and abstraction. 9. Democratic character structure. 10. Ability to love, etc. (*Toward a Psychology of Being*, 157).

Erik Erikson's definition of a healthy person is one who actively masters his environment, shows a certain unity of personality, and is able to perceive the world and himself correctly (*Identity, Youth and Crisis*, 92). Erikson states that anything which grows has a ground plan. Erikson's own ground plan involves negotiating the following stages. 1. Infancy: trust vs. mistrust. 2. Early childhood: autonomy vs. shame and doubt. 3. Play age: initiative vs. guilt. 4. School age:

industry vs. inferiority. 5. Adolescence: identity vs. identity diffusion. 6. Young adulthood: intimacy vs. isolation. 7. Adulthood: generativity vs. self-absorption. 8. Old age: integrity vs. disgust.

Lawrence Kohlberg has endeavored to work out a ground plan with regard to the formation of values: I. Pre-conventional level, stages 1 and 2: values judged from hedonistic consequences of action or from physical power of those who enunciate rules. II. Conventional level, stages 3 and 4: values judged according to norms of a group or according to loyalty to the social order; "good boy-nice girl" orientation, "law and order" orientation. III. Post-conventional level, stages 5 and 6: values based on principles related to a group or on a universal ethical principle orientation.

James W. Fowler of the Harvard Divinity School, while making use of some of the ideas we have just mentioned, has worked out a "structural developmental" approach to the stages of faith. After describing the research on which his position is based, in the following excerpt he describes the stages of faith.

*   *   *

THE STAGES: A BRIEF OVERVIEW

In our effort to give a structural-developmental account of faith we have identified six stages—moving from more simple and undifferentiated structures to those that are more complex and differentiated. Faith manifests growing self-awareness as you move through the stages. The ages given with each of these stages represent an average *minimal* age. Many persons attain them, if at all, at later chronological ages. Stage attainment varies from person to person and equilibrium of a stable sort may occur for different persons or groups at or in different stages.

Stage one—Intuitive-Projective Faith

The imitative, fantasy-filled phase in which the child can be powerfully and permanently influenced by the examples, moods, actions and language of the visible faith of primal adults (age 4).

Stage two—Mythic-Literal Faith

The stage in which the person begins to take on for himself/herself the stories and beliefs and observances that symbolize belonging to his/her community. Attitudes are observed and adopted; beliefs are appropriated with literal interpretations, as are moral rules and attitudes. Symbols are one-dimensional and literal. Authority (parental) and example still count for more than those of peers ($6\frac{1}{2}$–8).

Stage three—Synthetic-Conventional Faith

The person's experience of the world is now extended beyond the family and primary social groups. There are a number of spheres or theaters of life: family, school or work, peers, leisure, friendship, and possibly a religious sphere. Faith must help provide a coherent and meaningful synthesis of that now more complex and diverse range of involvements. Coherence and meaning are certified, at this stage, by either the authority of properly designated persons in each sphere, or by the authority of consensus among "those who count." The person does not yet have to take on the burden of world-synthesis for himself/herself (12–13).

Stage four—Individuating-Reflexive Faith

The movement or break from Stage Three to Stage Four is particularly important for it is in this transition that the late adolescent or adult must begin to take seriously the burden of responsibility for his/her own commitments, life-style, beliefs, and attitudes. Where there is genuinely a transition to Stage Four the person must face certain universal polar tensions which Synthetic-Conventional faith allows one to evade:

individuality	v. belonging to community
subjectivity	v. objectivity
self-fulfillment	v. service to others
the relative	v. the absolute

Often Stage Four develops under the tutelage of ideologically powerful religions, charismatic leadership, or ideologies of other kinds. It often finds it necessary to collapse these polar tensions in one direction or the other. Stage Four both brings and requires a qualitatively new and different kind of self-awareness and responsibility for one's choices and rejections (18–19).

Stage Five—Paradoxical-Consolidative Faith

In Stage Four the person is self-aware in making commitments and knows something of what is being *excluded* by the choices he/she makes. But for Stage Four, the ability to decide is grounded, in part at least, on the fact that one set of commitments is overvalued at the expense of necessarily viewing alternatives to it in a partial and limiting light.

Stage Five represents an advance in the sense that it recognizes the integrity and truth in positions other than its own, and it affirms and lives out its own commitments and beliefs in such a way as to honor that which is true in the lives of others without denying the truth of its own. Stage Five is ready for community of identification beyond tribal, racial, class or ideological boundaries. *To be genuine, it must know the cost of such community and be prepared to pay the cost.* A true Stage Five requires time and testing and regard for those who are different and who oppose you which Stage Four does not have. In a true Stage Five *espoused values and beliefs are congruent with risk, and action taken* (30–32).

Stage Six—Universalizing Faith

Stage Five's commitment to inclusive community remains paradoxical. To affirm others means to deny oneself. Defensiveness and egocentrism make the affirmation of others' truth difficult and threatening. One's own interests and investments in tribe, class, religion, nation, region, etc., still constitute biasing and distorting loyalties, which have to be struggled with and overcome continually.

Stage Six Universalizing Faith *is rare.* At this stage what Christians and Jews call the Kingdom of God is a live, felt reality for the person of faith. Here one dwells *in* the world as a transforming presence, but is not *of* the world. The sense of the oneness of all persons is not a glib ideological belief but has become a permeative basis for decision and action. The paradox has gone out of being-for-others; at Stage 6, one is being most truly oneself. Stage Six's participation in the Ultimate is direct and immediate. Their community is universal in inclusiveness. Such persons are ready for fellowship with persons at any of the other stages and from any other faith tradition. They seem instinctively to know how to relate to us affirmingly, never condescendingly, yet with pricks to our pretense and with genuine bread of life (38–40). . . .

STAGE ONE—INTUITIVE-PROJECTIVE FAITH
(AVERAGE AGES: 4–7)

A. Locus of Authority

Fundamental dispositions and their expression depend principally on relations to "primal" others (parents, family or surrogates). These persons represent power, nurturance and security. The child's dependence on and affectional ties with them makes them prime authorities or references in his/her construction of a meaningful world. They convey both consciously and subliminally their own basic outlooks and commitment toward the ultimate conditions of life.

Where the faith of primal others is expressed congruently in the language, symbol, and ritual of a religious tradition, those media may take on a character of authority for the child, though the child's reliance on them is derivative and second-hand.

B. Criteria and Modes of Appropriation

Manifest interest in a child and the possession of visible (surface) qualities that attract the child's imagination and interest are required to qualify adults as faith models at this stage. Children attend to and imitate the moods, gestures and visible practices of such primal persons. The "forms" so observed stimulate and give channels for the children's own projections of numinous intuitions and fantasies with which they try to come to terms with a world as yet unlawful, magical and unpredictable. Cognitive understanding of the language and actions of commitment of significant others is limited, but affective investment in such often give them formative power in the child's normative awareness of ideal responsibility or adulthood.

C. Symbolic and Conceptual Functioning

Thinking is *pre-operational* (Piaget), marked by egocentrism, and by the use of symbols and concepts (or pre-concepts—Vygotsky) in labile and fluid fashion. Typically there is little concern to separate fantasy from fact. Narrative ability is limited. Causal relations are vague to the child and notions of effectance in the world tend toward magical explanation.

Symbols of deity, where used, are frequently preanthropomorphic with an effort to use such ideas as invisibleness, soul and air to depict a God who nonetheless acts physically and substantially on the world.

D. Role-Taking and Extensiveness of Identification

There is little ability as yet to take the role of others. The child is not yet able to construct and interpret the inner feelings, intentions or reasoning of other persons. Interaction with others therefore is largely a matter of moment-to-moment parallel behavior, as in playing.

Prime identity and attachment are to family or caring group. While there is little consistent awareness of one's differences from other persons or groups, a sense of sexual, racial and perhaps ethnic identity is already forming.

E. Prototypical Challenges with Which Faith Must Deal

A self-system is forming that begins to have both a conscious present and a vague futurity. With growing clarity about the self as separate from others comes a new kind of anxiety rooted in the awareness of death. Now the child knows that death threatens. Those on whom one is so vulnerably dependent can be removed by death. Faith, largely a matter of reliance on these others, needs to find a ground of hope and sustenance beyond them in order to "contain" the anxiety of possible abandonment through their death.

This is not to claim that the child is obsessed with these concerns. There are moments, of course, when they are obsessive, and for some children, actual. But they constitute an unavoidable shadow, an underside of life, which has to be dealt with in some fashion.

There must be some dim but potent locus for authority and forces beyond the immediate, tangible presence of parents or other significant adults. Death, sickness, bad luck as well as their opposites are not totally under control of those who "control" the child. Parents or their substitutes often give evidence of acknowledging power(s) and authority(s) beyond themselves. Some sort of deference must be paid to these powers that transcend and hold even parents in their grip and sway.

STAGE TWO—MYTHIC-LITERAL FAITH
(AVERAGE AGES: 6½–11)

A. Locus of Authority

The realm of worthy authority now extends beyond primal others to include teachers, religious leaders, customs, traditions, the media, books, and the ideas of peers. The mythic lore, the ritual, the music and symbolism of a religious tradition can make powerful impressions on persons at this stage. As regards matters of perceptual experience the child's own logic and judgment are coming to be relied upon in a kind of empiricism.

Unless they have disqualified themselves, the primal-familial group, now extended to take in others "like us" (in religious, ethnic, social class and/or racial terms), typically still provide the most important models and validating sanctions for the form and content of faith.

B. Criteria and Modes of Appropriation

New role-taking ability enables one now to evaluate and respond to qualities in authorities that are no longer merely surface (as in Stage One). Potentially authoritative persons or sources for faith insights tend to be weighed by criteria like the following: (1) "Fit" with the values, style, tastes and commitments of those with whom one feels greatest emotional affinity and identification. (2) Consistency in expressing real regard for the person. (3) Appearance of competence and/or interesting qualities that promise access to a vaguely aspired to futurity. (4) "Orthodoxy" (the way "we" do it) as regards the style of religious action. The operation of such criteria is not self-conscious or self-aware at Stage Two, but is an implicit function of the person's belonging to a familial or extended-familial group.

C. Symbolic and Conceptual Functioning

Concrete operational thinking has developed. Fluidity of concepts and symbolism has diminished. The child is concerned to understand lawfulness and predictability in relations between persons and in conditions affecting one's life. There is a strong empirical bent fostering an experimental approach as regards the tangible world.

Symbols for deity, where used, are typically anthropomorphic. They have power to cause and make; but they also have feelings and will and are attentive to the intentions of humans.

Narrative ability is now well developed. There is interest in myths and heroic images. One-dimensionality and literalism mark efforts to "explain" that which myths and symbols try to convey.

D. Role-Taking and Extensiveness of Identification

The ability to take the perspective of the other has developed, though mutual role-taking (i.e., seeing myself as others are seeing me as we interact) is not yet possible. The person can take the role of the group, but does not see self through the eyes of the group. Interaction with others is now *cooperative* (H.S. Sullivan) in contrast to Stage One's parallelism.

The person's identity and faith still derive their parameters largely from ascriptive membership in the primal group and its ethnic, racial, social class and religious extensions, which now have considerable clarity for the person. Those who are "different" are characterized in Stage Two thinking by fairly undifferentiated stereotypical images.

E. Prototypical Challenges with Which Faith Must Deal

The person's world now has a kind of order and dependability about it which results from the experience of continuities and from new cognitive abilities (inductive and deductive logic, capacities for classifying and seriating, understanding of causal relations, and a sense of time as linear). No longer does the person experience the world as potentially so capricious, arbitrary or mysterious as before. The person operates with a more dependable understanding of the dispositions, intentions, motives and expectations of others—and of oneself. The orderliness or dependability of the (cognitively available) world makes possible a projection of order and intentionality onto a more cosmic theater. Reciprocity and fairness, lawfulness and respect for intentions characterize ideas of God at this stage.

There are still, however, arbitrary elements and forces impinging on life beyond the ordering capacities of the child. Death, illness, accidents, and the unfolding of the person's own physical characteristics and capacities come as contingent elements of experience.

Faith helps sustain a sense of worth and competence by investing in ideal self-images which, though largely private, do include identification and affiliation with ideal persons and groups. Religious symbols, myths, ritual, music, and heroic figures can provide (where accessible) important vehicles of identification and affiliation. Where effectively offered they can become means of evoking and expressing the child's or person's faith in a transmundane order or meaning, as well as being guarantors of present and future promise.

STAGE THREE—SYNTHETIC-CONVENTIONAL FAITH
(AVERAGE AGES: 12–ADULTHOOD)

A. Locus of Authority

Conventionally or consensually sanctioned authorities are relied upon in the various different spheres of one's life. Criteria for valid authority continue to be a blend of requirements of interpersonal virtues and competence, but now add credentialing by institutions, by custom, or through the ascription of authority by consensus. Authority tends to be external to self, though personal responsibility is accepted for determining the choice and weighing available sources of guidance or insight. Dissonances between valued authorities are solved either by compartmentalization or hierarchical subordination. Feeling tends to dominate conceptual reasoning.

B. Criteria and Modes of Appropriation

Criteria for truth are generated from what one feels or thinks on the basis of conventionally validated values, beliefs and norms. The examples and expectations of "collective others" constitute important sources of criteria. Stage Three differs from Stage Two in that there is now a "collective other" which includes institutional and civil doctrines and law (as well as significant persons) which constitute an implicit value system against which authorities and insights can be evaluated. But there is no ground for other criteria by which one's own most deeply felt and held commitments can be critically evaluated. There is implicitly a continuing reliance on a community (or communities) which sponsor or nurture one's beliefs, attitudes and values.

C. Symbolic and Conceptual Functioning

Early Formal Operational thinking is characteristic. Symbols are employed as having multiple levels of meaning, though there is little self-consciousness about this. There is a limited use of abstractions.

There is a tacit system to one's world-view, but this system is legitimated by external authorities and inner feelings and is not a matter of critical reflection *qua* system. The person's beliefs and concepts that are expressive of faith function not as theoretical ideas but as existentially valued orientations.

The person is prepared to make do with rather global and undifferentiated ideas and symbols. A penumbra of mystery and deference to qualified authority compensate for the lack of conscious internal linkages and integration.

D. Role-Taking and Extensiveness of Identification

Mutual role-taking has developed in interpersonal relations. One can now see himself/herself through the eyes of a group or groups. Interaction with others now can be collaborative (H.S. Sullivan), involving full mutuality of role-taking with each other and with groups to which there are common loyalties (though such loyalties as yet are not matters of critically self-conscious choice).

Role-taking or identification with individuals beyond one's group(s) shows a limited development, but the inability to take the role of groups different than one's own is marked. Their world-views are likely to be assimilated to one's own. Identity derives from *belonging* (family, ethnic groups, sex-role, work unit) and/or *possessing* (respectability, competence, children, etc.).

E. *Prototypical Challenges with Which Faith Must Deal*

The existential challenges dominating Stage Three derive primarily from new cognitive capacities underlying mutual interpersonal role-taking. The person, now able to see himself/herself *as being seen by a variety of significant others* who occupy a variety of disparate standpoints in his/her world, has the problem of synthesizing those mirror images. Moreover, congruence must be found between his/her own feelings and images of self and the world and those held by others.

An amalgam of conventional images, values, beliefs and attitudes is fashioned to orient and provide boundaries for an as yet incompletely differentiated faith. In theistic expressions of faith at this stage, God is often the bearer of the role of the "collective other" who sums up the legitimate expectations and the individual loyalties of the significant others and groups in one's life. Faith is *derivative* at this stage as is identity—a more or less promising variant of a larger group style. (*Group* may here be defined by any or all of the following: ethnic-familial ties, social-class norms, regional perspectives and loyalties, a religious system, a techno-scientific ethos, peer values and pressures, and sex-role stereotypes.)

Faith, so expressed and buttressed, serves to provide a kind of coherence and comprehensive unity to one's experience of a now much more complex and ambiguous world. It also functions to sustain ideal self-images and bonds of affiliation with those significant others or sources of values and insights whose expectations, examples and teachings provide orientation in a potentially overwhelming and chaotic world. By appropriating mainly *vicarious* solutions to life's besetting tensions, and by screening out a fair amount of dissonant data, this stage of faith can provide powerful sustenance and a basis for decisive initiatives and action in life. But it has little way other than denial or oversimplifying assimilation to meet and take account of world-views and life-styles different than its own.

STAGE FOUR—INDIVIDUATING-REFLEXIVE FAITH (AVERAGE AGES: 18–ADULTHOOD)

A. Locus of Authority

Charismatic representatives of ideological options, intensive (if selective) attention to the personal experience of oneself and peers, and/or the ideological consensus of intentional (as opposed to ascriptive) groups are typical loci of authority for this stage. Authority has begun to be internalized and criteria for its acceptance are no longer matters of convention. Loyalties are committed on the basis of the self's felt and ratified affinities of valuing, beliefs, style and need-fulfillment.

B. Criteria and Modes of Appropriation

Appropriation of truth or insight is guided by criteria of existential resonance and congruity with what one is becoming or has become. While previously one's world-view was part of a matrix of experiencing, authority and an implicit and assumed coherence, now there is awareness that one holds (as do others) a point of view. The reference point for validating explanations has shifted from assimilating them to a nurturing ethos (Stage Three) to measuring them and that ethos against one's own experience, values, and critical judgments.

C. Symbolic and Conceptual Functioning

Full formal operations are employed. The ability to reflect critically on one's faith has appeared. There is awareness that one's outlook is vulnerable and can shift, and also of the relativity of one's way of experiencing to that of others whose outlook and loyalties are different.

There is an awareness of one's world-view as an explicit system. There is a concern for inner consistency, integration and comprehensiveness. Stage Four typically has an ideological quality. There is an excess of assimilation over accommodation, of subjective over objective content. Differences with other world-views are sharply recognized and often dichotomized.

D. Role-Taking and Extensiveness of Identification

Subject has the ability to treat other groups or classes as objects of mutual role-taking. The continued existence and integrity of one's own group becomes an issue of concern, and conscious commitment is possible not only to other individuals (as in Stage Three) but also to norms, rules, and ideological perspectives that underlie groups or institutions.

Concern with group boundaries, exclusion and inclusion is typical. Purity and consistency are matters of both personal and group concern. Ideal patterns of relation, interpersonal and social-institutional, frequently are used to criticize existing patterns, with contrasts being sharply drawn. Derivative identity (Stage Three) has been supplanted by *awareness* identity.

E. Prototypical Challenges with Which Faith Must Deal

The existential challenges or crises activating Stage Four faith center around the issue of individuation. Telegraphically put, Stage Four develops in the effort to find or create identifications and affiliations with ideologically defined groups whose outlook is expressive of the self one is becoming and has become, and of the truth or truths which have come to provide one's fundamental orientation.

The transition to Stage Four involves becoming self-consciously aware of the boundaries of one's conventionally held outlook. This may arise either from confrontation with persons or groups who hold different coherent systems of belief and action, or it may come from experiencing the threatening of one's conventional synthesis under the impact of prolonged experiences of crisis that expose its limits. Or it may come from a combination of both these.

The hope and need is for affiliation with a group and its ideology that provides a style of living and seeing which both express and hold up models for further development of one's own individuating faith. Where this cannot be found or where a dominant ethos negates recognition of the need, many persons move into a potentially long-lasting transitional posture, dissatisfied with former Stage Three conventionalities, but without materials or models for construction of a Stage Four faith.

Stage Four faith provides channels and guidelines for religious or ideological orientation and for ethical and political responsibility in a world where the reality of relativism is threateningly real.

STAGE FIVE—PARADOXICAL-CONSOLIDATIVE FAITH
(AVERAGE AGES: MINIMUM CA. 30)

A. Locus of Authority

Authority has now been fully internalized. Insights are derived through a dialectical process of evaluation and criticism between one's most profound experiences and intuitions and such mature formulations of the human-ultimate relationship as are available. Multiple communities and points of view contribute to one's complex world-view, which is itself not reducible to any of these. While the normativity of tradition, scriptures, customs, ideologies and the like is taken seriously these no longer are solely determinative for the person. Personal methods and discipline have developed for maintaining a living relationship with, participation in, or deference to the transcendent of the ultimate conditions of life.

B. Criteria and Modes of Appropriation

Criteria for truth and adequacy of faith claims or insights now derive from a holding together of intentions for oneself and one's community (as in Stage Four) with intentions and hopes for a more inclusive community or humanity. There is tension between the claims of egocentric or "group-centric" loyalties and loyalties to a more comprehensive community; similarly between "objectivity" and "subjectivity" in the use of concepts and symbols. Stage Five embraces these tensions, accepting paradox when necessary, as essential characteristics of truth.

C. Symbolic and Conceptual Functioning

Stage Five affirms and incorporates existential or logical polarities, acting on a felt need to hold them in tension in the interest of truth. It maintains its vision of meaning, coherence and value while being conscious of the fact that it is partial, limited and contradicted by the visions and claims of others. It is not simply relativist, affirming that one person's faith is as good as another's if equally strongly held. It holds its vision with a kind of provisional ultimacy: remembering its inadequacy and open to new truth, but also committed to the absoluteness of the truth which it inadequately comprehends and expresses.

Symbols are understood as symbols. They are seen-through in a double sense: (1) their time-place relativity is acknowledged and (2) their character as relative representations of something more nearly absolute is affirmed.

D. Role-Taking and Extensiveness of Identification

The person has the ability not only to take the role of another person or group but also to take the role of another person's or group's world-view in its full complexity.

Stage Five must sustain political/ethical activity that has a more complex character than at Stage Four. It has a double consciousness not required of Stage Four. With opposing groups it must acknowledge a significant measure of identification—both in rights and wrongs—strengths and weaknesses. It has the burden of awareness of the degree to which "free will" or choice is always limited in fateful ways by a person's or group's history and situation. It must decide and act, but bears inevitable anguish due to a role-taking that transcends its own group's limits. Its imperatives of love and justice must be extended to *all* persons or groups.

E. *Prototypical Challenges with Which Faith Must Deal*

If Stage Four had to deal with the issues arising out of the individuation process, Stage Five's characteristic existential challenges grow out of the experience of finding the limits of one's Stage Four ideological and communal identifications.

First there is the issue of a loneliness now experienced as cosmic. One may have relationships with other persons or groups of great intimacy, yet there comes the recognition that one is never fully known nor capable of fully knowing others. Though one may work out patterns of loyalty and commitment with other person or persons, such loyalty is always limited either by will, capacity, or death. Great similarities and commonalities may be found or created with others, justifying celebrations; but even with those who are closest there may be deep-going differences which underscore the final aloneness and uniqueness of the person. One becomes aware of, and faith must deal with, the loneliness arising from the recognition of uncloseable gaps of experience, perspective and emotional structure between the self and even those who are closest.

Faith must come to grips with the tension of being ethically responsible but finite. Whereas Stage Four faith generally offers solutions that promise to solve the polar tensions between self-fulfillment and commitment to the welfare of others, Stage Five faith has to come to terms with the tragic character of that polar pull. Stage Five faith must sustain commitment to the worth of ethical action and its costliness even while accepting the realities of intractable ignorance, egocentricity, and limited abilities and interests—in oneself and in human beings generally.

Stage Five maintains its faith vision without the props of authority or ideological certainty that provide guarantees for Stages Three and Four respectively. Faith is a volitional act of paradoxical commitment at Stage Five. Stage Five is faith that has taken its own doubt and despair seriously.

STAGE SIX—UNIVERSALIZING FAITH
(AVERAGE AGE: MINIMUM CA. 40)

A. Locus of Authority

The matter of authority is now contained within a relationship of unmediated participation in and complementarity with the ultimate conditions of existence. There is a post-critical at-one-ness with the ultimate conditions of one's life and of being generally. The paradoxical quality of this in Five is overcome.

The ultimate conditions are differentiated from the mundane; they are kept in creative tension and interpenetration.

Usually some disciplined means is employed to restore a sense of participation in or permeation by the Transcendent.

B. Criteria and Modes of Appropriation

Criteria for truth now require incorporating the "truths" of many different standpoints into a synthesis that reconciles without negating their particular or unique contributions. In contrast to Stage Five this reconciliation of the one and the many is no longer paradoxical, but has a quality of simplicity. For these criteria to be fulfilled the person must have an identification with being in which love of self is genuinely incorporated and fulfilled in love of Being.

C. Symbolic and Conceptual Functioning

One is directly and nonmediately aware of the ultimate context of life. Symbols and concepts play a secondary function, making communication possible, though inevitably distorting. Stage Six draws on insights and vision from many sources, valuing them as helpful, if partial, apprehensions of Truth.

Conflicts and paradox are embraced as essential to the integrity of Being (similarly to Stage Five) but are unified in a no-longer-paradoxical grasp of the oneness of Being.

D. Role-Taking and Extensiveness of Identification

Stage Six has the ability to respond to and feel commonality with the concreteness and individuality of persons while also relating to and evoking their potential.

There is the capacity for a meaningful (i.e., tested and hard-won) taking the role of a universal community. Active compassion for a commonwealth of being is expressed, including but transcending group differences and conflicts.

E. *Prototypical Challenges with Which Faith Must Deal*

Faith at Stage Six must meet the temptation to transcend and give way to complete absorption in the *All*. Ethical and historical irresponsibility can result from a genuinely universalizing perspective. Too complete a merging with the Eternal Now can result in the abdication from time and concrete responsibility.

Stage Six bears the burden and challenge of relating to persons and issues concerned at quite other stages and levels of development. It must do so with patience, compassion and helpfulness. Faith at this stage must bear the pain and potential despair of seeing ethical causes and movements of compassion exploded or subverted by less universalizing interests.

There is a crucifixion involved in seeing and having to accept the inevitability of certain tragic denouements in history. Stage Six faith must cope with seeing and understanding more than others, and with the challenge and responsibilities of universal identifications.

Faith at Six must resist the subtle temptations to pride and self-deception and the danger of corruption by adulation.

Faith must overcome the danger of ethical and political paralysis while at the same time being a source of solutional approaches that introduce genuine novelty and transcendent possibilities into situations of conflict and bitterness and deeply contested interests.

Faith must endure the misunderstandings and slanders and violent potentials (and actualities) of those who cannot comprehend, or of those who do comprehend and are threatened to the core by the person's vision and way of being.

There is the burden of being a mediator, teacher or semi-divine model for others. Faith must maintain, generate and renew the vision of a cosmic meaning that will help sustain others. This is the frightful burden of being a "Savior of God" (Kazantzakis).

Fowler

James W. Fowler, *Stages of Faith.* N.Y.: Harper and Row, 1981.

Review Symposium on Fowler's *Stages of Faith, Horizons,* Spring 1982, 104–126.

Jim Fowler and Sam Keen, *Life Maps. Conversations on the Journey to Faith.* Minneapolis: Winston Press, 1980.

James W. Fowler, "Faith and the Structuring of Meaning," in *Toward Moral and Religious Maturity,* Christiane Brusselmans, convenor. Morristown, N.J.: Silver Burdett Co., 1980, 51–85.

James W. Fowler, "Stages in Faith: The Structural-Developmental Approach," in *Values and Moral Development,* Thomas C. Hennessy, S.J., ed. N.Y.: Paulist Press, 1976, 173–210; cf. critiques, 211–223.

Erikson and Kohlberg

Walter E. Conn, "Moral Development and Self-Transcendence," *Horizons,* Fall 1977, 189–206. Lonergan, Kohlberg, Erikson.

Walter E. Conn, *Conscience: Development and Self-Transcendence.* Birmingham, Ala.: Religious Education Press, 1981.

Ronald Duska and Mariellen Whelan, *Moral Development. A Guide to Piaget and Kohlberg.* N.Y.: Paulist, 1975.

Erik H. Erikson, *Identity, Youth and Crisis.* N.Y.: Norton, 1968.

Erik H. Erikson, *Identity and the Life Cycle.* N.Y.: Norton, 1980.

Richard I. Evans, *Dialogue with Erik Erikson.* N.Y.: Harper and Row, 1967.

Peter Homans, ed., *Childhood and Selfhood. Essays on Tradition, Religion and Modernity in the Psychology of Erik Erikson.* Lewisburg, Pa.: Bucknell University Press, 1978.

Lawrence Kohlberg, "The Cognitive-Developmental Approach to Moral Education," in *Readings in Moral Education,* Peter Scharf, ed. Minneapolis: Winston Press, 1978, 36–51; for a critique, see 250–263.

Brenda Munsey, ed., *Moral Development, Moral Education and Kohlberg.* Birmingham, Ala.: Religious Education Press, 1980; critique, 280ff.

Howard Muson, "Moral Thinking: Can It Be Taught?" *Psychology Today,* Feb. 1979, 48ff.

Paul Roazen, *Erik H. Erikson. The Powers and Limits of a Vision.* N.Y.: Free Press, 1976.

Ernest Wallwork, "Erik H. Erikson: Psychosocial Resources For Faith," in *Critical Issues in Modern Religion,* Roger Johnson, Ernest Wallwork, eds. Englewood Cliffs, N.J.: Prentice-Hall, 1973, 322–361.

XI.
C.G. Jung and the Religion of the Unconscious

Regina Bechtle, S.C.

Editor's Note

With C.G. Jung (1875–1961) we move to the area of transpersonal psychology. By transpersonal is meant a psychology whose point of stress is not on the ego and its development but on something beyond the ego. With Jung, the accent is placed on the unconscious and the transrational, the symbolical and the archetypal.

In Jung, one must distinguish between archetype and symbol. The archetype is a power or potency which is cross-cultural. It is not an innate idea but an a priori power of representation. The specific symbol is generally culturally determined and appears in the form of religious stories, myths, fairy tales and dreams (*Man and His Symbols*, 56–57).

The following essay presents an overview of Jung's religious thought. The author, Regina Bechtle, S.C., has specialized in the study of mysticism and in spiritual direction.

*　　*　　*

Born in 1875 in Switzerland, the son of a minister of the Swiss Reformed Church, Carl Gustave Jung studied medicine at the University of Basel and spent his first ten years as a doctor in a hospital in Burghölzli near Zürich, while also serving as professor in charge of the course in psychiatry at the university there. His experiments in "idea-association" led to collaboration with Sigmund Freud from 1907 to 1913, and

Jung's writings during this time evidence how profound was Freud's influence upon him. Initially he accepted Freud's theory of sexuality as the basic motivation behind man's conscious acts, but he soon discovered that a more comprehensive concept was needed, as well as a more dynamic theory which pointed ahead to a developmental process of self-realization rather than merely behind to the hidden and deeply-rooted causes of psychic disturbance. The publication in 1911–12 of Jung's *Wandlungen und Symbole der Libido* (translated as *The Psychology of the Unconscious*) marked his definitive break with the Freudian school.

In his second period, Jung left his teaching and medical positions to immerse himself in psychotherapy. He collected vast amounts of data from the dreams of his patients as well as from first-hand research into primitive cultures in Central Africa and North America. To trace similar patterns more thoroughly, he studied the religious and philosophical thought of the East, ancient Gnostic writings and medieval alchemical treatises. His 1937 Terry lectures at Yale entitled "Psychology and Religion" reflected his growing interest in religion and signaled the beginning of a new phase of work.

His post-war writings centered mainly on the nature and expressions of symbolism, especially in its religious manifestations, and specifically on the psychological meaning of Catholic doctrines such as the Mass, the Trinity, Christ and the Assumption of Mary.[1]

Our investigation of the work of Jung in relation to religion and revelation must begin with a brief exposition of his psychology—method, object and basic concepts. We will then be in a position to examine the origins, purpose and progress of his dialogue with religion. In particular, we will touch on his explanation of symbol in connection with the nature of religious experience and the function of dogma and myth. Finally, the charge of psychologism leveled against Jung will be evaluated, and his contribution to theology assessed.

I

JUNG'S PSYCHOLOGY

A. Use of Empirical Method

Influenced by the methodology of the natural sciences, as was almost inevitable for a man of his times, Jung was a thorough-going empiricist. This fact is important for understanding both his strictly psychological research and his observations of religious phenomena. He realized that absolute and unbiased objectivity was impossible to attain, especially when dealing with the complexities of the human psyche; the very act of determining an experimental procedure limited the phenomena to be observed and conditioned the results expected. Yet with these limitations, Jung tried to be as unprejudiced as possible as he formulated hypotheses based on the correlations between observed facts. Each patient he treated was a unique case, to be sure, yet over the years of his psychoanalytic practice, he perceived strikingly similar patterns of response, from which he could draw tentative conclusions as to the presence of some objective psychic reality. With admirable scientific detachment, he viewed a hypothesis as a mere tool to aid further research—thus his readiness to abandon one and to adopt another, perhaps contradictory to the first, if it offered a simpler and more complete explanation of the data. This factor adds to the unsystematic character of his work and has often been interpreted by philosophically-minded critics as symptomatic of confusion and lack of logic, whereas in reality it is but the natural outgrowth of his scientific procedure.[2]

The overriding characteristic of Jung's psychological methodology, then, is his commitment to empirical observation of data and to their interpretation in broad hypotheses which are always subject to modification and improvement.

B. Object: Psychic Reality

Jung's investigations cover all of psychic reality, a realm which he sees as qualitatively different from, and not to be reduced to, the physical, though its exact essence cannot be defined precisely.

In his earlier writing, Jung handled the problem of the

spiritual and material aspects of reality in a somewhat simplistic fashion, but one which nevertheless indicates the importance which he attached to the category of "psychic reality." He wrote:

> The conflict of nature and mind is itself a reflection of the paradox contained in the psychic being of man. This reveals a material and a spiritual aspect which appear a contradiction as long as we fail to understand the nature of psychic life.[3]

He proceeded to assert that only the psychic constitutes the realm of immediate experience. Even sense-impressions can be modulated or intensified by the psyche, and it is only these psychic images which form the immediate objects of consciousness. "We are in all truth so enclosed by psychic images that we cannot penetrate to the essence of things external to ourselves."[4]

If expressed in mutually exclusive terms—"Which principle alone explains reality: matter or spirit?"—the problematic admits of only unsatisfactory solutions. Jung preferred to view the physical and the mental as two distinct points of contact initiating the psychic process.

> If I change my concept of reality in such a way as to admit that all psychic happenings are real—and no other use of the concept is valid—this puts an end to the conflict of matter and mind as contradictory explanatory principles. Each becomes a mere designation for the particular source of the psychic contents that crowd into my field of consciousness.[5]

So reality in the psychological sense is affirmed of anything which exerts a psychic influence on a subject. Thus an "imaginary" voice which haunts a disturbed patient is psychically real and must be treated as such. So too the tremendous power and attraction of the idea of God throughout man's history points to the psychic reality of God. When indignant believers reacted against this as a reduction of God to the psychological, Jung took pains to assure them that the affirmation of the psychic existence of God was not a denial of his ontological reality but merely the only conclusion he could legitimately draw from his empirical observations; metaphysical proofs were not within his area of competence.[6]

After these somewhat abstract considerations, it might be well to make a few brief remarks on the nature of human knowing as an introduction to some of the fundamental concepts which Jung uses in his work. Contrary to the prophets of the Enlightenment and to modern rationalists, man's movement to comprehend reality is not exhausted by the intellectual activity of his consciousness.

> Do we ever understand what we think? We only understand that thinking which is a mere equation, and from which nothing comes out but what we have put in. That is the working of the intellect. But beyond that there is a thinking in primordial images—in symbols which are older than historical man; ... It is only possible to live the fullest life when we are in harmony with these symbols; wisdom is a return to them. It is neither a question of belief nor of knowledge, but of the agreement of our thinking with the primordial images of the unconscious.[7]

Neglect of this area of the unconscious has resulted in a psychologically unbalanced culture. Rational man, who should be master of his own fate, finds himself prey to irrational and destructive powers, which all his technological expertise cannot control; should modern man be tempted to consider himself the crown of the centuries, he need only recall the barbarism with which he still wages war on his fellows. Now that he has experienced the evil within himself, he can no longer trust in his own capabilities to realize any of the rosy visions of progress which earlier reformers dreamed, and neither can he project the cause of this failure onto the external world.

> Through his skepticism the modern man is thrown back upon himself; his energies flow towards their

source and wash to the surface those psychic contents which are at all times there, but lie hidden in the silt as long as the stream flows smoothly in its course.[8]

The myths and metaphysical systems which in earlier times objectified and thus dealt with their deepest human hopes, fears, longings and anxieties have disappeared; the hopes and fears have returned to the darkness within the self, and it is to this unknown territory that modern man is drawn.

C. Basic Concepts

1. *The Unconscious.* Jung's central thrust, as he expressed it, was "to penetrate into the secret of the personality."[9] That thrust took him below the surface of consciousness to the depths of the *unconscious,* the realm of psychic reality which influences consciousness yet is not identical with it, and which assumes an autonomous existence over against it. Jung's notion of the unconscious is unavoidably vague; it functions as a "boundary concept" (*Grenzbegriff*) to describe that non-conscious area whose boundaries are unspecified but which yet acts as though conscious, e.g., through all the manifestations attributed in other cultures to gods, demons, spirits and supernatural powers.[10]

In tracing the causes of psychological illness back to some aberration in sexual development, repressed into the unconscious, Freud linked the entire theory and practice of his psychotherapy to sexuality. Jung, though an early follower of Freud, was led to postulate a concept of psychic energy, or *libido,* broader than the merely sexual; for Jung, libido refers to the undifferentiated and uncontrolled psychic impulses and tendencies at the root of all human action. When its normal course is blocked, this energy is forced to backtrack, so to speak, and returns to regressive patterns of behavior. But this movement backwards has a positive side: it is an attempt, however unsatisfactory, to find some solution which will remove the inner obstacle.[11]

Phenomena such as dreams fantasies, hallucinations, etc. witness to the presence of unexplored, non-conceptualized and repressed aspects of our lives in the *personal unconscious.* Beyond

this, however, Jung's psychoanalytic research and his comparative studies in primitive religion and alchemy led him to the
conclusion that predispositions toward forming certain symbol-
patterns are found trans-culturally and trans-temporally. No
generation can consider itself psychologically severed from
previous ages.

> Our modern attitude looks back proudly upon the
> mists of superstition and of medieval or primitive
> credulity and entirely forgets that it carries the whole
> living past in the lower stories of the skyscraper of
> rational consciousness. Without the lower stories our
> mind is suspended in midair. . . . The true history of
> the mind is not preserved in learned volumes but in
> the living mental organism of everyone.[12]

Thus he postulated the *collective unconscious* as the sum total
of man's inherited psychic experience, shared by all men as a
transindividual psychological substratum of life.[13]

Among the contents of the unconscious are; the *shadow,* or
the dark and undeveloped side of one's personality, which must
be confronted if self-integration is to occur; the *anima* (*animus*),
or personification of feminine qualities in the male (masculine
in the female), complementing the conscious tendencies of the
person toward one sexual orientation rather than another.
These and other psychic realities can be subsumed under the
heading of *archetypes.*

2. *Archetypes of the Collective Unconscious.* The identity and
continuity of man's psychic structures is expressed in his innate
predispositions toward the formation of certain common images.

> In the mythology and folklore of different peoples,
> certain motives repeat themselves in almost identical
> form. I have called those motives archetypes and by
> them I understand forms or images of a collective

nature which occur practically all over the earth as constituents of myths and at the same time as autochthonous, individual products of unconscious origin.[14]

Examples of these primordial archetypal figures and patterns include the passage from darkness to light, or from death to rebirth; the Mother; the wise old man who mediates meaning; the dying god; the eternal child; the hidden treasure. As "organs of the prerational psyche," the archetypes are not encountered directly but only though the medium of symbols.

3. *Symbol.* In contradistinction to signs, symbols in Jung's terminology are not just convenient ways of expressing concisely something which is already known, much as a striped pole outside a shop stands for the presence of a barber within. Rather they are mediators of an unknown reality, polyvalent in meaning, capable of arousing many different thoughts and feelings because they arise spontaneously from the soil not only of past and forgotten consciousness but of the as-yet-unrealized unconscious.[15] Etymologically, symbol (from the Greek *sym-ballo*) connotes a process of totalizing or unifying, and herein lies its therapeutic power:

> As a uniter of opposites, the symbol is a totality which can never be addressed only to one faculty in a man —his reason or intellect, for example—but always concerns our wholeness, touches and produces a resonance in all four of our functions at once. The symbol as 'image' has the character of a summons and stimulates a man's whole being to a total reaction; his thought and feeling, his senses and his intuition participate in this reaction and it is not, as some mistakenly suppose, a single one of his functions that is actualized.[16]

We have attempted in this section to clarify several concepts basic to Jung's psychology—libido, unconscious, archetype, symbol—without defining them exhaustively. We will now study the application of these terms to the rhythm of human development.

D. *The Process of Individuation*

Jung believed that the psyche was oriented toward a state of dynamic self-fulfillment, toward a unified psychic totality which would integrate all the disparate components of the personality, both conscious and unconscious. This process of individuation has been described as "the systematic confrontation, step by step, between the ego and the contents of the unconscious,"[17] and more fully, as "the open conflict and open collaboration between the conscious and the unconscious by means of which the individual is forged into an indestructible whole."[18] Although this growth does occur naturally in some, many others shun the effort and discipline required, and so the individuation process must often be assisted by external means, such as psychoanalysis, in which the consciousness is summoned to intervene in the spontaneous movement of the psyche in order knowingly to accept and integrate its contents.[19] The dialectic between conscious and unconscious is bridged by symbols, and it is in symbolic terms that the conflicting claims of the various elements of the psyche are acted out.

> The symbols that rise up out of the unconscious in dreams point rather to a confrontation of opposites, and the images of the goal represent their successful reconciliation. Something empirically demonstrable comes to our aid from the depths of our unconscious nature. It is the task of the conscious mind to understand these hints.[20]

Whether in the first half of life, which could be described as a period of initiation into external reality, or in the second, a time of reduction to the essential, inner reality, an underlying dynamic toward wholeness is operative. "The goal of psychic development is the self. There is no linear evolution; there is only a circumambulation of the self."[21] The archetype of the Self, embodying this "ultimately unknowable, transcendent 'centre' of the personality," usually appears in dreams, legends, myths, fairy tales and fantasies under the guise of a *mandala* or symmetrical arrangement of elements in relation to a center. When the tension between conscious and unconscious is experienced as confusing, threatening or destructive, the emergence of such a symbol serves to reconcile the opposites and to restore psychic order, balance and security to the person.[22]

We might summarize this brief outline of the individuation process and set the stage for Jung's specific application of his psychological framework to the spiritual situation of modern man in the following words of Hostie:

> As long as the totality of the self remains hidden from the eyes of that inveterate rationalist, Western man, he goes on basking in the illusion that he can be a complete autocrat. Only the emergence into consciousness of this totality can bring him out of this dream state. If he does not allow it to emerge, the neglected psychic components go on tyrannizing over him as projections; a clear acceptance of it, however, leads to submission to the self and this in turn leads to a harmonious integration of all the psychic potentialities. And then, individuation, or the confrontation of consciousness and the unconscious, reaches its culmination.[23]

II
PSYCHOLOGY AND RELIGION

A. The Spiritual Situation of Modern Man

As long as man's conscious patterns of action and systems of thought harmonize with the archetypal structure of his unconscious, he can live in relative inner peace and security, guaranteed meaning by an objective world order which satisfies the projections of his psychic needs. In our day, however, the darkness of the unconscious is effectively ignored in the technology-centered day-to-day living of one-dimensional man; his ideals of wealth and progress seem to admit of no realization; his systems of belief and metaphysical certainties no longer

adequately express his experience.[24] The creative tension between the conscious and the unconscious, and the resolution of
that tension through meaningful symbols, has yielded to a
destructive polarization and fragmentation of self.

> As soon as [man] has outgrown whatever local form of
> religion he was born to—as soon as this religion can
> no longer embrace his life in all its fulness—then the
> psyche becomes something in its own right.[25]

> This 'psychological' interest of the present time shows
> that man expects something from psychic life which he
> has not received from the outer world: something
> which our religions, doubtless, ought to contain, but
> no longer do contain—at least for the modern man.
> The various forms of religion no longer appear to the
> modern man to come from within—to be expressions
> of his own psychic life; for him they are to be classed
> with the things of the outer world.[26]

Jung sees the current renewal of interest in the psychic
realm as a positive factor; it signals a rejection both of material-
ism and of pseudo-intellectualism, and a humble embracing of
the totality of life—spirit and instinct—which he describes as
profoundly "religious."[27]

B. Meaning and Function of Religion

Religion has indeed failed the man of today, in Jung's
opinion—but why should religion play any part at all in the life
of enlightened man? Departing from the Freudian school, Jung
repeatedly emphasized not only the psychological importance
of religion but also the irreducible religious orientation of man.
Even in his early writings, while refusing to grant any objective
reality to the concept of God, he nevertheless is forced to admit
the benefits which religion brings to mankind.

> The religious myth meets us here as one of the great-
> est and most significant human institutions which,
> despite misleading symbols, nevertheless gives man

assurance and strength, so that he may not be overwhelmed by the monsters of the universe. The symbol, considered from the standpoint of actual truth, is
misleading, indeed, but it is *psychologically true,* because
it was and is the bridge to all the greatest achieve-
ments of humanity.[28]

In a later development of his thought, Jung described religion
as "the attitude peculiar to a consciousness which has been
altered by the experience of the numinosum,"[29] that is, by a
dynamic factor outside the voluntary control of the subject.
And in a short work published in 1958, Jung further refined his
concept of religion in terms of its counterbalancing effect
against a totalitarian State:

> Religion means dependence on and submission to the
> irrational facts of experience. . . . Its evident purpose
> is to maintain the psychic balance, for the natural man
> has an equally natural 'knowledge' of the fact that his
> conscious functions may at any time be thwarted by
> uncontrollable happenings coming from inside as well
> as from outside.[30]

In essence, then, true religion participates in the numinous, the irrational, the experiential. Before we discuss the
objectification of religion in dogma, we must examine the
Jungian concept of God.

C. The Idea of God

Perhaps no position of Jung's has been so misunderstood
as his concept of God. True to his empirical and phenomenological methodology, he has repeatedly asserted that the
objective existence of God remains outside the scope of his investigation; all that he can study is the psychological effect of
subjective experience.

> The idea of God is an absolutely necessary psycholog-
> ical function of an irrational nature, which has nothing
> whatever to do with the question of God's existence.

The human intellect can never answer this question, still less give any proof of God. Moreover such proof is superfluous, for the idea of an all-powerful divine Being is present everywhere, unconsciously if not consciously, because it is an archetype.[31]

The archetypal character of the God-image is revealed most clearly in Christ. Christ lived a concrete historical existence which assumed earth-shaking significance because he participated so deeply in the archetypal life of mankind. In the life of Christ is reflected man's experience, his striving for self-integration and wholeness through the process of individuation.

Looked at from the psychological standpoint, Christ, as the Original Man ... represents a totality which surpasses and includes the ordinary man, and which corresponds to the total personality that transcends consciousness. We have called this personality the 'self'.[32]

The Self is the transcendent center of the personality, which organizes and guides all the psychic functions, the unknown yet beneficent power to whom the person must submit himself in order to achieve wholeness.[33] Christ then becomes for man a symbol of the Self, his incarnation a paradigm of self-realization, and his passion a prototype of the suffering involved in the task of individuation: the submission of the ego to the wider dimension of the Self. In summary,

the drama of the archetypal life of Christ describes in symbolic images the events in the conscious life—as well as in the life that transcends consciousness—of a man who has been transformed by his higher destiny.[34]

In a passage reminiscent of Tillich, Jung wrote: "Psychologically the God-concept includes every idea of the ultimate, of the first or last, or the highest or lowest. The name makes no difference."[35] No matter what its ultimate reference or meaning, the fact of man's innate orientation towards "God," as a primordial psychic structure, cannot be arbitrarily ignored. From his observations of patients during a 30-year span of time, Jung concluded:

> Among all my patients in the second half of life . . . there has not been one whose problem in the last resort was not that of finding a religious outlook on life. It is safe to say that every one of them fell ill because he had lost that which the living religions of every age had given to their followers, and none of them has really been healed who did not regain his religious outlook.[36]

What function did these "living religions" perform for man? Why does modern man reject the systems of belief which his predecessors found adequate? Is his "religious outlook" to be regained apart from, or even in opposition to, the structures of the established religions? An answer to these questions demands an examination of the roles of religious experience and of dogmatic formulation in Jung.

D. Religious Experience and Objectification

It comes as no surprise to find that for Jung, the experience of the numinous comprised the essence of religion, as well as its starting-point. In this connection Jung likened our times to the first and second centuries A.D., when Gnostic thought attained its peak. Distrust of reason, expectation of a heavenly revelation, exaltation of inner awareness and participation in the arcane mysteries characterized the Gnostic reaction to the over-rational atmosphere of late Greek culture. So too modern man only accepts common formulations of belief when they correspond to his own psychic experience.[37]

Creeds and dogmas merely codify and systematize the original religious experience. Even revelation, for Jung, is not primarily a transmission of knowledge about God, but a discovery of what lies within the person.

Revelation is an unveiling of the depths of the human soul first and foremost, a 'laying bare,' hence it is an essentially psychological event, though this does not of course tell us what else it could be.[38]

In some instances, Jung criticizes the established religions for preserving systems "no longer based on their own inner experience but on *unreflecting belief.* . . . Belief is no adequate substitute for inner experience. . . . People call faith the true religious experience, but they do not stop to think that actually it is a secondary phenomenon arising from the fact that something happened to us in the first place which instilled πίστις into us—that is, trust and loyalty."[39]

On the other hand, dogma exercises a positive function in that it "shields" the believer from the unknown dangers of an immediate experience of the divine or else serves as a criterion by which his experience can be judged as coming from God or the devil. Dogma protects because it reflects the workings of the unconscious (here Jung is referring to archetypal patterns which Christianity expresses in such doctrines as the Incarnation of the God-Man, the Virgin Birth, the Trinity, the Redemption, etc.); once a ritual has been formulated, whether in words or in actions, the dark and lurking powers of the unconscious can be dealt with harmlessly.[40] "The whole life of the collective unconscious has been absorbed without remainder, so to speak, in the dogmatic archetypes, and flows like a well-controlled stream in the symbolism of ritual and of the church calendar."[41]

Yet the indictment remains: the religious bodies of today have ceased to incarnate meaning for man.

Since they are compromises with mundane reality, the creeds have accordingly seen themselves obliged to undertake a progressive codification of their views, doctrines and customs and in so doing have externalized themselves to such an extent that the authentic religious element in them—the living relationship to and direct confrontation with their extra-mundane point of reference—has been thrust into the back-ground.[42]

Since dogmas no longer act as "reconciling symbols" between the conscious and the unconscious, the psyche must retrace its steps inward, back to the primal experience which alone can make it whole.

> No matter what the world thinks about religious experience, the one who has it possesses the great treasure of a thing that has provided him with a source of life, meaning and beauty. . . . Where is the criterium by which you could say that such a life is not legitimate, that such experience is not valid and that such pistis it mere illusion? Is there, as a matter of fact, any better truth about ultimate things than the one that helps you to live?[43]

E. The Role of Christianity[44]

Lest we begin to think of Jung as a cynical anti-institutionalist, we must recall the high regard in which he held Christianity both from the historical and the psychotherapeutic perspectives. The inadequacy of the Christian symbol in expressing the deepest needs of modern man does not signal irreversible defeat.

> It is not Christianity, but our conception and interpretation of it, that has become antiquated in face of the present world situation. The Christian symbol is a living thing that carries in itself the seeds of further development. It can go on developing; it depends only on us, whether we can make up our minds to meditate again, and more thoroughly, on the Christian premises.[45]

One of these "Christian premises" is at the same time a contribution and a burden to mankind: centered on Jesus, the Word made flesh, Christianity has become the "religion of the word," and has specified our civilization by the supremacy and autonomy which it accords to the word, and the consequent rupture it promotes between faith and knowledge.[46]

F. Religion in East and West

It is understandable that those to whom Christian symbols no longer speak meaningfully should, in their journey back along the paths of the psyche, discover the attraction of the East. According to the psychological law of *enantiodromia* (the tendency against a one-sided orientation of the psyche because of which its opposite emerges) an overemphasis on the materialistic and rational provokes a reaction favoring the other-worldly and intuitive—and this is precisely the experience of many today.[47] Yet Jung wonders whether modern man can with impunity abandon the tradition of his own symbols in favor of those of the East. Neither matter nor spirit suffices in itself to embrace the totality of reality, just as neither the conscious nor the unconscious can be allowed to tip the balance of the person if wholeness is to be won.

> When the primitive world disintegrated into spirit and nature, the West rescued nature for itself. It was prone to a belief in nature, and only became the more entangled in it with every painful effort to make itself spiritual. The East, on the contrary, took mind for its own, and by explaining away matter as mere illusion (*maya*), continued to dream in Asiatic filth and misery. But since there is only *one* earth and *one* mankind, East and West cannot rend humanity into two different halves.[48]

Perhaps the East—in the sense of contemplative reflection, detachment and stability—is within our very selves.[49]

In the first part of this essay, we have attemped to sketch the basic points of Jung's analytical psychology, noting his empirical-phenomenological method, his investigation of psychic rather than ontological reality, his conceptual framework and his key developmental category of "individuation." Next we addressed ourselves to his religious concerns, rooted in the spiritual crisis of modern man, and viewed religion, God, dogma and religious experience from his perspective. We now propose to discuss the main criticism brought against Jung's approach—that of "psychologism."

III
CRITICISMS

It was inevitable that Jung's treatment of religious themes from a psychological point of view should leave him open to the charge of "psychologism." According to his own understanding of the term as any theory in which religion is merely the projection or transformation of an instinct, Jung is exonerated from this charge, since he maintains that religion is irreducible and non-derivative.[50]

Hostie feels that, while Jung, especially in his later period, rejected the idea that God was nothing more than a psychic reality, his sketchy knowledge of, and his aversion to, metaphysics and theology prevented him from grappling more satisfactorily with the problem. Jung's own attitude is revealed in a remark he made to Hostie: "It is quite clear that God exists but why are people always asking me to prove this psychologically?"[51]

In this connection, the question of methodological consistency has been raised by Hostie, who takes issue with Jung's assertion that his empiricism does not allow him to make any statements whatsoever about the existence of the non-observable, specifically, God. In actual fact, Hostie feels, Jung overstepped the limits he set for himself for he repeatedly shifts his argumentation, especially in his earlier works, from: "It is impossible *for me* to know or prove *scientifically* that God exists," to: "It is impossible to know or prove that God exists," a statement which completely discounts the validity of philosophical or theological knowledge.[52] On this basis, we would concur with Hostie in Goldbrunner's evaluation of Jung as an "agnostic positivist" up until 1940.

Jung's later work in religious symbolism does give evidence of a growing recognition of the validity of "the religious point of view," but for him this classifies metaphysics, faith and theology alike under the one rubric: acceptance of something as true on the basis of a subjective conviction.[53] Jung wrote in 1944: "The religious-minded man is free to accept whatever metaphysical explanations he pleases . . . ; not so the intellect, which must keep strictly to the principles of scientific interpretation."[54]

We feel that Jung does at times seem to over-generalize his assertion that he can say nothing at all about ontological reality. This lack of methodological precision must be acknowledged. He grappled constantly with what he perceived as the conflicting paths of faith and knowledge:

> I do not fiddle with dogma. In my eyes it has the highest authority, but I try to *understand* it, since unfortunately I cannot believe anything I do not understand, and in this I am like many other people today. If it were otherwise, I should only be believing in empty words, and this surely cannot be the meaning of belief . . .[55]

It is strange that Jung who always upheld the primacy of subjective experience disliked the word "faith." Faith, for him, seems to have connoted an externally imposed belief bereft of the inner experience. Perhaps his usage merely reflects his own personal struggle to reconcile scientific method and religious experience. Be that as it may, we feel that on no account can the later Jung, at least, be accused of agnosticism in the usual sense of the word. As he wrote in his autobiography. "The decisive question for man is: Are you related to something infinite or not?"[56]

IV
JUNG'S CONTRIBUTIONS

This essay has barely skimmed the surface of the Jungian corpus of writings. We have not treated such topics as his concept of evil within God, or his analysis of the Trinity. These conclusions, therefore, are based not on specific points but on a general overview of Jung's attempt to achieve a *rapprochement* between psychology and religion.

A. Synthesis of Opposites

Valuable as a model for Christian revelation is Jung's synthetic approach. Beginning with the fundamental duality of conscious and unconscious in the personality, and the need to integrate them under the guidance of the Self-archetype in order to achieve wholeness, Jung showed himself deeply aware of the principle that truth is many-sided and that a narrow insistence on either end of a mutually exclusive polarity could only result in an impoverishment of the truth; thus the creative tension between causality and finality, psychic structure and external images, personal and collective unconscious.[57]

In its applications to religion, the method of synthesis offers a hermeneutic for understanding modern culture with its emphasis on the body:

> If we are still caught by the old idea of an antithesis between mind and matter, the present state of affairs means an unbearable contradiction; it may even divide us against ourselves. But if we can reconcile ourselves with the mysterious truth that spirit is the living body seen from within, and the body the outer manifestation of the living spirit—the two being really one —then we can understand why it is that the attempt to transcend the present level of consciousness must give its due to the body.[58]

Frei comments:

> On his way towards the 'self' man must not restrict himself by being solely a creature of instinct nor solely a disembodied mind, but seek to be a complete human being, combining both spirit and matter. He must accept the tension between mind and flesh as his

cross, and must endeavour through this Golgotha to attain to the Easter resurrection. . . . The shell of our small 'I' must be broken and an existential link forged with God and the cosmos, in a union which emanates both from within and from without.[59]

Jung's own words with regard to the culmination of the individuation process reiterate the profound significance of synthesis: "The self then functions as a union of opposites and thus constitutes the most immediate experience of the Divine which it is psychologically possible to imagine."[60]

B. Respect for the Irrational

The concept of the unconscious, autonomous in its own sphere over against the ego, has provided a counterbalance to the tyranny of the intellect. Jung has shown that, severed from its instinctual roots, consciousness becomes sterile and thinks itself sufficient. Recognition of the independence of the unconscious, both personal and collective, leads to an attitude of humility before reality that allows us to relinquish our desperate hold on life and to stand before it in awe and wonder, as did primitive man, knowing that the ultimate decisions lie outside our control. Such a stance is similar to the believer's, who "is accustomed to the thought of not being sole master in his own house."[61]

With all of his emphasis on the non-rational, however, Jung cannot be accused of being anti-rational. For him, the distinguishing characteristic of man is his consciousness, and with all the infinite complexity of the archetypal and symbolic depths of man,

> it is the task of the conscious mind, as the ordering and understanding principle in man, to help one or the other of these aspects to become operative, and to add its sense- and form-giving energy to the indifferent sway of our primordial psychic nature, in order that neither instinct nor intellect, but a spirit that surveys them both, may keep the psychic balance.[62]

V

CONCLUSION

To ask whether Jung has succeeded or failed in his attempt
to illuminate religion in the light of psychology is, we think, to
pose the wrong question. Inevitably there are points at which
his theories cast doubt on and even contradict traditional interpretations of Christian dogma. Yet does not the revelation of
man to himself play a role in preparing him for the revelation
of God? The incarnational principle of Christianity affirms that
God communicates himself through the structures of man's
consciousness and history, and it is this belief which must
ultimately condition our acceptance of the valid findings of
every human science.

With regard to revelation, Jung's contribution is to be
found primarily in his elucidation of the human pole of the
divine-human dialogue. For him, as for Karl Rahner, man is a
being open to the transcendent, but not only because of the
thrust of human knowing. Jung saw the traces of the divine
imprinted on the hiddenmost layers of the psyche as its origin,
and as the symbol of wholeness towards which it strives.

Notes

1. Raymond Hostie, *Religion and the Psychology of C. G. Jung*
(New York: Sheed and Ward, 1957), pp. 1–2, 111. Jung's autobiography is found in *Memories, Dreams, Reflections,* ed. by Aniela Jaffé, trans.
by Richard and Clara Winston (New York: Pantheon Books, 1963).
2. For a fuller discussion of Jung's use of empirical method, see
Hostie, pp. 7–14, upon which the above analysis has drawn.
3. C. G. Jung, *Modern Man in Search of a Soul,* trans, by W. S.
Dell and Cary F. Baynes (London: Kegan Paul, Trench, Trubner &
Co., 1933), p. 219.
4. *Ibid.,* p. 220.
5. *Ibid.*
6. Hostie, pp. 14–17. Cf. especially *Psyche & Symbol.* Ed. by
Violet de Laszlo. N.Y.: Doubleday, 1958, pp. 344, 349–350.
7. Jung, *Modern Man,* pp. 129–130.

8. *Ibid.*, p. 235.

9. Jung, *Memories, Dreams, Reflections,* p. 206.

10. Victor White, O.P., *God and the Unconscious* (Chicago: Henry Regnery, 1953), p. 37.

11. Hostie, p. 33.

12. C. G. Jung, *Psychology and Religion* (New Haven: Yale University Press, 1938), p. 41.

13. Gebhard Frei, "Appendix—On Analytical Psychology: the Method and Teaching of C. G. Jung" in White, *God and the Unconscious,* p. 238. The following outline of Jungian concepts owes much to Frei's clear exposition.

14. Jung, *Psychology and Religion,* p. 63.

15. CF. C. G. Jung, *Psychological Types,* trans. by H. G. Baynes (London: Kegan Paul, 1923): "The symbol is alive only so long as it is pregnant with meaning." (p. 602); also White, p. 221; Hostie, pp. 41–43.

16. Jolande Jacobi, *Complex-Archetype-Symbol in the Psychology of C. G. Jung,* trans. by Ralph Manheim, Bollingen Series LVII (New York: Pantheon Books, 1959), p. 88. Cf. also Hostie's remark: "The symbol . . . understands both conscious and unconscious, past and future, unifying them in an actualized present. . . . It likewise totalizes the rational and the irrational in man." (p. 42)

17. Jolande Jacobi, *The Way of Individuation,* trans. by R. F. C. Hull (New York: Harcourt, Brace & World, 1967), p. 34. This section on Jung's theory of individuation depends to a great extent on Jacobi's perceptive analysis, both in this work and in *Complex-Archetype-Symbol,* cited above.

18. Frieda Fordham, *An Introduction to Jung's Psychology* (Penguin Books, 1966), p. 77.

19. Jacobi, *Individuation,* pp. 12–20.

20. C. G. Jung, *Answer to Job,* trans. by R. F. C. Hull (London: Routledge and Kegan Paul, 1954), p. 460.

21. Jung, *Memories, Dreams, Reflections,* pp. 196–7. Jacobi comments: "In this sense one can regard the individuation process as a growing of the ego out of the Self and as a re-rooting in it." (*Individuation,* p. 42).

22. Jacobi, *Individuation,* pp. 57–8.

23. Hostie, p. 83.

24. June K. Singer, "Religion and the Collective Unconscious: Common Ground of Psychology and Religion," *Zygon* 4 (1969), 329: "In his mad dash toward the materialistic goals of our time, man has

destroyed the symmetry between his intrinsic nature and his striving after personal growth."

25. Jung, *Modern Man*, p. 233.

26. *Ibid.*, p. 237.

27. Jacobi, *Individuation*, pp. 107–8.

28. C. G. Jung, *The Psychology of the Unconscious*, trans. by B. M. Hinkle (London: Kegan, Trench, Trubner and Co., 1919), p. 39.

29. Jung, *Psychology and Religion*, p. 6.

30. C. G. Jung, *The Undiscovered Self*, trans. by R. F. C. Hull (Boston: Little, Brown and Company, 1958), pp. 19, 26.

31. C. G. Jung, *Two Essays in Analytical Psychology*, trans. by H. G. Baynes (London: Baillière, 1928), p. 70.

32. C. G. Jung, *Psychology and Religion: West and East*, Bollingen Series XI (New York: Pantheon Books, 1958), p. 273. Cf. also p. 88.

33. Hostie feels that Jung was forced by his scientific method to postulate the Self as the totality *within the psyche* (though at the same time beyond it) because this was the only way Jung could reconcile the observable effects of the attraction of the numinous upon man (the "religious attitude") with his empiricism which prohibited him from asserting anything about an unobservable in a realm beyond the subject. (Hostie, p. 145) For a different view, cf. Jacobi, *Individuation*, pp. 51–7, 108–9.

34. Jung, *Psychology and Religion: West and East*, p. 157.

35. *Ibid.*, p. 455. Hanna comments: "For Jung the experience of God was the impact of totality upon the soul." [*The Face of the Deep: The Religious Ideas of C. G. Jung* (Philadelphia: Westminster Press, 1967), p. 37.] Cf. also Jung, *Psychology and Religion*, p. 75; Jacobi, *Individuation*, p. 56.

36. Jung, *Memories, Dreams, Reflections*, p. 69.

37. Jung, *Modern Man*, pp. 238–9; White, pp. 192–5.

38. Jung, *Psychology and Religion: West and East*, p. 74.

39. Jung, *The Undiscovered Self*, pp. 36–7.

40. Jung, *Psychology and Religion*, pp. 52–8.

41. C. G. Jung, *The Integration of the Personality*, trans. by S. Dell (New York: Farrar and Rinehart, 1939), p. 60.

42. Jung, *The Undiscovered Self*, p. 21.

43. Jung, *Psychology and Religion*, pp. 113–14.

44. Rather than discuss the parallels which Jung finds between Christian symbols and archetypal myth patterns, I prefer to present here some general remarks of Jung on Christianity as a symbol system.

45. Jung, *The Undiscovered Self,* pp. 62–3.

46. *Ibid.,* pp. 73–77.

47. Jung, *Modern Man,* pp. 241–2.

48. *Ibid.,* p. 221.

49. *Ibid.,* p. 250.

50. Hostie, p. 160.

51. *Ibid.*

52. Hostie, pp. 131–5. Cf. a typical example of Jung's position at this time: "The human intellect can never answer this question [of God's existence], and still less can it give any proof of God. . . . Our intellect has long known that one cannot think god, much less conceive in what fashion he really exists, if indeed at all."(*Two Essays,* p. 73)

53. Hostie, pp. 156–9.

54. C. G. Jung, *Psychology and Alchemy,* trans. by R. F. C. Hull, Bollingen Series XII (New York: Pantheon Books, 1953), p. 14.

55. Letter dated 13 January 1948, cited in White, p. 261.

56. Jung, *Memories, Dreams, Reflections,* p. 325.

57. Hostie, pp. 86–7.

58. Jung, *Modern Man,* pp. 253–4.

59. White, pp. 248–9.

60. Jung, *West and East,* p. 261.

61. Jung, *The Undiscovered Self,* p. 86.

62. Jacobi, *Complex-Archetype-Symbol,* p. 124. Cf. also Jung, *Psyche and Symbol,* p. 314.

Works By Jung:
cf. readings in Chapter XII.

Lives of Jung

Vincent Brome, *Jung.* N.Y.: Atheneum, 1978. Sympathetic, yet critical.

Marie-Louise von Franz, *C.G. Jung: His Myth in Our Time.* Boston: Little, Brown, 1975. By a disciple.

Barbara Hannah, *Jung. His Life and Work.* N.Y.: Putnam's, 1976. By a pupil.

Paul Stern, *C.G. Jung. The Haunted Prophet.* N.Y.: Braziller, 1974. Sharply critical.

Laurens van der Post, *C.G. Jung. Jung and the Story of Our Time.* N.Y.: Putnam's, 1975. By a friend.

Works on Jung

Clifford A. Brown, *Jung's Hermeneutic of Doctrine.* Chicago: Scholars Press, 1981.

David B. Burrell, C.S.C., *Exercises in Religious Understanding.* Notre Dame: U. of Notre Dame Press, 1974. Section on Jung.

Edward Edinger, *Ego and Archetype.* N.Y.: Viking, 1972. Religious symbolism.

Frieda Fordham, *Introduction to Jung's Psychology.* N.Y.: Penguin, 1953. A good introduction.

Andrew Reid Fuller, *Psychology and Religion: Eight Points of View.* Washington, D.C.: University Press of America, 1977, 21–47. Fine synthesis.

Peter Homans, *Jung in Context. Modernity and the Making of a Psychology.* Chicago: University of Chicago Press, 1979. Theory in the context of his life.

George B. Hogenson, *Jung's Struggle With Freud.* Notre Dame: U. of Notre Dame Press, 1983.

Raymond Hostie, S.J., *Religion and the Psychology of Jung.* N.Y.: Sheed and Ward, 1957. Good, but somewhat dated.

Jolande Jacobi, *The Psychology of C.G. Jung.* New Haven: Yale, 1968. Good introduction.

Jolande Jacobi, *The Way of Individuation.* N.Y.: Harcourt, Brace and World, 1965. Clear synthesis.

Walter Kaufmann, *Discovering the Mind.* Volume Three. *Freud Versus Adler and Jung.* N.Y.: McGraw-Hill, 1980, 289ff.

Morton Kelsey, "Jung as Philosopher and Theologian," in *The Well-Tended Tree,* Hilde Kirsch, ed. N.Y.: Putnam's, 1971, 184–196.

Antonio Moreno, O.P., *Jung, Gods and Modern Man.* Notre Dame: U. of Notre Dame Press, 1970.

John A Sanford, *Healing and Wholeness.* N.Y.: Paulist Press, 1977. On Jung.

Ann Ulanov, *The Feminine in Jungian Psychology and in Christian Theology.* Evanston: Northwestern U. Press, 1971.

Ann and Barry Ulanov, *Religion and the Unconscious.* Phila.: Westminster Press, 1975.

XII.
The Archetype of the Self and the God Image

C.G. Jung

(Excerpts from: (1) *Psychology and Religion.* New Haven: Yale University Press, 1938, pages 4–6, 72–73, 97–99, 114; (2) *Aion. Researches into the Phenomenology of the Self.* Princeton, N.J.: Princeton University Press, second edition, translated by R.F.C. Hull, pages 36–39.)

Editor's Note

Jung believed that religion is a natural function in human beings. Its base cannot be proved logically and rationally. It is an a priori datum. The only test is pragmatic: Does it work? Does it lead to health?

For Jung, religion arises in the unconscious. Its source is that part of the unconscious wherein is found the God image or the God archetype. This is an elusive concept in Jung and it cannot be understood apart from the Archetype of the Self.

There is some power in us which generates all the other archetypal images (the motif of the journey, the hero, death and rebirth, the wise old man, the earth mother, the eternal child as well as the trickster and the shadow). This is the ultimate archetypal power. Jung calls it the Archetype of the Self. It should not be thought of as an image. More correctly, it is an experience, the central experience of the Self. The Archetype of the Self is the experience of my genuine present and future possibilities. It is my ideal Self, my hero Self, my highest Self (not the Self of my neurotic shoulds, however). When you are "right with the world," you are living out your archetype, you are "on your stream."

Jung called the Archetype of the Self "the inner empirical deity." He was not denying a God beyond man. Jung said that the psycholo-

164

gist speaks of the "Imprint," the theologian speaks of the "Imprinter" (*Psychology and Alchemy,* 17). "We find numberless images of God, but we cannot produce the original. There is no doubt in my mind that there is an original behind our images, but it is inaccessible" (*The Symbolic Life,* 706). He called the Archetype of the Self the "inner empirical deity" to signify that it was the empirical print of God.

Why did Jung identify the Archetype of the Self with the God Archetype? There are a number of reasons. 1. The archetype of the Self has a certain numinosity attached to it. The word "numinosity" is from the Latin root, *nuo,* to bow in awe. Whatever is numinous is the object of our ultimate concern. Inside of us there are structures arising from the Archetype of the Self, like the journey, the hero, etc., to which we accord the highest concern as structures for our spiritual development. (This is true also for atheists.) In them, we find the will of God written in the psyche. (However, some of these structures can be demonic and ego is needed for discernment.) 2. The archetype of the Self represents psychological and spiritual wholeness in which our sense perceptions, intellect, feelings and intuitive powers are ideally developed. For Jung, this represents our "God-manship," God's will for us. 3. Jung believed that our Archetype of the Self is always involved in the projections of our God image. Freud said that our God image was deeply influenced by our father (others emphasize the mother). Jung accepted this but he placed more emphasis on the Archetype of the Self as coloring the God image. In *Answer to Job,* he saw the Archetype of the Self of people at a primitive stage as projecting into God a type of arbitrary omnipotence. God commanded wars, seemed to have little concern for justice, etc. Later, with the Book of Job, a softening of the God image occurred. Finally with the incarnation another revolution occurred in the God image when Jesus is seen as the incarnation of God and his love. Jesus reconciles God and man.

At times Jung gives the impression that the content of Jesus as the Christ, the God-man, was projected upon him from the believers' God image, a position which is contrary to Christian belief. At other times he implies that Jesus actually lived out the God-man archetype and thus was God-man in Jung's terms. Jung was ambivalent about Jesus. He wrote, "One is tempted to attach greater importance to the immediate and living presence of the archetype than to the idea of the historical Christ." Jung said that a central figure in history could be an instrument of revelation for others whose personal experience of wholeness did not share that same degree. He mentions Jesus and

Buddha as examples. History is a revelation of the person of God when it manifests the archetype of wholeness.

The thought of Jung resembles a dense jungle with much undergrowth. Apart from his popular works, he writes in a circling style much less structured than Freud's. Consequently, excerpts representative of his religious thought are difficult to isolate. The following excerpts are from *Psychology and Religion* and *Aion*.

*   *   *

I

In speaking of religion I must make clear from the start what I mean by that term. Religion, as the Latin word denotes, is a careful and scrupulous observation of what Rudolf Otto[1] aptly termed the "numinosum," that is, a dynamic existence or effect, not caused by an arbitrary act of will. On the contrary, it seizes and controls the human subject, which is always rather its victim than its creator. The numinosum is an involuntary condition of the subject, whatever its cause may be. At all events, religious teaching as well as the consensus gentium always and everywhere explains this condition as being due to a cause external to the individual. The numinosum is either a quality of a visible object or the influence of an invisible presence causing a peculiar alteration of consciousness. This is, at least, the general rule. . . .

Religion appears to me to be a peculiar attitude of the human mind, which could be formulated in accordance with the original use of the term "religio," that is, a careful consideration and observation of certain dynamic factors, understood to be "powers," spirits, demons, gods, laws, ideas, ideals or whatever name man has given to such factors as he has found in his world powerful, dangerous or helpful enough to be taken into careful consideration, or grand, beautiful and meaningful enough to be devoutly adored and loved. In colloquial language one often says of somebody who is enthusiastically interested in a certain pursuit, that he is almost "religiously devoted" to his cause; William James, for instance, remarks that a scientist often has no creed, but "his temper is devout."[2]

I want to make clear that by the term "religion"[3] I do not mean a creed. It is, however, true that on the one hand every confession is originally based upon the experience of the numinosum and on the other hand upon Πίοτις, the loyalty, trust, and confidence toward a definitely experienced numinous effect and the subsequent alteration of consciousness: the conversion of Paul is a striking example of this. "Religion," it might be said, is the term that designates the attitude peculiar to a consciousness which has been altered by the experience of the numinosum.

Creeds are codified and dogmatized forms of original religious experience.[4] The contents of the experience have become sanctified and usually congealed in a rigid, often elaborate, structure. The practice and the reproduction of the original experience have become a ritual and an unchangeable institution. This does not necessarily mean a lifeless petrification. On the contrary it can become the form of religious experience for ages of time and for millions of people without there being any vital necessity for alterations. Although the Catholic church has often been blamed for a particular rigidity, it admits nevertheless that the dogma has its life and hence is capable of undergoing change and development. . . . What one could almost call a systematic blindness is simply the effect of the prejudice that the deity is *outside* man. Although this prejudice is not solely Christian, there are certain religions which do not share it at all. On the contrary they insist, as do certain Christian mystics, upon the essential identity of God and man, either in the form of an a priori identity, or of a goal to be attained by certain practices or initiations, as we know them, for instance, from the metamorphoses of Apuleius, not to speak of certain yoga methods.

The application of the comparative method indubitably shows the quaternity as being a more or less direct representation of the God manifested in his creation. We might, therefore, conclude that the symbol, spontaneously produced in the dreams of modern people, means the same thing—*the God within.* Although the majority of cases do not recognize this analogy, the interpretation might nevertheless be true. If we take into consideration the fact that the idea of God is an "unscientific" hypothesis, we can easily explain why people have forgotten to think along such lines. And even if they cherish a certain belief in God they would be deterred from the idea of God within by their religious education, which always depreciated this idea as "mystical." Yet it is precisely this "mystical" idea which is enforced by the natural tendencies of the unconscious mind. I myself, as well as my colleagues, have seen so many cases developing the same kind of symbolism that we cannot doubt its existence any longer. My observations, moreover, date back as far as 1914 and I waited fourteen years before I alluded publicly to them.

It would be a regrettable mistake if anybody should understand my observations to be a kind of proof of the existence of God. They prove only the existence of an archetypal image of the Deity, which to my mind is the most we can assert psychologically about God. But as it is a very important and influential archetype, its relatively frequent occurrence seems to be a noteworthy fact for any *theologia naturalis*. Since the experience of it has the quality of numinosity, often to a high degree, it ranks among religious experiences. . . .

When we find a triumphant Christ in the rose window of a medieval church, we assume rightly that this must be a central symbol of the Christian cult. At the same time we also assume that any religion which is rooted in the history of a people is as much an expression of their psychology as the form of political government, for instance, that the people have developed. If we apply the same method to the modern mandalas that people have seen in dreams or visions, or have developed through "active imagination," we reach the conclusion that the mandalas are expressions of a certain attitude which we cannot avoid calling "religious." Religion is a relationship to the highest or strongest value, be it positive or negative. The relationship is voluntary as well as involuntary, that is, you can accept, consciously, the value by which you are possessed unconsciously. That psychological fact which is the greatest power in your system is the god, since it is always the overwhelming psychic factor which is called god. As soon as a god ceases to be an overwhelming factor, he becomes a mere name. His essence is dead and his power is gone. Why have the antique gods lost their prestige and their effect upon human souls? It was because the Olympic gods had served their time and a new mystery began: God became man.

If we allow ourselves to draw conclusions from modern mandalas we should ask people, first, whether they worship stars, suns, flowers or snakes. They will deny it and at the same time they will assert that the globes, stars, crosses and the like are symbols for a center in themselves. And if asked what they mean by that center, they will begin to stammer and to refer to this or that experience which may be something very similar to the confession of my patient who found that the vision of his world clock had left him with a wonderful feeling of perfect harmony. Others will confess that a similar vision came to them in a moment of supreme pain and distress. To others again it is a remembrance of a sublime dream or of a moment when long and fruitless worries came to an end and a reign of peace began. If you sum up what people tell you about their experience, you can formulate it about in this way: They came to themselves, they could accept themselves, they were able to become reconciled to themselves and by this they were also reconciled to adverse circumstances and events. This is much like what was formerly expressed by saying: He has made his peace with God, he has sacrificed his own will, he has submitted himself to the will of God.

A modern mandala is an involuntary confession of a peculiar mental condition. There is no deity in the mandala, and there is also no submission or reconciliation to a deity. The place of the deity seems to be taken by the wholeness of man. . . .[5]

Nobody can know what the ultimate things are. We must, therefore, take them as we experience them. And if such experience helps to make your life healthier, more beautiful, more complete and more satisfactory to yourself and to those you love, you may safely say: "This was the grace of God."

Notes

I

1. Rudolf Otto, *Das Heilige* (1917).

2. "But our esteem for facts has not neutralized in us all religiousness. It is itself almost religious. Our scientific temper is devout" (William James, *Pragmatism* [1911], p. 14 *et seq.*).

3. "Religio est, quae superioris cujusdam naturae (quam divinam vocant) curam caerimoniamque affert" (Cicero, *De invent. Rhetor.*, Lib. II); "Religiose testimonium dicere ex jurisjurandi fide" (Cicero, *Pro Coel.*, 55).

4. Heinrich Scholz (*Religionsphilosophie*, 1921) insists upon a similar point of view; see also H. R. Pearcy, *A Vindication of Paul* (1936).

5. *Two Essays*, p. 202 *et sqq.*; *Psychological Types* (1923), pp. 588, 593 *et sqq.*; "Ueber die Archetypen des collectiven Unbewussten," *Eranos-Jahrbuch 1934*, p. 204 *et sqq.*; "Ueber den Archetypus mit besonderer Berücksichtigung des Animabegriffes," *Zentralblatt für Psychotherapie*, IX (1936), 259 *et sqq.*

II

Why—my reader will ask—do I discourse here upon Christ and his adversary, the Antichrist? Our discourse necessarily brings us to Christ, because he is the still living myth of our culture. He is our culture hero, who, regardless of his historical existence, embodies the myth of the divine Primordial Man, the mystic Adam. It is he who occupies the center of the Christian *mandāla*, who is the Lord of the Tetramorph, i.e., the four symbols of the evangelists, which are like the four columns of his throne. He is in us and we in him. His kingdom is the pearl of great price, the treasure buried in the field, the grain of mustard seed which will become a great tree, and the heavenly city.[1] As Christ is in us, so also is his heavenly kingdom.

These few familiar references should be sufficient to make the psychological position of the Christ symbol quite clear. *Christ exemplifies the archetype of the self.*[2] He represents a totality of a divine or heavenly kind, a glorified man, a son of God *sine macula peccati*, unspotted by sin. As Adam *secundus* he corresponds to the first Adam before the Fall, when the latter was still a pure image of God, of which

Tertullian says: "And this therefore is to be considered as the image of God in man, that the human spirit has the same motions and senses as God has, though not in the same way as God has them." Origen is very much more explicit: The *imago Dei* imprinted on the soul, not on the body, is an image of an image, "for my soul is not directly the image of God, but is made after the likeness of the former image. Christ, on the other hand, is the true image of God, after whose likeness our inner man is made, invisible, incorporeal, incorrupt, and immortal. The God-image in us reveals itself through *prudentia, iustitia, moderatio, virtus, sapientia et disciplina.*"

The God-image in man that was damaged by the first sin can be "reformed"[3] with the help of God, in accordance with Rom. 12:2: "And be not conformed to this world, but be transformed by the renewal of your mind, that you may prove what is . . . the will of God" (R.S.V.). The totality images which the unconscious produces in the course of an individuation process are similar "reformations" of an a priori archetype (the *mandāla*).[4] As I have already emphasized, the spontaneous symbols of the self, or of wholeness, cannot in practice be distinguished from a God-image. Despite the word *metamorphousthe* ("be transformed") in the Greek text of the above quotation, the "renewal" (*anakainosis, reformatio*) of the mind is not meant as an actual alteration of consciousness, but rather as the restoration of an original condition, an apocatastasis. This is in exact agreement with the empirical findings of psychology, that there is an ever-present archetype of wholeness[5] which may easily disappear from the purview of consciousness or may never be perceived at all until a consciousness illuminated by conversion recognizes it in the figure of Christ. As a result of this *anamnesis* the original state of oneness with the God-image is restored.

Notes

1. For "city" cf. *Psychology and Alchemy* (Coll. Works, Vol. 12), pp. 104ff.

2. Cf. my observations on Christ as archetype in "A Psychological Approach to the Dogma of the Trinity," in *Psychology and Religion* (Coll. Works, Vol. 11).

3. Augustine, *De Trinitate*, XIV, 22.

4. Cf. "Concerning Mandāla Symbolism" in *Archetypes and the Collective Unconscious* (Coll. Works, Vol. 9, Part I).

5. *Psychology and Alchemy* (Coll. Works, Vol. 12), pp. 207ff.

Some Pertinent Works of Jung

Memories, Dreams, Reflections. N.Y.: Random House, 1961. Jung's autobiography.

The Symbolic Life. Collected Works, Vol. 18. Princeton, N.J.: Princeton University Press, 1976. Best for Jung's personal religious beliefs.

Man and His Symbols. N.Y.: Dell, 1968, 1–94. A good introduction, Jung's last synthesis.

Psychology and Religion. New Haven: Yale University Press, 1938.

Aion. Research into the Phenomenology of the Self. Princeton, N.J.: Princeton University Press, 1959. The Self, the Christ image, God image.

Answer to Job. Princeton, N.J.: Princeton University Press, 1969. A difficult work on the evolution of the God image.

Psychology and Alchemy. Collected Works, Princeton, N.J.: Princeton University Press, Vol. 12, 1968. 1–46, God image and mandala symbols.

Mandala Symbolism. Princeton, N.J.: Princeton University Press, 1972.

The Undiscovered Self. Boston: Little, Brown and Co., 1957. General cultural and religious ideas.

XIII.
Martin Buber:
God as "Thou"

John J. Heaney

Jung's thought has evoked much enthusiasm and much criticism. Some critics feel that Jung's symbolical approach is more dangerous to religion than Freud's critical stance. Others believe that Jung assists the believer to get beyond rote belief to a deeper level of religious experience.

Martin Buber (1878–1965) insisted that in Jung's thought there is no relation of an I to a Thou. "This is, however, the way in which the unmistakably religious of all ages have understood their religion even if they longed most intensely to let their I be mystically absorbed into that Thou" (*Eclipse of God*, 79). Buber also believed that Jung had a reductionist tendency in which religion became simply the relation of the ego to the soul (i.e., the unconscious). However, this seems to be a misunderstanding of Jung. It is due in part to Jung's unclarity about the relationship between the domains of theology and psychology. However, Jung did admit that "the Imprint" implied an "Imprinter." Lastly, Buber felt that the social aspect of religion was absent in Jung and that he too easily believed that the voice of the unconscious was the voice of conscience. But the unconscious can be demonic. Buber, more than Jung, accents the conscious and ethical components of religion.

In the following essay, the editor offers a reflective synthesis of Martin Buber's thought on the I-Thou relationship and its implication of the Eternal Thou. (The apparent sexist usage of "man" instead of "humans" in this essay arises out of reference to Buber's own vocabulary.)

173

"Thou" and "relationship" are central symbols for Buber's thought. The word "Thou" is rich with connotations and allusions. A seemingly simple word, it carries with itself an extremely subtle and creative system of thought.

"Man with man—the unity of I and Thou—is God."[1] This quotation is not from Buber but from Feuerbach. Buber was strongly influenced by Feuerbach whom he resembles and from whom he radically differs. The difference is that Feuerbach inverted theology into anthropology. That is, he said that statements about God are really statements about man. He made this move in order to save the dignity of man who, he thought, had alienated the best in himself by projecting his highest ideals into "God." But Buber preserves human dignity without rejecting theology through the use of the "Thou" model. Feuerbach and Buber are similar in that, unlike Kant, they wish to found philosophy on the whole being of the person, and not simply on human cognition.[2]

A person's key metaphors and models direct the cast of his or her thought. Buber draws his main model from interpersonal relations. "Thou" is a term of address. Evidently, then, human relations can never fade into the background in his system. Nor can the unconscious, as with Jung, rule supreme.

What is this "Thou"? If "all real living is meeting,"[3] then thou is not an object or a person in isolation,. Thou does not exist except in combination. Man has two "primary words" or "attitudes."[4] Both attitudes or primary words are combination words, I-Thou and I-It. "Primary words do not signify things, but they intimate relations."[5]

Thou in the I-Thou combination cannot be separated from the I. "If Thou is said, the I of the combination is said along with it."[6] Similarly there is no I taken in itself. There is only I of the primary word I-Thou and the I of the primary word I-It. "As I become I, I say Thou."[7] It is a relationship of suffering and action.

Buber says that the primary word I-Thou can be spoken only with the whole being. The primary word I-It can never be spoken with the whole being. This latter statement of Buber can be misunderstood. It does not mean that man cannot relate to even the non-personal with his whole being. It does not mean that man cannot relate to *nature* with his whole being. As we will see, man can say Thou to a tree or a cat. Thus *It* does not signify primarily a thing but an attitude (of accumulation of information, of mastery, of use, of isolating aspects).[8] If this is true of It, it must also be true of Thou. Thou does not signify an object, or even exclusively a person. It signifies primarily an attitude *of relationship.*

To understand Buber's primary words, let us look first at how they fit into man's relationship with nature and with man. Man looks at a tree. He can look at it as an object for a photograph, as something to be cut for lumber, as a thing to be classified. In all this there is an I-It relationship. But with this tree I can also have an I-Thou relation. Without rejecting all the former objective elements, I can "become bound up in relation with it." I can be seized by the power of its exclusiveness.

This is a difficult concept in Buber's thought. It is close to poetic intuition. It is important to notice that Buber dislikes the word "experience" to describe relationship. As he sees it, experience depends on my moods. But a tree, for example, is before me despite my moods. I am caught up in the exclusiveness of the tree. I let it "step forth in its singleness." The only word for the event in Buber's vocabulary is relation. Yet how is this relation mutual? Precisely because the tree reveals itself always to one who has the I-Thou attitude.

When I face a human being with the I-Thou attitude, the other is not a "he" or a "she." Notice that in writing about someone, when we say "he" or "she," we are immediately brought into the "I-it" atmosphere. The Thou is not a thing, an object (he, she), nor a thing among things. Early in his book, *I and Thou,* Buber makes a remarkable statement. He says that the Thou "fills the heavens."[9] Does the Thou in Buber mean more than the other person? It includes the other person but it is primarily *an attitude.* The quotation about the Thou filling the heavens implies that there are intimations of an Absolute in the Thou. We will return to this point shortly.

To say the primary word "Thou" to another does not mean for Buber "to experience" another person. As we mentioned, Buber dislikes the word "experience" to express relationships. For Buber, to experience another means to move out of relation, to become centripetal, to use, to measure another exclusively according to one's feelings. "In the act of experience, Thou is far away."[10] But to take my stand in relation involves risk and sacrifice since I speak the relational word with my whole being. "Thou" means not experience but knowledge. Experience is self-isolation for Buber and knowledge involves a relational web which is concrete and existential. In knowledge of the Thou, "we know nothing isolated about it anymore."

The relation to the Thou is not in a kind of Platonic timelessness. It exists always in time, but always in the present, not in chronological time but in the real, filled present as actual presentness, meeting and relation. Jung has been accused by some critics of using others as fodder for an archetypal machine. But this could never be a criticism made of Buber. For Buber, present time exists only because the Thou becomes present. The Thou does not exist in time but time exists in the Thou since "the heaven of Thou spreads out over all."[11]

The Thou relation is not simply an idea, for that would lead only to expressing an idea, an abstraction, an I-it word. Nor is the Thou relation mediated by fantasy, as in romantic love, for example. Neither lust nor goals intervene between the I and the Thou.

Since the Thou relation is direct, it would seem to be essentially a feeling. But Buber says: "Feelings accompany the metaphysical fact of love, but they do not constitute it."[12] The Thou relation is love-as-*responsibility* of an I for a Thou. In this, not in feeling, is how I recognize the Thou—though feeling is there.

The Thou relationship actually forms the I or the person. An I-Thou relationship precedes the recognition of self as self, as when the child sees the mother's face. "Through the Thou a man becomes I."[13]

But the direct Thou relation cannot permanently persist. It falls back again into He, She, or It. But the impersonal attitude is the "eternal chrysalis" of the Thou. When the I of the relation steps forth and takes on a separate existence, it moves in a strange, reduced, tenuous, functional activity. We might object here that even I-it involves relation. Buber would say yes, but only as experiencing, using, relieving and equipping human life.[14]

Buber connects feeling to the I-Thou relation in a subtle and revealing manner. "Living mutual relation includes feelings but does not originate with them." Yes, but human relationships often are generated through feeling and that feeling is at times quite selfish. How can a man's whole being become involved in the I-Thou relation? Buber explains this by using the Hasidic idea of "the evil impulse" in human beings. If one wishes to find his central wish, that which stirs his inmost being, the recognition comes in the form of "the evil urge" which seeks to lead him astray. Man has become so alienated from his strongest feelings that he knows them only hidden in what can lead him astray.[15] "The man who lets the abundant passion of what is rejected invade the growth to reality of what is chosen—he alone serves God with the evil impulse."

The evil impulse then is the feeling, the passion, which is guided by and into relation. It gives the relation power but it serves it, and always accompanies it but does not primarily constitute it.

Our relations in charity often seem dead and without feeling. This problem becomes most acute and most clear when the I-Thou relation moves out to world community. As Buber puts it, the Thou relation has "a dreadful point of climax—to love all men."[16] When men realize that I-it relationships to institutions yield no life, they try to loosen them asunder by the introduction of freedom of feeling. They think that the community of love will arise out of free abundant feeling.

But Buber says: "The true community does not arise through peoples having feelings for each other (though indeed not without them) but through, first, their taking their stand in living, mutual relation with a living Center, and second their being in living, mutual relation with one another."[17]

This is a crucial sentence. Buber has not *logically* justified his introduction of the "Center" which is the builder of community. That is, he has no strict natural theology. It seems that he begins from a biblical faith while using Hasidic tradition.[18] God, he says, is not an idea as for Kant.[19] The "Center" arises from a biblical faith which is not primarily conceptual, but concrete and existential. However, Buber considered himself not a theologian, nor even a philosopher of religion, but a philosophical anthropologist, an investigator of the problem of man.[20] Thus Buber's source for the Center is *both* a philosophical anthropology *and* biblical faith.

How does the Center arise from Buber's philosophical anthropology? Robert Johann in *The Pragmatic Meaning of God* shows that since relationships are not always reciprocal, a Personal Center, God, who responds in relationships, is needed to sustenance love.[21] Buber's approach is somewhat similar to this. But Buber does not use a pragmatic approach. He finds God implicated in the mystery of the Thou attitude. Relation, as in its best example in marriage, arises from "the revealing by two people of the Thou to one another."[22] The Thou which is revealed goes beyond the other; it fills the heavens. "The extended lines of relation meet in the Eternal Thou."[23] It is "the condition for the possibility of all authentic living." (Here Buber alludes to and widens Kant. For Kant, the condition for the possibility of knowing anything is the a priori categories. However, for Buber, the condition for the possibility of not just knowing anything but for having any relationship at all is, not the categories, but the inborn Thou.) As we said, the model one chooses influences the whole of one's thought. When Buber chose the model of Thou and relationship, it was inevitable that "Thou" and "relationship" would be found at the heart of the universe.

Thus, Buber moves to his silent, dynamic base, God, the Eternal Thou. This is not a move to mysticism. Buber rejected mysticism in his later years because he believed that, in insisting on union, it did not respect otherness. For Buber, God is always "other." But this "Other" does not alienate human beings from themselves, a point so feared by Fromm. For Buber, God is not "Big Brother." Buber avoids human alienation in speaking of the Eternal Thou. For him, there is even no alien norm of morality. No one has ever understood the Ten Commandments, he said, unless he has heard the Thou of command as addressing himself in *his particular situation.*[24] As he put it so memorably, "He who approaches the Face has indeed surpassed duty and obligation."

When Buber returns to human love, he says that a man who loves a woman "is able to look in the Thou of her eyes into the beam of the Eternal Thou." But a man would be coarse, he says, who while love-making tells his woman that he sees the eternal Thou in her. It would be foolish because "there is nothing in which God cannot be found." Furthermore, unlike Kierkegaard who rejected Regina Olsen for God, Buber says that God wants to come to us by means of the Reginas he has created and not by renunciation of them.[25]

God then is the Thou present to the spirit from the beginning. This Thou is the source of mystery and relation. However Buber's anthropology does not tell him what God is in himself, but only how we are related to him. He is not an idea. He cannot be experienced but he can be "done."[26] He cannot be logically inferred. He yields himself as there from the beginning. He is the Absolute Person whom we know only in relation to us. He cannot be understood. He can be addressed, "Thou." God cannot be comprehended but he can be embraced. God cannot be expressed but only addressed. In one sense, this is the "death of God," the death of all images.

The pre-condition of the I-Thou relation is the Eternal Thou, the eternal face in every face. It does not alienate us from the world because "meeting with God does not come to man in order that he may concern himself with God, but in order that he may confirm that there is meaning in the world."[27]

In one sense Buber's Eternal Thou is in process. But he opposes the idea of a God becoming. This is perverted, he says, because "only through the primal certainty of divine being can we come into contact with the mysterious meaning of divine becoming. . . . If God were entirely in process, man could not know where the process might lead." "What turgid and presumptuous talk that is about 'the God who becomes,' but we know unshakably in our hearts there is a becoming of the God that is."[28] Buber thus opposes the concept of God as pure becoming but not a becoming of God in the world, his ripening in man. (In Jungian terms, this would be the evolution of the God image.) But Buber says that we must avoid the pretension that we have exact knowledge of God in himself. Man cannot know God but can imitate him. Man can know God only in relation. But in relation the Eternal Thou co-suffers in every face.

What does Thou mean in Buber? Thou can only be indicated or suggested. Thou cannot be expressed. Yet Thou can be addressed, "Thou." God in Buber's thought must be described as a person, an Other, for he says he does not mean by God an idea or a principle, but "who—whatever else he may be—enters into direct relation with us men in creative, revealing and redeeming acts, and thus makes it possible for us to enter into a direct relation with him. This ground and meaning of our existence constitutes a mutuality, arising again and again, such as can subsist only between persons." Since the concept of the personal cannot fully adequate God's essential being, Buber says that it is "both permitted and necessary to say that God is *also* a Person."[29]

Buber means that God infinitely transcends human personality. "God comprises, but is not my Self." God, for Buber, is the wholly Other, the mystery that appears and overthrows. But he is also the wholly Same, the wholly Present, nearer to me than my own I. The unity of these contraries is "the mystery at the innermost core of the dialogue" between God and man. "Thou" is said to God as to Someone who transcends me and yet is intimate to my being. God is not my unconscious nor the collective unconscious. And "Thou" is said to God not merely as a word from my unconscious, but as an address from the center of my conscious, ethical responsibility for the other.

Notes

1. L. Feuerbach, *The Essence of Christianity.* Tr. by George Eliot. N.Y.: Harper Torchbook, 1957. Quotation from introduction by Karl Barth, p. xiii.

2. M. Buber, *Between Man and Man.* N.Y.: Macmillan, 1965, p. 146. On Buber and Feuerbach, cf. M. Friedman, *Martin Buber. The Life of Dialogue.* N.Y.: Harper Torchbook, 1960, pp. 29, 48, 128, 164.

3. M. Buber, *I and Thou.* N.Y.: Scribner's, 1958, 2nd ed., p. 11.

4. *Ibid.,* p. 3.

5. *Ibid.*

6. *Ibid.*

7. Friedman, *op. cit.,* p. 59.

8. *Ibid.,* pp. 64, 68.

9. *I and Thou,* p. 8.

10. *Ibid.,* p. 9.

11. Cf. p. 9.

12. *I and Thou,* p. 14.

13. *Ibid.,* p. 29.

14. *Ibid.,* p. 38.

15. For a good treatment of the evil urge, see M. Friedman, *To Deny Our Nothingness.* N.Y.: Delta, 1967, pp. 302ff.

16. *I and Thou,* p. 15.

17. *Ibid.,* p. 45.

18. Cf. Friedman, *Martin Buber,* pp. 16–26.

19. *The Eclipse of God.* N.Y.: Harper, 1952, p. 54.

20. Cf. *Between Man and Man* where the statement by Buber is mentioned in Friedman's introduction, p. xviii.

21. *The Pragmatic Meaning of God.* Milwaukee: Marquette U. Press, 1966, pp. 51ff.

22. *I and Thou,* pp. 46, 81.

23. *Ibid.,* p. 76.

24. *To Deny Our Nothingness,* p. 290.

25. *Between Man and Man,* p. 52.

26. *I and Thou,* p. 110.

27. *Ibid.,* p. 115.

28. Friedman, *Martin Buber,* pp. 52–53.

29. *I and Thou,* p. 135.

Readings

Martin Buber, *Eclipse of God.* N.Y.: Harper and Row, 1957. See critique of Jung, 78–92, 133–137.

Maurice Friedman, *To Deny Our Nothingness.* N.Y.: Delta Books, 1967, esp. 146–167.

Peter Homans, *Jung in Context: Modernity and the Making of a Psychology.* Chicago: U. of Chicago Press, 1979.

Robert C. Smith, "Empirical Science and Value Assumptions: Lessons from C.G. Jung," *Journal of Religion and Health,* Vol. 16, 2, 1977, 102–109. A good critique of Jung's methodology.

Paul J. Stern, *C.G. Jung: The Haunted Prophet.* N.Y.: Braziller, 1974. A driving attack on Jung.

XIV.
Peak-Experiences and Religion

Abraham Maslow

(Excerpt from Abraham Maslow, *Religions, Values, and Peak-Experiences.* Ohio State University Press, 1964. pages xi–xiv, 58–68.)

Editor's Note

Abraham Maslow (1908–1970) saw himself as a member of "the third force" in psychology, that is, a humanistic psychology which is neither behaviorist-determinist, nor Freudian in the orthodox sense. However, he also saw his ideas as part of a new, transpersonal psychology. "I should say that I consider Humanistic Third Force Psychology to be transitional, a preparation for a still 'higher' Fourth Psychology, transpersonal, transhuman, centered in the cosmos rather than in human needs and interest, going beyond humanness, identity, self-actualization and the like. . . . Without the transcendent and transpersonal, we get sick" (1968, iv).

Biographical. Maslow's father was a Russian Jew who moved to the United States from Kiev. His mother came from Russia to marry his father. Abraham was the first of seven children, born in Brooklyn. He said that his mother was a good childbearer but her maternal feelings were not highly developed. "She was a pretty woman but not a nice one" (Wilson, 131). He said she was of the schizophrenogenic type, that is, "the type who makes crazy children." He was curious why he didn't go insane. His father stayed away from home as much as possible. "A very vigorous man who loved whiskey and women and fighting," he was liked by his son but also feared by him. Early in life, Abraham met anti-Semitism. During his first twenty years, he said he was extremely neurotic, very depressed, very lonely, isolated and self-rejecting. But he was to become an immensely genuine human being.

His Religious Position. At thirteen he declared himself "a fighting atheist." He seems to have identified with his free-thinking father and reacted against his mother who was a very orthodox Jew and extremely superstitious. He saw theistic religions as "crap" (Lowry, 14). However, he accepted the "holy" in Otto's sense. He had had, he thought, the experience that generations of theists had mistaken for God.

In a sense he had a lover's quarrel with religion. He found repellent what he called "superstition" and "supernaturalism." As a student he wrote: "Any external agency such as God or (the) Absolute can be tossed off without consideration as improbabilities. For me, the historical account of the evolution of the idea of God is enough to show that I ought not to take it seriously as a cosmological explanation." On the other hand, he was gradually attracted to religion. He ultimately claimed that religion and religious drives were deep-rooted in human nature, and that religion was as necessary for health as Vitamin B-12.

What principally attracted him to religion was: (1) "a Jewish passion for ethics and utopianism"; (2) its "gnostic revelation," that is, the glimpse of reality it gave as reality truly is behind the veil; (3) its damnation of being mere average human beings; the self-actualized man was akin to the righteous, perfected man of the Talmud; (4) its essence which he saw as lonely, private illumination of the "B-values," a revelation of the values of Being inherent in religion itself (Lowry, 68).

In late life Maslow wrote: "The word 'god' is being defined by many theologians today in such a way as to exclude the conception of a person . . . If God gets to be defined as 'Being Itself', or as 'the integrating principle of the universe', or as 'the whole of everything', or as the meaningfulness off the cosmos, or in some other non-personal way, then what will we atheists be fighting against?" (1964, 45).

His Taoistic Approach. Maslow's notion of Being runs parallel to certain religious notions of God—self-sustaining, the ground of all existence and the source of all goodness. But Maslow said that "the supernaturalists" conceived God as a person, while he insisted that Being is "just impersonally what it is" (Lowry, 71). In a perceptive sentence, his interpreter, Lowry, suggests that the difference seems more of degree than of kind, "for it is difficult to see how Being could contain its values rather than our own unless it were capable of *valuing,* which is to say, unless it had at least this one attribute of a 'person'."

His wife Bertha said that Abe believed in knowledge through the greater perception of loving, and this he called "Taoistic knowledge" (Bertha Maslow, 42). The simple model of Taoistic objectivity comes from the phenomenology of disinterested love and admiration for the being of the other person. For instance, Maslow wrote, loving one's baby, or one's friend, or one's profession, or even one's problem, in the scientific sense, one's field of science, can be so complete and accepting that it becomes non-interpreting, non-intrusive. In this sense, he wrote, "I remain modestly open to the truth, objective and disinterested in this new Taoistic sense of refusing to prejudge the truth or to tamper with it, as our scientists and politicians are now doing."

We might say, then, that Maslow's absolute base is the Tao or way. He seems to have espoused the aspects of Taoism as described in Taoistic commentaries (Kao, 97). Tao produced all things, and is the ground of all things. It enables one to see life, self and death from a higher point of view. The Tao is the harmony and orderliness displayed in heaven and on earth. It is the result of the cosmic energy of the way or road (Tao), the way of going of the universe. Fullness of life is present harmony with the Tao. Impersonal conformity to the Tao is a species of mysticism (1966, 95–101).

Is Maslow's idea of the Tao similar to God? (Note that when the Bible was translated into Chinese, the Logos in John's Gospel was translated as Tao: "In the beginning was the Tao." The Tao is the undifferentiated oneness behind all.) I think that the chief ways in which Maslow's Tao differs from the Christian God is that it does not intervene in personal dealings, nor probably in self-giving love, nor does it remain in relationship with persons beyond death.

Maslow and Freud. Freud interpreted "the oceanic experience" as a regression to infancy. Maslow, who uses the term "peak experiences," says that there is a quest for peak experiences which is a regression. He calls this "a low nirvana." This occurs when one seeks transcendence without negotiating the demands of ego-formation. But if these demands are met, the result is what he terms "a high nirvana."

Freud and Maslow also differ on the notion of pleasure and value. Freud said that we all act exclusively for pleasure; even the reality principle was merely a delaying of pleasure. Maslow shows that there are many degrees of pleasure or gratification. They range from lower to higher, from the relief of pain to the enjoyment of friends, to the bliss of having a child, to the fusion of "B-values" (Being values) such as beauty, truth and goodness. Thus we cannot say that biological pleasure is the sole goal of human beings.

Maslow sees the person as growing from *lower-need* hedonism (biological), to *higher-need* hedonism (pleasure in *needing* love, *needing* people), to *meta-need* hedonism ("meta" means beyond needs). Meta-need hedonism is pleasure that comes from *giving* or *being*. On the third and highest level, we find altruism where pleasure and value coincide. "At this level there is no contradiction between pleasure and duty since the highest obligations of human beings are certainly truth, justice, beauty."

The Basic Needs. Maslow held that, apart from heroic exceptions, one must satisfy the lower needs before the higher needs can be fulfilled. His list of needs is as follows: (1) Hunger needs: including self-preservation, etc. (2) Safety needs: the need for order and predictability, a regular routine, regular employment, protection from criminals. (3) Love needs: friends, one to be affirmed by, wife or children. (4) Esteem needs: stable evaluation from others, self-respect. (5) The need for self-actualization: to become everything one is capable of, an ideal mother, an ideal person, perfection at a job. #1 to 4 are deficiency needs ("D values"). #5 is a "B value," a being something and capable of full giving.

No one ever achieves full self-actualization. However, it is when one is working on this level that self-transcendence takes the form of "peak experiences." (Cf. the excerpt which follows.) Maslow believed that these are very important for health. He also saw them as secular mystical experiences, the raw materials out of which religions can be built. At times, Maslow spoke as if these experiences were the essence of religion. However, he also saw that certain types did not have peak experiences, people whose character structure was extremely rational, obsessive-compulsive types (1964, 22; 1971, 87). There were self-actualized transcenders or "peakers" (e.g., Schweitzer, Buber, Einstein) but there also were self-actualized non-transcenders (Mrs. Roosevelt, Truman, Eisenhower). Certainly he would not deny that this last type could be religious. Maslow distinguished two types of people: (1) prophets and discoverers; (2) organizers and conservers. His point seems to be that religion begins with a peak experience had by a prophet, as with Moses on Sinai or with Jesus' experience of "Abba" or "Father." Organized religion, then, becomes the effort to communicate peak experiences to non-peakers. Often, this results in what has been called "the routinization of charisma."

The question which arises from the phenomenology of peak experiences presented by Maslow is whether this touches the heart of mysticism. This question we will return to in the next chapter.

*   *   *

It has been discovered that this same kind of subjective experiential response (which has been thought to be triggered only in religious or mystical contexts, and which has, therefore, been considered to be only religious or mystical) is also triggered by many other stimuli or situations, e.g., experiences of the aesthetic, of the creative, of love, of sex, of insight, etc. If we insist on calling the peak-experience a religious experience, then we must say that religious experiences can be produced by sexual love, or by philosophical insight, or by athletic success, or by watching a dance performance, or by bearing a child. This inevitably means, as James and Dewey both saw, that we must take the word "religious" out of its narrow context of the supernatural, churches, rituals, dogmas, professional clergymen, etc., and distribute it in principle throughout the whole of life. Religion becomes then not one social institution among others, not one department of life distinct from others, but rather a state of mind achievable in almost any activity of life, if this activity is raised to a suitable level of perfection.

Peak-experiences, as I have defined them for this analysis, are secularized religious or mystical or transcendent experiences; or, more precisely, peak-experiences are the raw materials out of which not only religions can be built but also philosophies of any kind: educational, political, aesthetic, etc. Not only are these experiences not dependent on churches or specific religions, as James and Dewey saw, they do not necessarily imply any supernatural concepts. They are well within the realm of nature, and can be investigated and discussed in an entirely naturalistic way. . . .

This thesis that religious experiences are natural experiences could be seen by churchmen with dismay, as simply and only a further instance of science carving another chunk out of the side of organized religion—which, of course, it is. But it is also possible for a more perceptively religious man to greet this development with enthusiasm, when he realizes that what the mystics have said to be essential to the *individual's* religion is now receiving empirical support and no longer needs rest only on tradition, blind faith, temporal power, exhortation, etc. If this development is a secularizing of all religion, it is also a religionizing of all that is secular. This lecture is a critique, not only of traditional, conventional religion, but also of traditional and conventional atheism. As a matter of fact, I am addressing myself much more to the latter than to the former. Religion is easy to criticize but difficult to explain. It begins to be clear to me that in throwing out *all* of religion and everything to do with it, the atheists have thrown out too much. Also, religion has been "reduced" too much, e.g., by Freud, by Feuerbach, etc. Undoubtedly correct to a large extent, yet they went too far in their generalizations and, in any case, were, I think, attacking organized religions more than private, transcendent experiences. (See also Allport on "growth-religion" vs "safety-religion.")[1] Also, it is clear that they didn't realize, as we do today, how deep and possibly even "instinctoid" is the need for a framework of values (Fromm), for meaning (Frankl), for understanding (Maslow). Nor did they anticipate that a psychology of ends (an ontopsychology, a psychology of Being) could become possible, offering us in the distance not too far ahead the possibility of a "scientific" or objective value system. (In a fuller treatment I would also bring up the possibility of a "need for transcendence" beyond the need for understanding, as Fromm has.) . . .

RELIGIOUS ASPECTS OF PEAK-EXPERIENCES

Practically everything that happens in the peak-experiences, naturalistic though they are, could be listed under the headings of religious happenings, or indeed have been in the past considered to be only religious experiences.

1. For instance, it is quite characteristic in peak-experiences that the whole universe is perceived as an integrated and unified whole. This is not as simple a happening as one might imagine from the bare words themselves. To have a clear perception (rather than a purely abstract and verbal philosophical acceptance) that the universe is all of a piece and that one has his place in it—one is a part of it, one belongs in it—can be

so profound and shaking an experience that it can change the person's character and his Weltanschauung forever after. In my own experience I have two subjects who, because of such an experience, were totally, immediately, and permanently cured of (in one case) chronic anxiety neurosis and, in the other case, of strong obsessional thoughts of suicide.

This, of course, is a basic meaning of religious faith for many people. People who might otherwise lose their "faith" will hang onto it because it gives a meaningfulness to the universe, a unity, a single philosophical explanation which makes it all hang together. Many orthodoxly religious people would be so frightened by giving up the notion that the universe has integration, unity, and, therefore, meaningfulness (which is given to it by the fact that it was all created by God or ruled by God or *is* God) that the only alternative for them would be to see the universe as a totally unintegrated chaos.

2. In the cognition that comes in peak-experiences, characteristically the percept is exclusively and fully attended to. That is, there is tremendous concentration of a kind which does not normally occur. There is the truest and most total kind of visual perceiving or listening or feeling. Part of what this involves is a peculiar change which can best be described as non-evaluating, non-comparing, or non-judging cognition. That is to say, figure and ground are less sharply differentiated. Important and unimportant are also less sharply differentiated, i.e., there is a tendency for things to become equally important rather than to be ranged in a hierarchy from very important to quite unimportant. For instance, the mother examining in loving ecstasy her new-born infant may be enthralled by every single part of him, one part as much as another one, one little toenail as much as another little toenail, and be struck into a kind of religious awe in this way. This same kind of total, non-comparing acceptance of everything, as if everything were equally important, holds also for the perception of people. Thus it comes about that in peak-experience cognition a person is most easily seen per se, in himself, by himself, uniquely and idiosyncratically as if he were the sole member of his class. Of course, this is a very common aspect not only of religious experience but of most theologies as well, i.e., the person is

unique, the person is sacred, one person in principle is worth as much as any other person, everyone is a child of God, etc.

3. The cognition of being (B-cognition) that occurs in peak-experiences tends to perceive external objects, the world, and individual people as more detached from human concerns. Normally we perceive everything as relevant to human concerns and more particularly to our own private selfish concerns. In the peak-experiences, we become more detached, more objective, and are more able to perceive the world as if it were independent not only of the perceiver but even of human beings in general. The perceiver can more readily look upon nature as if it were there in itself and for itself, not simply as if it were a human playground put there for human purposes. He can more easily refrain from projecting human purposes upon it. In a word, he can see it in its own Being (as an end in itself) rather than as something to be used or something to be afraid of or something to wish for or to be reacted to in some other personal, human, self-centered way. That is to say, B-cognition, because it makes human irrelevance more possible, enables us thereby to see more truly the nature of the object in itself. This is a little like talking about god-like perception, superhuman perception. The peak-experience seems to lift us to greater than normal heights so that we can see and perceive in a higher than usual way. We become larger, greater, stronger, bigger, taller people and tend to perceive accordingly.

4. To say this in a different way, perception in the peak-experiences can be relatively ego-transcending, self-forgetful, egoless, unselfish. It can come closer to being unmotivated, impersonal, desireless, detached, not needing or wishing. Which is to say, that it becomes more object-centered than ego-centered. The perceptual experience can be more organized around the object itself as a centering point rather than being based upon the selfish ego. This means in turn that objects and people are more readily perceived as having independent reality of their own.

5. The peak-experience is felt as a self-validating, self-justifying moment which carries its own intrinsic value with it. It is felt to be a highly valuable—even uniquely valuable—experience, so great an experience sometimes that even to at-

tempt to justify it takes away from its dignity and worth. As a matter of fact, so many people find this so great and high an experience that it justifies not only itself but even living itself. Peak-experiences can make life worthwhile by their occasional occurrence. They give meaning to life itself. They prove it to be worthwhile. To say this in a negative way, I would guess that peak-experiences help to prevent suicide.

6. Recognizing these experiences as end-experiences rather than as means-experiences makes another point. For one thing, it proves to the experiencer that there are ends in the world, that there are things or objects or experiences to yearn for which are worthwhile in themselves. This in itself is a refutation of the proposition that life and living is meaningless. In other words, peak-experiences are one part of the operational definition of the statement that "life is worthwhile" or "life is meaningful."

7. In the peak-experience there is a very characteristic disorientation in time and space, or even the lack of consciousness of time and space. Phrased positively, this is like experiencing universality and eternity. Certainly we have here, in a very operational sense, a real and scientific meaning of "under the aspect of eternity." This kind of timelessness and spacelessness contrasts very sharply with normal experience. The person in the peak-experiences may feel a day passing as if it were minutes or also a minute so intensely lived that it might feel like a day or a year or an eternity even. He may also lose his consciousness of being located in a particular place.

8. The world seen in the peak-experiences is seen only as beautiful, good, desirable, worthwhile, etc. and is never experienced as evil or undesirable. The world is accepted. People will say that then they understand it. Most important of all for comparison with religious thinking is that somehow they become reconciled to evil. Evil itself is accepted and understood and seen in its proper place in the whole, as belonging there, as unavoidable, as necessary, and, therefore, as proper. Of course, the way in which I (and Laski also) gathered peak-experiences was by asking for reports of ecstasies and raptures, of the most blissful and perfect moments of life. Then, of course, life *would* look beautiful. And then all the foregoing might seem like

discovering something that had been put in a priori. But observe that what I am talking about is the perception of evil, of pain, of disease, of death. In the peak-experiences, not only is the world seen as acceptable and beautiful, but, and this is what I am stressing, the bad things about life are accepted more totally than they are at other times. It is as if the peak-experience reconciled people to the presence of evil in the world.

9. Of course, this is another way of becoming "god-like." The gods who can contemplate and encompass the whole of being and who, therefore, understand it must see it as good, just, inevitable, and must see "evil" as a product of limited or selfish vision and understanding. If we could be god-like in this sense, then we, too, out of universal understanding would never blame or condemn or be disappointed or shocked. Our only possible emotions would be pity, charity, kindliness, perhaps sadness or amusement. But this is precisely the way in which self-actualizing people do at times react to the world, and in which all of us react in our peak-experiences.

10. Perhaps my most important finding was the discovery of what I am calling B-values or the intrinsic values of Being. (See Appendix G.) When I asked the question, "How does the world look different in peak-experiences?", the hundreds of answers that I got could be boiled down to a quintessential list of characteristics which, though they overlap very much with one another can still be considered as separate for the sake of research. What is important for us in this context is that this list of the described characteristics of the world as it is perceived in our most perspicuous moments is about the same as what people through the ages have called eternal verities, or the spiritual values, or the highest values, or the religious values. What this says is that facts and values are not totally different from each other; under certain circumstances, they fuse. Most religions have either explicitly or by implication affirmed some relationship or even an overlapping or fusion between facts and values. For instance, people not only existed but they were also sacred. The world was not only merely existent but it was also sacred.

11. B-cognition in the peak-experience is much more pas-

sive and receptive, much more humble, than normal perception is. It is much more ready to listen and much more able to hear.

12. In the peak-experience, such emotions as wonder, awe, reverence, humility, surrender, and even worship before the greatness of the experience are often reported. This may go so far as to involve thoughts of death in a peculiar way. Peak-experiences can be so wonderful that they can parallel the experience of dying, that is of an eager and happy dying. It is a kind of reconciliation and acceptance of death. Scientists have never considered as a scientific problem the question of the "good death"; but here in these experiences, we discover a parallel to what has been considered to be the religious attitude toward death, i.e., humility or dignity before it, willingness to accept it, possibly even a happiness with it.

13. In peak-experiences, the dichotomies, polarities, and conflicts of life tend to be transcended or resolved. That is to say, there tends to be a moving toward the perception of unity and integration in the world. The person himself tends to move toward fusion, integration, and unity and away from splitting, conflicts, and oppositions.

14. In the peak-experiences, there tends to be a loss, even though transient, of fear, anxiety, inhibition, of defense and control, of perplexity, confusion, conflict, of delay and restraint. The profound fear of disintegration, of insanity, of death, all tend to disappear for the moment. Perhaps this amounts to saying that fear disappears.

15. Peak-experiences sometimes have immediate effects or aftereffects upon the person. Sometimes their aftereffects are so profound and so great as to remind us of the profound religious conversions which forever after changed the person. Lesser effects could be called therapeutic. These can range from very great to minimal or even to no effects at all. This is an easy concept for religious people to accept, accustomed as they are to thinking in terms of conversions, of great illuminations, of great moments of insight, etc.

16. I have likened the peak-experience in a metaphor to a visit to a personally defined heaven from which the person then returns to earth. This is like giving a naturalistic meaning to the

concept of heaven. Of course, it is quite different from the conception of heaven as a place somewhere into which one physically steps after life on this earth is over. The conception of heaven that emerges from the peak-experiences is one which exists all the time all around us, always available to step into for a little while at least.

17. In peak-experiences, there is a tendency to move more closely to a perfect identity, or uniqueness, or to the idiosyncracy of the person or to his real self, to have become more a real person.

18. The person feels himself more than at other times to be responsible, active, the creative center of his own activities and of his own perceptions, more self-determined, more a free agent, with more "free will" than at other times.

19. But it has also been discovered that precisely those persons who have the clearest and strongest identity are exactly the ones who are most able to transcend the ego or the self and to become selfless, who are at least relatively selfless and relatively egoless.

20. The peak-experiencer becomes more loving and more accepting, and so he becomes more spontaneous and honest and innocent.

21. He becomes less an object, less a thing, less a thing of the world living under the laws of the physical world, and he becomes more a psyche, more a person, more subject to the psychological laws, especially the laws of what people have called the "higher life."

22. Because he becomes more unmotivated, that is to say, closer to non-striving, non-needing, non-wishing, he asks less for himself in such moments. He is less selfish. (We must remember that the gods have been considered generally to have no needs or wants, no deficiencies, no lacks, and to be gratified in all things. In this sense, the unmotivated human being becomes more god-like.)

23. People during and after peak-experiences characteristically feel lucky, fortunate, graced. A common reaction is "I don't deserve this." A common consequence is a feeling of gratitude, in religious persons, to their God, in others, to fate or to nature or to just good fortune. It is interesting in the

present context that this can go over into worship, giving thanks, adoring, giving praise, oblation, and other reactions which fit very easily into orthodox religious frameworks. In that context we are accustomed to this sort of thing—that is, to the feeling of gratitude or all-embracing love for everybody and for everything, leading to an impulse to do something good for the world, an eagerness to repay, even a sense of obligation and dedication.

24. The dichotomy or polarity between humility and pride tends to be resolved in the peak-experiences and also in self-actualizing persons. Such people resolve the dichotomy between pride and humility by fusing them into a single complex superordinate unity, that is by being proud (in a certain sense) and also humble (in a certain sense). Pride (fused with humility) is not hubris nor is it paranoia; humility (fused with pride) is not masochism.

25. What has been called the "unitive consciousness" is often given in peak-experiences, i.e., a sense of the sacred glimpsed *in* and *through* the particular instance of the momentary, the secular, the worldly.

Note

1. Gordon Allport, *The Individual and His Religion* (N.Y.: Macmillan Co., 1950, paperback).

(*Editor's note:* in the second edition to *Religions, Values and Peak Experiences,* Maslow added an important preface in which he listed some correctives to a possible over-emphasis on peak experiences. Seeking peak experiences, he wrote, may cause one to turn from the world, to use others as triggers for peak experiences, to become selfish, anti-rational, anti-empirical, anti-verbal. Consistently seeking peak experiences might bring about the need to escalate triggers, through drugs for example. It might cause one to rely too heavily on inner voice experiences, to lose sight of the sacred in the ordinary, to become individualistic and lose sight of the value of organizations and communities. Lastly, Maslow said that he would also see more value now in nadir ("dark night") experiences and "plateau experiences." The latter are more cognitive and more casual, arising perhaps out of a personal philosophy.)

Works by Maslow

Religions, Values and Peak Experiences, 1964; 2nd ed. N.Y.: Penguin, 1976.
The Psychology of Science. Chicago: Regnery, 1966.
Toward a Psychology of Being. Chicago: Regnery, 1968.
Motivation and Personality. N.Y.: Harper and Row, 1970.
The Farther Reaches of Human Nature. N.Y.:Viking, 1971.

Other Readings

Andrew Reid Fuller, *Psychology and Religion: Eight Points of View.* Washington, D.C.: University Press of America, 1977.
Frank Goble, *The Third Force.* N.Y.: Pocket Books, 1970. On Maslow.
Charles C. Kao, *Search for Maturity.* Phila.: Westminster, 1975. Taoism.
Richard J. Lowry, *A.H. Maslow, An Intellectual Portrait.* Monterey, Calif.: Brooks/Cole, 1973.
Bertha G. Maslow, *Abraham Maslow. A Memorial Volume.* Monterey, Calif.: Brooks/Cole, 1972.
Salvatore R. Maddi, Paul T. Costa, *Humanism in Personology.* N.Y.: Aldine-Atherton, 1972. Section on Maslow.
April and Vincent O'Connell, *Choice and Change.* Englewood Cliffs: Prentice-Hall, 1980. The growth model may not be for everyone; 10ff.
Karl Rahner, S.J., 'Self-Realization and Taking Up One's Cross," *Theological Investigations,* Vol. IX. N.Y.: Seabury, 1972, 253–262.
Colin Wilson, *New Pathways in Psychology. Maslow and the Post-Freudian Revolution.* N.Y.: Taplinger, 1973.

XV.
Transpersonal States
and Chemical Ecstasy

David R. Crownfield

(Excerpt from David R. Crownfield, "Religion in the
Cartography of the Unconscious: A Discussion of Stanislav
Grof's *Realms of the Human Unconscious*," *Journal of the Ameri-
can Academy of Religion*, 44/2 [1976], 309–315.)

Editor's Note

Similarities have often been noted between the peak experiences
described by Maslow, the transpersonal states triggered by physiological techniques (LSD, meditation and isolation), and the experiences
of many mystics. Similarities in phenomenology include a quality of
ineffability, a noetic intuitive sense, a feeling of timelessness and
passivity, a consciousness of the oneness of everything, and a conviction that the familiar phenomenal ego is not the center of the real I
(Happold, 45).

Masters and Houston in their classic, *The Varieties of Psychedelic
Experience*, presented a model exhibiting four levels of experience
traversed during their studies of manipulative techniques: (1) the
sensory level: an altered perception which can be very pleasant or
very frightening; (2) the recollective-analytic level: introspective, early
personal life problems are examined, somewhat as in Freudian analysis; (3) the symbolical level: archetypal images such as death and
rebirth prevail, as in Jungian theory; (4) the integral level: an experience of total self-understanding, an experienced confrontation with
the Ground of Being, God, Mysterium, Ultimate Reality (148).

Only eleven out of two hundred and six subjects reached the
integral level. This shows that drugs or various techniques are not the
causes of the religious experience on the integral level. Rather, they

197

act as triggers. The outcome is determined more by "set and setting," that is, one's spiritual and psychic state, prior training, and the methods of control (Barr, 164).

Scholars generally distinguish between two types of mysticism, the extrovertive type and the introvertive type. The extrovertive type looks outward into the physical world and finds a Oneness there of which the mystic is a part. Teilhard de Chardin had this experience in the Egyptian desert. The introvertive type turns inward and finds the One at the depth of the self (Wainwright, 87). The basic apprehension is an ultimate non-sensuous unity in all things.

The introvertive type is usually divided into three or four classes. 1. Soul mysticism: the experience of the deeper self and of eternity. 2. Nature mysticism: experience of nature and its central force (usually this is extrovertive but its emphasis can also be introvertive). 3. Religious mysticism: (a) experience of Absolute Consciousness, or (b) experience of God. Many authors call the first "monistic" and the second "theistic." (4) Christ mysticism: Paul—no longer I but Christ lives within me (Happold, 43).

As psychology has moved into the domain of the transpersonal and to the study of consciousness, difficult questions arise in the dialogue between psychology and theology. How is the transpersonal experience related to theistic religion, and to Christianity in particular? Is it a type of soul mysticism? Is the experience of Absolute Consciousness the experience of God? With regard to this question, while the subject has not been studied in great depth by theology, one can imagine a broad spectrum of opinions. (a) There is no connection whatever between the Christian God and the experience of Absolute Consciousness (the Barthian school). (b) This experience might stand as a symbol of God but God infinitely transcends it. (c) This experience *may be* a dim experience of God but it lacks the depth and richness of the experience of God mediated through Jesus. (d) It *is* an experience of God, mediating implicitly what is mediated explicitly in the life of Jesus.

The author of the following excerpt, David R. Crownfield, professor of religion and philosophy at the University of Northern Iowa, says, "Metaphysically, the origin and basis of such experiences is a complete mystery." In what follows, Crownfield presents an overview of the work of Stanislav Grof, *Realms of the Human Unconscious.*

*   *   *

"In my experience, everyone who has reached these levels develops convincing insights into the utmost relevance of the spiritual and religious dimensions in the universal scheme of things. Even hardcore materialists, positivistically oriented scientists, skeptics and cynics, and uncompromising atheists and antireligious crusaders such as the Marxist philosophers suddenly became interested in a spiritual search after they confronted these levels themselves."[1]

In *Realms of the Human Unconscious: Observations from LSD Research,* Stanislav Grof offers a model of the levels and dynamics of human experience and symbolization that appears to invite a far-reaching reassessment of the roots of myth, ritual and religious experience. A beautifully written interpretive report on nearly two decades of psychiatric research with LSD, the book not only provides extensive documentation and useful classification of the often discussed analogies between psychedelic states and religious phenomena; its theoretical structure and the scope and nature of its generalizations on human experience at large are rich with hermeneutical resources for the interpretation of religion generally.

The research on which the book is based was chiefly carried out in Prague, where Grof personally supervised several thousand LSD sessions, in a psychiatric setting, with subjects whose psychiatric history and profile were known in advance. The primary purpose of the research was to assess the usefulness of the drug as an aid to psychoanalytic therapy. In Grof's view, the therapeutic value of LSD is potentially great, under properly controlled conditions. But the scope and quantity of the religious and mythological material, and the centrality of its function in the therapeutic process itself, give the work potentially great importance for the phenomenology of religion as well.

The ability to generalize from LSD research to theory of religion does not depend merely on analogy. The specific psychological contents of a session derive not from its pharmacology, but from the basic materials of the life of the subject.

Whatever psychological agendum is dominant in the subject is the determinant of the session. When sessions are run basically without cues and other input from the therapist or the environment, the results are essentially an amplification of processes that are already operative. As such, they are indicative of general human phenomena, rather than simply the special milieu of drug experience. This assumption is supported by the extent to which similar results are found in non-drug states, including meditation, dying, prolonged isolation, and controlled conditions of sensory deprivation and overload. The function of the religious materials in the sessions is thus taken to be indicative of their function at deep levels of human experience generally.

I

Grof finds four levels of phenomena in his material. While they are not absolutely discrete or sequential, they involve different basic processes, and they tend to be distributed in a rough temporal order, both within a session and over a series of sessions. The first level is abstract and aesthetic, characterized by sensory distortion and, with the subject's eyes closed, complex and intricate visual patterning. These phenomena appear to have no psychological or existential importance; they do not function as symbols or expressions but simply as perceptual events.

The second level Grof calls the *psychodynamic*. At this level the material has the familiar Freudian characteristics. Repressed memories, symbolic expression of conflicts and wishes, Oedipal material, infantile traumas, are common. Grof reports that sessions tend to center on memories and symbols related to the same Gestalt or complex, passing through many aspects and episodes, until eventually, in classic psychoanalytic fashion, the subject relives the original traumatic experience in the session, after which that material ceases to appear. Later sessions may focus around other unresolved problems, but once its nuclear experience is relived and discharged, each ceases to recur.

Religious material occurs at the second level in standard

psychoanalytic ways. Subjects may remember experiences in which religion was a factor, or they may symbolize their conflicts and fantasies in a religious form. The dynamics of these processes are well understood in general, and Grof breaks no new ground here.

The third level, the *perinatal*, is another story. The central issue of this level is the problem of death. Fear of death, revaluation of life in the face of death, suicidal and murderous feelings, and undergoing what the subject experiences to be his own actual death, are common. This level also involves experiences of lost paradise, of no exit, of *Anfechtung*, of struggle and quest, or orgiastic and scatological scenes, and, climactically, rebirth or resurrection. Subjects frequently associate these events with a sense of reliving their own birth. Grof finds confirmation in this level of Otto Rank's thesis of the centrality of the birth trauma. But Grof goes far beyond Rank in developing organizing principles for this material, in grounding it in the specific somatic patterns of the birth process, and in connecting (as Rank supposed it was impossible to do) the material relating to death with the birth experience.

Before developing in more detail the structures of the perinatal level, and their import for the question of religion, let us complete this survey of the four levels with a consideration of the *transpersonal*. Transpersonal experiences can occur in any session, but once the core perinatal experience of one's own death and rebirth has occurred, they tend to be the dominant content of the sessions. These experiences as reported by subjects include clairvoyance and "out-of-body" phenomena, ancestral and previous-incarnation memories, identification with other individuals or with a group or race, or mankind, or another species. There are accounts of cellular consciousness, of memory of embryonic beginnings. There are Jungian archetypes of the Mother, the Outcast, the Fool, and others, and mythic and fairy-tale material. A culminating experience of this level is that of cosmic unity, and, beyond it, the void.

Grof does not propose to take the transpersonal material ontologically at face value. But neither does he reduce it to psychopathology in the usual sense. It does not conform to the patterns of delusion and of Freudian dream-symbols. Its emergence appears to be largely dependent on resolution of any typical psychoneurotic systems. And its emergence, and especially the experience of cosmic unity, appears to be of great therapeutic value. Grof does not offer a genetic model here, as he does with the perinatal level. What he does, over and above the reporting of the phenomena, is to make a useful taxonomic separation of this more Jungian material from the Freudian and Rankian and to show its close connection with psychiatric healing, rather than disease. When the theoretical puzzles about the genesis of this material are unraveled, we should be able to learn much about some of the most baffling phenomena of religion.

II

Let us return now for a more detailed look at the perinatal level of material. Grof subdivides this material in accordance with the various stages of the birth process. The *first perinatal matrix* includes experiences patterned on intrauterine life: enclosed, secure, tranquil. The "oceanic feeling" of which Freud speaks is, for Grof, a basic first-matrix experience. Imagery of paradise and of primeval innocence and tranquility express mythically and symbolically the quality of experience in this matrix.

The *second perinatal matrix* corresponds to the first clinical stage of delivery, in which labor has fully begun, but dilation of the cervix is incomplete, so there is no movement of the infant through the birth canal. The transition between the first and second matrices is experienced in terms of the fall, the loss of paradise, the introduction of suffering into the idyllic experience. The Four Passing Sights, through which the Buddha's secure life in the palace is spoiled by the awareness of suffering, old age, and death, give legendary expression to the experiential type characteristic of this transition.

The second matrix itself is grounded in a time in which the benign womb-environment has turned hostile, and is a source of great compression and pain from which no escape can be anticipated. Grof reports that patients frequently undergo an existential crisis of nothingness and despair, a "no-exit" experience, which they associate with this aspect of birth experience. Overwhelming and hopeless experiences of all sorts, passive depressions, despair, apathy, and images of the grave and of hell are characteristic of the second matrix.

(It is, of course, usually impossible to check the clinical details of the experience of birth to ascertain whether the dominance of one or another matrix in adult LSD experience correlates systematically with a specific difficulty in the individual's delivery. In the few instances where information was available, it appeared to confirm the clinical association of these experiences with those aspects of birth. But Grof is very clear about the fragility of such accidentally-available evidence, and scrupulously avoids asserting a strict causal correlation. The correlation is between the symbolic and existential content of the patient's psychedelic experience and the aspect of birth the patient spontaneously reports as an experience or apparent recollection in conjunction with the symbolic content, rather than with hypothesized facts about the past. We are dealing, as it were, with the existential *Geschichte* of birth, rather than with its *Historie*.)

The *third perinatal matrix*, corresponding to the progress of the infant through the birth canal, is the most complex. Its dominant motif is struggle. Here are evoked mythic images of cosmological conflict, of wrestling with demons, of combat against monsters, dragons, constricting serpents or the forces of evil. Sometimes the subject is engaged in struggle, and sometimes he or she is observer, with deep emotional involvement, as the armies of good and evil engage as though at Armageddon.

Temptation-experiences, like Jesus in the wilderness, or St. Anthony in the desert, or the Buddha in conflict with Mara, are another facet of this matrix. The myths of a long and arduous quest, whether of Gilgamesh or Orpheus or Beowulf, associate with this family as well.

Sometimes the violent dimensions of the third matrix are escalated to a kind of cosmic sado-masochistic dimension.

Bloody Aztec sacrifices, the Nazi holocaust, the destruction of
Sodom and Gomorrah, incredible cataclysms and conflagrations, scenes of torture and murder, are common, with the
subject variously the agent, or victim, or spectator of the horrible scene. The picture of the Charles Manson gang presented
in *Helter Skelter,* seen from the perspective of Grof's work, is an
astonishingly coherent story of enactment in the external world
of the symbols and myths of this aspect of the third matrix.

An orgiastic sexual phase is also found in the third matrix,
again with the subject variously in active, passive, and observer
roles. This facet does not find a great deal of precedent in
Judaeo-Christian materials, but elements of cosmic eroticism
elsewhere in the religions of the world are not hard to find.
There is less widespread expression of scatological elements in
religious imagery, though scatology is another major facet of
Grof's third matrix. The labors of Hercules are perhaps an
easier source here, though Luther, in particular, does provide
some evidence for correlating this dimension with Christian
experience.

Third-matrix imagery frequently moves toward a sense of
ultimate judgment. Sometimes this may take the form of a quiet
weighing in the scales, as in the Egyptian Papyrus of Hunefer.
Or it may involve the precarious passage of the narrow bridge,
as in Zoroastrian eschatology. Jesus or Yahweh on a throne of
judgment is not uncommon, or scenes like that of the judgment
portrayed at the bottom of a Tibetan Wheel of Life may occur.

Apocalyptic themes abound in this critical transition experience. The destructive aspect of Shiva or Kali, the shattering
of the whole cosmic order in an ultimate clash of good and evil,
or vast volcanic or thermonuclear conflagrations in which everything is annihilated, can characterize this crisis. Subjects
report a sense of literally experiencing personal and cosmic
death, the final surrender and overcoming of everything to
which they could cling. The psychological core of this transition is the death of the ego, and its etiology appears to lie in the
final defeat and destruction of the embryonic life and identity
which is all the infant has known or presumably can conceive.

The *fourth perinatal matrix* emerges from the crisis of the death of the ego. It is birth, resurrection, salvation, rapture, Clear Light, beatific vision, the blessed surcease from strife and sorrow. (The fourth matrix can have a negative aspect, involving cold, choking, abdominal or genital pain, fears of mutilation or abandonment; but Grof does not report mythic and religious correlates of this facet, and implies that such negative aspects can be resolved, through LSD therapy, in such a way as to lead into the beatific aspect.)[2]

When an LSD subject has experienced ego-death and re-birth, frequently there follows regression to the untroubled intrauterine world of the first matrix. The eschatological paradise turns out to be identical with the primeval garden, except that it is now larger, richer, more secure than before.

Grof reports that, just as subjects reliving Freudian psychodynamic traumas thereby free themselves from the accompanying symptoms and symbols, so one who fully undergoes the death-and-rebirth crisis of the perinatal experience is freed from the repetition of these struggles, and can move fairly directly in subsequent sessions into transpersonal experiences. There is here a strong suggestion of a microcosmic analogy to Buddhist doctrine: when one finally achieves enlightenment, one is freed from the wheel of rebirth and suffering.

The therapeutic power of the death-rebirth experience, Grof indicates, is tremendous. He does not present here the quantitative results, but he asserts that this experience has a profound releasing power for many deep psychiatric difficulties.

III

The critical importance of Grof's results, if sustained by the work of others, will lie in a revolutionary shift in the relation between psychiatric and religious understanding of the human condition. For Freud, and, indeed, at the psychodynamic level of traumatic and childhood-based neurosis in Grof's results as well, religion has a defensive, regressive function. It is a cosmic fantasy, a wishful falsification of the world to main-

tain the dimensions of childhood experience. Even when one
enlarges the scope of psychoanalytic interpretation of religion
to make allowance for maternally-oriented fantasy as well as the
patriarchal structures Freud recognized, the interpretation of
religion remains negative—it continues to function essentially
as a mode of unrealism, regression, neurosis, as inimical to
health.

Jung, of course, long disputed this interpretation. But,
despite some remarkable interpretations of religious images
and myths as progressive and transformative, Jung's view has
never acquired the hermeneutical authority granted to Freud's.
This may be, in part, because the two were regarded as com-
petitors, and the evidence for Freud's view is considerable, and
fairly clearly accessible. Freud also provides a simpler and
more comprehensive view of the etiology of religion; Jung's
talk of "archetypes" and "collective unconscious" has appeared to many speculative and uneconomical. By grounding
some of the Jungian materials in concrete body-experience,
infantile and traumatic to a degree that out-Freuds Freud, Grof
has made possible a theoretical overview, correlating both in a
way not previously available.

(Otto Rank's *The Trauma of Birth* is only a minor precedent
for Grof's work. For one thing, Rank deals almost exclusively
with the trauma of simply changing from uterine to mundane
existence, to the neglect of the somatic traumatization which is
the focus of Grof's interpretation. For another, Rank understands religion in classic Freudian terms, as originating in
postnatal relations to parents. He assumes, too, that a child
learns of death at second hand, several years after birth, while
Grof assumes the newborn infant has already experienced
"death" in an overwhelmingly devastating way.)

While the religious symbols of the psychodynamic, Freudian level are involved primarily with defense and unreality,
those of the perinatal level are integrally and affirmatively
related to the process of transformation. Inasmuch as the reliving of the birth experience as a death-rebirth or death-resurrec-
tion crisis has a profoundly liberating and healing power, the
symbols drawing us back into these primordial matrices are

inherently thereby also drawing us forward, toward transformation, resurrection, new life.

With characteristic moderation, Grof does not assert that the personal reliving of the birth trauma as an experience of death and rebirth is, as such, the reality denoted by religious symbols. Material that would suggest at least a hypothesis in this direction is available and impressive. But Grof has learned enough about the impoverishment of understanding by the reductionisms of the past to know better than to institute a new one at the first opportunity. He does, however, recognize a strong analogy and powerful alliance between the transformative power of religious initiation, conversion, rebirth, and the like and the healing transformation through reexperiencing the birth process which is the culmination, at this level, of his psychedelic therapy.

In the realm of "transpersonal" experiences, the issues are much less clear. Grof has amply documented and usefully sorted out various such experiences. The archetypal, mythical and theological character of many experiences at this level seems well established. And Grof claims, here, too, that a profound psychedelic experience of cosmic unity and/or encounter with the ultimate abyss has deeply transformative and regenerative power. Such experiences play a critical part in liberating psychotics and severely addicted patients; here, as on the perinatal level, there is a positive correlation between core religious motifs and core psychiatric processes. Unfortunately, we are totally in the dark about the genesis and ontological status of these experiences. Pragmatically, transpersonal experiences of the One and the Abyss have decisive healing and reconciling power. Metaphysically, the origin and basis of such experiences is a complete mystery.[3]

IV

The scope of Grof's theoretical model for interpreting his material makes imperative a thorough scrutiny of the grounds of its credibility. Until there has been extended discussion and comparison of Grof's results with those of others, and of the relative power and simplicity of his and other models, this question must be kept clearly in view. I judge that credibility provisionally affirmatively for a number of reasons. Grof is an internationally recognized researcher in the field. Pharmacological studies of LSD appear to agree with his premise that the drug amplifies existing processes in individually-varied ways rather than inducing specific effects common to diverse users.

More important, the model preserves and relativizes the work of his predecessors and illuminates some of their unresolved problems, e.g., Freud's basic work is assumed, but his inability to deal adequately with depression seems to be overcome. The paradigm of the birth process integrates economically a wide variety not only of LSD material but of cultural phenomena of comparable structure. This integration is respectful of the diversity of the data and illuminates rather than suppresses their inherent dynamics and impact. And the model identifies areas of unsolved problems and is open to revision and extension.

Whether these provisional grounds for the credibility of Grof's work stand up under scrutiny remains, of course, to be seen. Until a substantial body of critical challenge and response has accumulated, judgments on a thesis of this magnitude are, perforce, tentative. The apparent competence, simplicity, inclusiveness and openness of the work, meanwhile, invite the preliminary judgment that it is an event of major importance.

In conclusion, I should underscore the point that the origins of Grof's results in psychedelic research are essentially accidental to their significance. It is the intensity and efficiency of the psychedelic process in psychotherapy which has made these materials available. But all the elements of perinatal and transpersonal experience have been and continue to be accessible through non-chemical processes, including ritual, asceticism, meditation, dreams and fantasies as well as through sensory isolation, hypnosis, and other external agencies. The specific intensity and amplification provided by a decade of carefully controlled psychiatric use of drugs served the heuristic purpose of making levels, patterns, and relationships evident. Grof's work asserts that these levels, patterns and relationships are matrices of human experience generally.

*   *   *

Editor's Comment

Two questions arise from the previous presentation. (1) Do such states offer us meaning? (2) Are such states mysticism? The answer to the first question depends on whether we believe that patterns embedded in human experience are roads to meaning.

With regard to the second question, the study of chemical or other manipulative techniques is a good point of departure for the study of the essence of Christian mysticism. Most secular writers approach the subject from a strictly *phenomenological* perspective. They imply that the phenomenological typology includes the heart of mysticism, theistic or non-theistic. However, both the Eastern traditions and Christianity have warned about taking the phenomena for the essence. For example, St. John of the Cross said that in a deeply spiritual communion with God there is often an *overflow* into the imagination and feelings, but that these are not the heart of the experience (Johnston, 1970, 78). "God communicates Himself most to the soul that has progressed farthest in love" (Granfield, 109).

Some authors like Stephen Katz in *The Philosophy of Mysticism* and Peter Donovan in *Interpreting Religious Experience* claim that mysticisms differ not because of the experience but because of differing interpretations, different doctrinal systems. The religious "set and setting" defines what is found. Krippner and Brown believe that similarities in mystical experience derive from activity on the subcortical level while differences of interpretation derive from neo-cortical activity, or varying symbol systems (101).

However, whatever the case may be, for the Christian mysticism is fundamentally a union of wills from which awareness comes. Thus there is no short-cut in this mysticism other than conformity of our wills to the will of God (Granfield, 109).

A rough definition of mysticism might be the art of union with the real (Underhill), or the consciousness of the really Real, or the contemplation of an "embracing-Something" (Egan, 27). In Christian thinking, mysticism as altered states of consciousness is not a necessary part of Christian life (Rahner, 1981, 98). Mysticism in the wider, more ordinary sense of union with God is part of Christian life. (Cf. Chapter VI.) The mysticism of unusual mental states seems to belong to the natural psychic set-up of an individual (though this too can be a grace) since it cannot transcend in any essential way the experience of the Spirit in faith (Rahner, 1975, 1010). Thus mystical experiences do *not* differ from normal Christian existence *because* they are of a higher nature by being mystical. They differ because their natural substratum (e.g., suspension of the powers of the mind) is different from the psychological circumstances of everyday life.

Finally, I wish to conclude by offering for the reader's reflection a few very tentative conclusions about drug experience and ordinary religious experience, as contrasted with mystical states in the unusual sense:

1. If a person begins with faith in a personal God, this often shows up in these experiences. If a person begins without such a faith, the experiences seem to be of symbols in the unconscious, which *may* help in the integration of self with others or with nature. However, some atheists in these experiments have developed a strong sense of personal immortality or even of an Absolute. I would think that this latter would be a manifestation of "the unconscious God" in Frankl's sense.

2. In themselves, these experiences are not conclusive demonstrations of the claims of monotheistic religion. Psychic experiences are experiences of *the-self-in-relation*—in relation to whom or what? One's answer will depend on one's philosophy and theology, on one's experience of coherence, on faith.

3. Psychedelic experiences seem to perform the important function of releasing feeling. Thus they may be valuable for uniting religious feeling with cognitive meaning. This would harmonize with Paul Tillich's idea of "meaning," as a sense of direction plus feeling-power.

4. Mystical experience must always be balanced by prophetic and social religion. "Let me have no more of the din of your chanting, no more of your strumming on harps. But let justice flow like water, and integrity like an unfailing stream" (Am 5:23–24). Western prophetic religion, while it has included strong mystical spirits, has generally mistrusted an exclusively mystical approach. It has emphasized justice, charity, and belief in a personal God. Christian guides have always rated mysticism positively or negatively precisely insofar as it has or has not promoted growth in charity.

5. Judaeo-Christian faith itself *is* an experience, but it is an experience of being transcended by what one experiences.

Readings

Walter Houston Clark, *Chemical Ecstasy.* N.Y.: Sheed and Ward, 1969.

Peter Donovan, *Interpreting Religious Experience.* N.Y.: Seabury, 1979.

Harvey D. Egan, S.J., *What Are They Saying About Mysticism?* N.Y.: Paulist, 1982. Fine introduction.

Daniel Goleman and Richard Davidson, eds., *Consciousness: Brain, States of Awareness and Mysticism.* N.Y.: Harper and Row, 1979.

David Granfield, "Can Physiological Techniques Lead To Christian Mysticism?" *Proceedings, Catholic Theological Society,* June 1978, 97–109.

Andrew Greeley, *Ecstasy.* Englewood Cliffs, N.J.: Prentice-Hall, 1974.

L. Grinspoon and J.B. Bakalar, *Psychedelic Drugs Reconsidered.* N.Y.: Basic Books, 1979.

Stanislav Grof, *Realms of the Human Unconscious.* N.Y.: Viking, 1975.

Stanislav Grof, *Principles of LSD Psychotherapy.* Pomona, Calif.: Hunter House, 1980.

Stanislav and Christina Grof, *Beyond Death.* London: Thames and Hudson, 1980.

F.C. Happold, *Mysticism.* Baltimore: Penguin, 1964.

William Johnston, *The Inner Eye of Love. Mysticism and Religion.* N.Y.: Harper and Row, 1978.

William Johnston, *The Still Point.* N.Y.: Harper and Row, 1970.

Steven Katz, ed., *Mysticism and Philosophical Analysis.* N.Y.: Oxford University Press, 1978.

Stanley Krippner and Daniel P. Brown, "Altered States of Consciousness and Mystical-Religious Experience," *Journal of the Academy of Religion and Psychical Research,* July 1979, 93–110.

Karl Rahner, S.J., "Mystical Experience and Mystical Theology," *Theological Investigations,* Vol. XVII. N.Y.: Seabury, 1981.

Karl Rahner, S.J., "Mysticism," *Encyclopedia of Theology.* N.Y.: Seabury, 1974.

William A. Richards, "Mystical and Archetypal Experiences of Terminal Patients in DPT-Assisted Therapy," *Journal of Religion and Health,* April 1978, 117–126.

Huston Smith, *Forgotten Truth. The Primordial Tradition.* N.Y.: Harper and Row, 1976.

Walter Stace, *The Teachings of the Mystics.* N.Y.: New American Library, 1960.

William Wainwright, *Mysticism.* Madison: University of Wisconsin, 1981.

Richard Woods, O.P., ed., *Understanding Mysticism.* Garden City, N.Y.: Doubleday, 1980. An anthology of readings.

Notes

1. Stanislav Grof, *Realms of the Human Unconscious: Observations from LSD Research* (New York: Viking Press, 1975), pp. 95–96.

2. After I first publicly summarized Grof's work, one of my students read to me her journal of her first LSD experience. She felt secure but separated from the group she was with by an unclear barrier, with muffled sound and little sense of personal contact. Anxiety increased, and the barrier became a red film. As she began to fear something was radically wrong, the film dispersed, she breathed fully, all was light and open and she was back in contact with others and felt reborn. I confessed that her story did not conform to Grof's model, in that it lacked both the no-exit experience and the struggle. She responded, "Would it make any difference that I was born by elective Caesarian section?" As the missing elements are, according to Grof, directly attributable to the experience of labor, the story becomes confirmatory, rather than anomalous. It is not hard evidence, but it illustrates one sort of material on which, carefully developed and sifted, the model must stand or fall.

3. But see the appendix, "The Psychedelic Evidence," in Huston Smith, *Forgotten Truth: The Primordial Experience* (New York: Harper & Row, 1976), which focuses on just this question.

XVI.
Transpersonal States and Near-Death Experiences

John J. Heaney

(Reprinted from the *Journal of Religion and Health* Summer 1973.)

Recent studies have disclosed that a significant number of people undergo altered states of consciousness in near-death experiences. Are these experiences hallucinations, archetypal experiences or literal experiences of a life beyond death? The editor of this volume believes they are probably archetypal experiences accompanied by paranormal ESP phenomena.

The general public first became aware of research in the area of near-death experiences with the publication of Dr. Raymond Moody's book, *Life After Life,* in 1975.[1] Moody had gathered information on about one hundred and fifty cases of people who either had been declared clinically dead or had come very close to physical death. Of these he interviewed some fifty persons in great detail. He found a pattern in the cases, but he does not tell us how many people experienced each category of the pattern. However, no one person experienced all of the following categories:

    (a) a feeling of ineffability, of peace and serenity;

    (b) a noise (buzzing, clicking, roaring, banging, whistling, music);

    (c) an out-of-the-body experience (OBE) from which vantage point one can look back and see his or her own body, occasionally while it was being operated upon;

(d) other spirit-like persons are met, often deceased parents or friends;

(e) there is a meeting of a being of indescribable light, known as personal, with whom a direct transfer of thoughts takes place; this being is not identifiable; some Christians identify it as Christ, Jews as an angel, etc.;

(f) an intense review of one's life;

(g) an experience of a border or limit of some sort that cannot be passed; at times, a loved one who died unbeknown to the person is seen beyond it;

(h) there is a generally reluctant return to one's body;

(j) a change is effected in one's life: a growth in love for others and in a desire for knowledge, less fear of death, less of a reward/punishment model of afterlife; the being responded not with anger, but with understanding, even humor;

(k) a corroboration of details seen during the OBE, especially of technical details of medical operations, etc.

Subsequently, Dr. Moody published another book entitled *Reflections on Life After Life*.[2] In this book he added more material to his investigation and also endeavored to make a defense against some of the objections that were being made to his study. These objections we will handle shortly.

Osis. Few people knew that certain researchers had already been at work on these experiences long before Moody's book appeared, for example, William Barrett in England and Hornell Hart at Duke. However, I wish to center on recent research concerning near-death experience (NDE), and I will begin with the studies of Dr. Karlis Osis of the American Society for Psychical Research. During 1959–1960 Dr. Osis had made a pilot survey of six hundred and forty medical personnel.[3] From 1961 to 1964 he surveyed one thousand and four doctors and nurses in America. Then, in 1973–1974, Osis, with the Icelandic parapsychologist Dr. Erlendur Haraldsson, made a cross-cultural study in the United States and in India. The combined data for these studies appeared in the book, *At the Hour of Death*.[4] Some patients had disjointed hallucinations. Some had patterned experiences. There were three types of patterned experiences: (1) visions of people; (2) visions of places; (3) elevation of mood. I will place the patterned and hallucination-type experiences below in parallel columns for clarity of contrast, a technique used by Osis.

Near-Death Experiences

There was some ESP. People correctly mentioned details of the room they were in and of the environment outside of it.

Hallucinogenic Type of Experiences

There was a sick-brain type of delusion. There was also malfunction of the nervous system.

Hallucinogenic Factors

The use of hallucinogens did not increase the frequency of these patterned visions. In fact ESP decreased with drug usage.

The more hallucinogens used, the more rambling were the visions. There was no ESP.

Content

Relatively coherent. Oriented to transition; "take-away" figures often appeared.

These visions portrayed only memories stored in the brain and expressed as desires; the beliefs were characteristic of the culture.

Psychological Factors

The fewer drugs used, the greater clarity of consciousness, the more patterned visions.

Clarity of consciousness was less conducive to hallucinations.

The expectation of dying didn't influence the occurrence of the patterned vision.

Expecting to recover led to this-life figures; expecting to die led to hallucinations of the afterlife.

Stress did not increase frequency.

Stress increased frequency.

Content Variability

Little variability. Content was of visions of another life; essentially similar for old, young, men, women, Christian, non-Christian.

There was much variability. It varied widely with disposition and culture.

OTHER MISCELLANEOUS DATA
ON THE PATTERNED EXPERIENCES

1. The patients' normal perception of the room was intact in eighty-three percent of the cases.

2. Experiences were had against their expectations; occasionally they saw friends or relatives who they thought were still living but who had died. Desired living persons were conjured up in only thirteen of four hundred and seventy-one cases.

3. Those who had the patterned type of experience often saw "take-away" figures, while the rambling type of hallucinations which the others had manifested no purpose. In the latter, hospital visitors were taken for strange characters, while those who had the near-death experience saw the visitors as who they were, just visitors to the hospital. (Incidentally, Elisabeth Kübler-Ross described a similar episode as she visited her dying father. She wrote, "My own father talked to his father, who had been dead thirty years, and then turned back and spoke rationally to me.")[5]

4. If wish-fulfillment were the explanation, it is strange that the messengers did not come more often to those expecting to die and less often to those not so expecting.[6] In India, some even screamed and were opposed to being taken away.

5. What happened was not due to their religious expectations, at least if we take these from the Bible or the Bhagavad Gita. However, Christ was not seen by Hindus, nor Krishna nor a Yamdoot by a Christian.

At the beginning of their work, Osis and Haraldsson had presented two opposing hypotheses. The first hypothesis was that the experience was a transition experience to another life. The second hypothesis was that it was the beginning of an experience of extinction. The authors claimed that the data were more consistent with the hypothesis of a transition experience to a life beyond death than with the extinction hypothesis. However, the authors did not claim, just as Moody had not, that they had proved that there was life after death. They admitted that there were subjective differences in their cross-cultural study. However, they insisted that the cross-cultural *pattern* suggested a meaningful transition experience.

In this study there is no mention of OBEs nor of the being of indescribable light. Dr. Osis has told me that there is no real discrepancy here between this study and Moody's. The questions in this study were so framed that they were unlikely to bring forth these experiences. And, furthermore, there was specific reference to religious figures such as Christ or God, the common denominator being the religious apparitions that possess qualities of a numinous experience of varying degrees of intensity.

Noyes. A different interpretation of the experience is presented by Dr. Russell Noyes, associate professor at the University of Iowa College of Medicine, who had collected one hundred and fourteen cases.[7] He also found the experience of the life-review and the experience of the transcending of the body. But he believes that the life-review could be the result of a rapid regression to prior life to escape a frustrating reality, and thus to reach an intrinsically pleasant state. The experience of body transcendence would be the result of a type of dissociation (depersonalization) through which the reality of death would be excluded from consciousness. This allows one to pretend that he or she is witnessing it only as a spectator. Freud said that our death is unimaginable and we have to perceive it as a spectator, for in the unconscious every one of us is convinced of his or her own immortality.

However, Noyes' position does not account for the paranormal perceptions of the patients in Moody's work (seeing one's medical operation while lying with eyes closed, and the deceased who were not known to be dead). Noyes admits definite mystical overtones in the experience, and his subtle explanation stops short of Freudian reductionism according to which all "mystical" experiences or "the oceanic experience" are regressions to the security of early infancy. He endeavors to remain more open and presents an excellent phenomenological description. This type of description may be very helpful as we endeavor to come to definite conclusions about the nature of the experience.

Rawlings. Meanwhile, a book by Maurice Rawlings, M.D., *Beyond Death's Door,* appeared in 1978.[8] Rawlings claimed that he was particularly qualified to speak on deathbed experiences because he is a cardiologist who is a member of a resuscitation team. Furthermore, he recounts a number of experiences of "hell" which were recorded by patients who survived "clinical death." But he discovered that, while the "heavenly" scenes were remembered, the "hellish" scenes were *not long remembered* and were totally repressed by the patients later on. His conclusion was, "I feel assured that there is life after death, and not all of it is good." Rawlings said that he had always thought of death as "painless extinction," but that contact with these patients occasioned a conversion experience. Rawlings' book has been criticized for its careless, popular and non-scientific treatment. The book is also colored by a kind of evangelical, fundamentalist missionary tone. For example, he wrote of "our need for missionary work at home." Rawlings' claim to be the only investigator who actually has resuscitated patients is no longer true in view of subsequent studies.

As an example of the more *positive* or heavenly scenes, he tells us of a man who is looking for Jesus and sees a huge building. He said to his deceased parents who were with him, "What is that?" They said, "In there is God." In many of the positive experiences there is a flooding light which is identified by the person as Christ. In one of the *negative* visions of "hell," a woman who had attempted suicide saw a huge forbidding cave. Inside, "the beings had tails and slanted eyes," she said, "and looked horrible." From a philosophical-theological point of view, these scenes are certainly not literal transcriptions of the beyond. They are, at the most, symbolical. The question is: Are these symbols only of one's psyche, or are they symbols of some transcendent reality? Second, some of the visions of hell imply notions which are radically different from those of traditional Christianity, a point which Rawlings does not make. For example, a lumberjack had a vision in which he stood near a lake of fire. There he sees a youth who died at thirteen with cancer of the jaw. Christ comes and beckons him out. Thus, "hell" is not eternal. Again, a staunch Christian, a founder of a Sunday school, had a vision of hell during cardiac arrest. He then had two further experiences of cardiac arrest in which, "without any apparent reason, unless some secret transformation or dedication occurred (of which I am unaware), the patient's subsequent two experiences during other deaths were beautiful."[9] As Rawlings is unaware of any conversion, the notion of an experience of hell followed by an experience of heaven without any apparent life change seems to suggest something that is symbolic only of the state of the subject's own psyche.

Ring. In 1980, Dr. Kenneth Ring, professor of psychology at the University of Connecticut, published a work, *Life at Death: A Scientific Investigation of Near-Death Experience.*[10] This represents a well-written and seriously critical effort to investigate NDEs. Ring had one hundred and two formal interviews with near-death survivors, in addition to informal contacts with almost a hundred other persons. Forty-eight percent had experiences that conformed at least in part to Moody's model. However, Ring found that the earlier stages of Moody's experience were most common and that the later stages manifested themselves with decreasing frequency. In other words, more people experienced peace and bodily separation than the later stages. More than a third of the dying had distinct out-of-the-body experiences, but progressively fewer entered the darkness, saw the light, and entered the light. One-sixth saw the light, but only one-tenth entered the light. This is the stage in which deceased relatives are seen and greeted. Ring notes that there was no conjunction between seeing spirits or relatives and encountering the light-presence. Illness victims appear most likely to have near-death experiences; accident victims are next; and suicide victims are least likely. Many suicide victims are left with no recall.[11] Ring found that religious persons are not more likely to have near-death experiences than those who are non-religious. Religiosity may well be a determinant of the *interpretation* that the individual places on his or her experience, but religiosity does not affect either the likelihood or the depth of a near-death experience.

Ring ruled out explanations like depersonalization, wishful thinking, psychological expectations, dreams or hallucinations, and pharmacological explanations. He found the experience to be different from temporal lobe involvement and cerebral anoxia (lack of oxygen). Basically, he holds that we do not as yet have a fully satisfying explanation. Ring notes that in his study, as in Moody's, people had no feeling of guilt with regard to their mistakes. It was as if they were watching their lives like objective spectators. As with Moody, if judgment was made, it was self-judgment. But he adds an interesting fact with regard to the life review. Some people who experienced this had not only flashbacks but also "flash-forwards." This unusual fact eliminates many psychological and neurological theories as a total explanation of the experience. Ring holds with a number of investigators today that for many people there is a *transpersonal* experience at death. Tentatively, he favors the hypothesis that in these experiences there is a genuine out-of-the-body experience or a separation of consciousness from the known body. He hypothesizes that the transpersonal experience may well be one of another dimension of time-space. He speculates that the "voice of God" that is heard at times is not so much the voice of God but the voice of one's total self or what some traditions call the higher self.

Ring believes that dying brings a change of consciousness, a movement to a new "frequency domain." This shift of consciousness is gradual—the tunnel, the friends, the light, etc. As a paradigm to clarify his position, Ring uses the model of a hologram. A hologram is an image that is the result of lensless photography and light techniques. If part of the image is broken off, the broken fragment continues to contain the entire image. Similarly, in NDEs one taps into that order of reality that is behind the world of appearances. The fragmentary experience taps into the whole.

Some people experience a most pleasant transpersonal experience ("heaven") because they have negotiated the change of consciousness or frequencies. Some "get stuck," as it were, in the lower frequencies. This accounts for the "hellish" experience and visions where drooping and depressed people are seen wandering around. The reason one becomes "stuck" is not clear, but it seems to be related to the state of mind previous to the experience. Furthermore, these experiences

always change from "bad" to "good," a fact that suggests a
gradual change of consciousness.

Ring has presented an intriguing and rich interpretation of
the experience. Admittedly, much is very tentative. Also, his
concept is close to Jung's idea of the "collective unconscious."
We will add some thoughts on this point later.

Sabom. In 1982, another fine work on near-death experiences was published by Michael D. Sabom, M.D., *Recollections of
Death: A Medical Investigation.*[12] Sabom studied one hundred
hospital patients. Thirty-nine of these recalled nothing during
the period of unconsciousness. Sixty-one had definite recollections. Surprisingly consistent details came forth. There were
three types of experience: self-visualization from a position of
height, often called "autoscopy" (sixteen patients), passage of
consciousness into a foreign region or dimension (thirty-two
patients), or a combination of autoscopy and this change of
consciousness (thirteen patients). We will not analyze these
data in detail. However, Sabom, working at times with Sarah
Kreutziger, a psychiatric social worker, clearly ruled out anoxia
or loss of oxygen to the brain as an explanation. There were no
illusions of people as distorted or flat, no sudden feelings of
despair, no olfactory experiences, such as occur in anoxia.
Drugs were not an explanation. Several patients indicated no
drug usage. The depersonalization experience mentioned by
Noyes also does not explain the experience. It requires, Noyes
admits, *perception* of imminent death, as with people who *consciously* face "psychological" death just before a car crash. But
many of Sabom's patients were already unconscious, and Noyes
himself admits that this seems to be a different kind of experience. Also Sabom noted there was no lack of emotion in his
patients, lack of which is a characteristic of depersonalization.
Sabom also clearly distinguished "autoscopic" hallucinations,
which are described in psychiatric literature, from NDE self-
visions. In the NDE vision there is a perception *of the physical
body by consciousness outside of it.* In the psychiatric experience
there is a vision *from the physical body of a self-image outside.*

Sabom said that his own beliefs in this matter are leaning
in the direction of a genuine out-of-the-body experience. The

accuracy of the "visual"observations while a person is unconscious helped him to come to this conclusion. Sabom made it
quite clear that we have in no way as yet solved the meaning of
near-death experiences. However he does wonder whether the
split of the mind from the physical body that happens at death
could be the soul, which continues to exist after final bodily
death according to many religious doctrines. This, of course,
raises an enormous problem of dualism for philosophical and
Christian thought, a point which must be treated elsewhere.

Other studies have been made on near-death experiences,
as, for example, those done by the Kansas psychiatric team of
Glen Gabbard, Stuart Tremlow, and Fowler Jones, by Dr.
Charles Garfield of the University of California, Dr. Bruce
Greyson of the University of Michigan, Dr. Paola Giovetti of
Italy, and recently a survey by George Gallup, Jr.[13] For brevi-
ty's sake, let me merely mention that the frequency of NDEs
runs from about twenty-one percent to as high as fifty-nine
percent, but the existence of a core pattern is the common
thread.

Siegel. There have been a number of serious, even vehe-
ment, attacks made on the very tentative conclusions of the
authors I have mentioned. Perhaps the most important of these
attacks was made by Dr. Ronald K. Siegel of the Department of
Psychiatry and Behavioral Sciences at the University of California, Los Angeles.[14] Siegel ranges widely, comparing the death
rituals of animals like elephants to that of man, dismisses recent
apparition study with a wave of the hand, and rejects Dr. Ian
Stevenson's incredibly detailed work on reincarnation as a
study of the reveries of children. In his main point, he com-
pares near-death experiences to subjective hallucinations associated with depersonalization or dissociative experiences.

To set the context of Siegel's approach, one must be aware
that he does not accept the existence of ESP, "an untestable
construct." Second, he seems eager to show that there is no life
after death. "The most logical guess is that consciousness
shares the same fate as that of the corpse." His article in
Psychology Today ends as follows: "But, for the living, may the
life after death rest in peace." I will present a brief but necessarily inadequate summary of some of Siegel's main points.

There are certain "form-constants" in hallucinations: a bright light in the center of a visual field, a tunnel-like perspective, cartoon-like people. He also lists: lattice-tunnel forms, red colors, exploding rotational movements; a change of imagery so rapid that it is difficult to maintain a running commentary; things seen in caricature; pulsating scenes; a floating feeling, depersonalization during which a person feels as if he or she is seeing himself or herself from a distance, a feeling of unreality.[15]

Siegel holds that the light is caused by phosphenes, visual sensations arising from discharges of neurons in the structure of the eye. The experiences are due to common biological structures in the brain and nervous system. Siegel also wrote for *The UFO Handbook,* where he sees UFO abduction experiences as similar to NDEs in having abduction-like phenomena, travel in tunnels, sensations of floating, and glowing objects.[16]

While a bright light and tunnel-forms are found in NDEs, I find no cartoon-like people, no constant red forms, and no exploding rotational movements or pulsating scenes. There may be a floating feeling but it is often accompanied by paranormal knowledge, a point which Siegel would probably reject. In NDEs a person sees himself from a distance but, according to Sabom, there is no depersonalization which is usually accompanied by automatic movements, lack of affectivity and anxiety. To include "feelings of unreality" in NDEs is arbitrary. In NDEs, patients describe them as their most real moments, unless of course Siegel means here reality as he defines it.

Yet, as an expert on hallucinations, Siegel deserves a hearing. The patterns in his book on hallucinations, however, are random and haphazard and unlike the patterned experiences in NDEs, except for the light, occasionally a city of lights, and the tunnel effect.[17] He does point out, however, that in hallucinations the rest of the room is not always distorted, a position differing from that of Osis.

Grof. Siegel alludes to Grof and Halifax[18] as if supporting his position that these experiences "are related to stored memories of biological events that are activated in the brain." Grof and Halifax had, indeed, held that dying or near-death experience, in Siegel's words, "triggers a flashback or retrieval of an

equally dramatic and emotional memory of the birth exper-
rience." In the article cited by Siegel and in their later work,
they present LSD experiences as at times re-enacting the birth
experience. The feelings of peace may be related "to the original state of intrauterine existence," as Siegel puts it, and "the
experience of moving down a dark tunnel may be associated
with the clinical stage of delivery," and "the border or limit
may be associated with the experience of incipient emergence
from the mother." Grof and Halifax see the psychological
death of the ego as followed by a rebirth and resurrection.[19]

But Grof and Halifax do not treat the experience in a
reductive fashion. The LSD experiences with dying cancer
patients, they wrote, "can function as triggers of unconscious
matrices." There are biological, emotional, intellectual, transpersonal, religious, and metaphysical components in the experiences. In fact, Grof later writes, ". . . biological death is the
beginning of an adventure in consciousness."[20] Neither Grof
nor Halifax see the NDE as exclusively a recall of birth memories. Rather Grof sees in the death experience a relationship to
Jung's archetypes and the collective unconscious. Grof and
Halifax, however, do make the point that psychedelic sessions
with dying cancer patients did not differ substantially from
psychedelic sessions with those who are not dying, e.g., alco-
holics.[21]

On the other hand, Grof does not tell us, to my knowledge, what proportion of his patients who were not dying
underwent an experience similar to near-death patients. For all
patients, the more advanced stages, similar to those reached in
NDEs, came only after repeated administration of LSD. This
agrees with R.E.L. Masters and Jean Houston in their classic,
The Varieties of Psychedelic Experience.[22] There it is shown that one
needs preparation if one is to reach stages beyond that of mere
memory retrieval. In that study, only about forty percent of the
sample reached the second highest stage, the symbolical, which
involves archetypal imagery and death-rebirth experiences.
(Only eleven out of two hundred and forty-six reached the
"highest" stage, the integrative-mystical stage.)

On the other hand, I find no problem in principle in
finding a similarity between LSD experiences in people who are

not dying, but who are advanced and ready for ego loss, and near-death experiences. Preparation may do for these people what near-death itself does in near-death experiences. In *The Human Encounter with Death* Grof describes one man who had the same experience twice, once with LSD and once while really dying.[23] However, this man in both cases knew he was dying because he was terminally ill. Perhaps proximity to death was the cause and not simply the LSD. This is a rich field for more research.

Conclusion. I will now, at some risk, offer a tentative position on near-death experiences, a very difficult endeavor in view of the fact that the mass of data are, at times, conflicting. If, of course, one believes that life becomes extinct at death, one cannot discuss near-death experiences as pointers to the beyond. However, whether life continues after death is not principally solved by the study of near-death experiences. One's belief or disbelief in life beyond death is connected with previous philosophical and religious positions.

My own belief, shared by Christians and countless others, is that death is not the end. However, many who share this belief hold that NDEs are purely subjective hallucinations. Yet this position does not seem to be consonant with the evidence we have assessed. Do we, then, have no option left but to consider NDEs as definite transition experiences to another life? Is there another option? Yes, I believe there is. Near-death experiences may be *archetypal* and *symbolical* experiences, deep experiences of the individual and collective psyche, *combined with some ESP phenomena.* These experiences are not of themselves immediately self-validating. A further judgment as to the validity of their sign value is needed.

In order to demonstrate the difficulty of coming to the conclusion that NDEs are symbolical and archetypal rather than literal transition experiences, and in order to show why I lean to the archetypal theory, I will place two columns below. The first column represents the archetypal position (a cross-cultural or transpersonal symbolism whose origin is in the collective psyche). The second column represents the literal transition position (also involving some subjective and cultural embroidering).

Archetypal Experience

A Literal Transition Experience With Some Symbolism

• In the work of Osis, persons are sent back as if a mistake had been made. This seems implausible if we are dealing with literal experiences of the beyond. Osis himself believes there may be hallucinatory elements in these cases.

• We might well guess at some good purpose for this, e.g., a purposeful pre-experience of death for growth or insight. If this element is hallucinatory, there is still the core pattern to account for.

• But one person died only two minutes after having this "send-back" experience! (p. 154)

• This may have been a hallucination.

• Subjective symbolism certainly is involved, e.g., Christ appears only to Christians, Krishna to Hindus.

• We admit the presence of subjective cultural conditioning, but the cross-cultural pattern suggests something objective.

• Rawlings' account has many strange caves, unusual animals, God in a big building, etc. These all are definitely symbolical.

• We can picture what is really beyond space and time only through this-world symbols.

• Rawlings speaks of a man who had a "hell" experience; then, without any apparent conversion he saw two beautiful scenes. This implies an archetypal picture not necessarily connected with one's afterlife state.

• Rawlings implies that what one sees is what one receives. But he seems to have missed the point that this does not come from his material. Two of his patients saw "hell," but Christ brought them out. The experience may have had a purpose.

• Moody mentions that a few patients who had attempted suicide had negative experiences. Osis mentions a case of a woman who saw "hell." But the woman had a prior guilt feeling. Those who attempted suicide also may have had prior depression. The prior subjective state rather than a semi-literal experience of an afterlife may account for this.

• But these may have been experiences of a genuine future life. After all, what the woman felt guilty about was an extramarital affair and illegitimate children. As to the attempted suicides, we have no study of their prior state. Most attempted suicides experienced only the earliest stages of the NDE, and no judgment on them is manifested.

Archetypal Experience	A Literal Transition Experience With Some Symbolism
• But "nasty, mean" people, in Osis' description, often view beautiful scenes. Love and ethics don't seem to affect what is seen, a strange point if this is a literal picture of afterlife.	• But we do not know the inner conscience of these people. More research is needed on whether genuine theological guilt feelings bring experiences that are different from those who die with antecedent neurotic or immature guilt feelings.

The fact that one can go back and forth in this way shows how difficult it is to come to a decision on this issue. However, this brief sampling suggests to me, at least, that the literalist position has many weaknesses. The two positions are, as a matter of fact, quite close to each other. The more literal position holds that NDEs are *genuine transition experiences* to another life but woven through with symbolism. The archetypal-experience interpretation hypothesizes that NDEs are archetypal and symbolical experiences which *may point* to another life, but without informing us of its real nature. They might be "bridge" experiences, as it were.

I chose the archetypal-symbolical position as the most plausible interpretation of near-death experiences because (a) it covers all the data, (b) it does not go beyond the data as does the other position, and (c) it prevents *premature foreclosure* of the question.

Archetypes and the Real. The problem now shifts its focus to this question: Are archetypal symbols genuine pointers to the real? This question leads us, of course, to C.G. Jung and his theory of the archetypes and the collective unconscious.

Many mistakenly believe that in his theory of the archetypes Jung held that all people are born with *innate images*. He certainly made his rejection of this interpretation clear in his later writings. There are two elements in archetypal theory: (1) an innate patterning power, which has a tendency to form motifs, and (2) specific images or experiences which are *a posteriori* and drawn from one's culture (e.g., in NDEs the appearance of Christ or Krishna). Jung has been criticized

rightly for too casually listing various images as archetypal.[24]
Yet, it is becoming clear that the main lines of his theory are
receiving support from converging investigations, such as
Grof's LSD work, studies of specific states of consciousness,
investigations in transpersonal psychology, and from its fruitful
application to dream study and to schizophrenic drawings, and,
last, by its evident usefulness in explaining certain paranormal
events in parapsychology.

But do archetypal experiences and images point to the real
beyond phenomena? Here one must make an option. Jung, in
Memories, Dreams, Reflections, wrote, "A man should be able to
say that he has done his best to form a conception of life after
death. Not to have done so is a vital loss. For the question that
is posed to him is the age-old heritage of humanity, an archetype rich in secret life, which seeks to add itself to our own
individual life to make it whole. . . . The unconscious helps by
communicating things to us, or making figurative allusions. It
too has other ways of informing us of things which by all logic
we could not possibly know."[25] He finally called them "hints."
"He [Jung] believed that electing a course of action that results
in permanent healing, in human wholeness, comes closest to
living with reality as it is."[26] Ira Progoff, who was influenced by
Jung, put it this way, "The messages to the ego from the larger
transpersonal consciousness contain larger principles which
give intimations of the meaning of life to us."[27]

Rollo May calls myths a "clue to reality." (NDEs can be
seen as myths in the positive sense.) "Myth," he says, "is a
description of a position of life arising out of the unconscious,
that carries the values for a society and gives a person the
ability to handle anxiety, to face death, to deal with guilt. It
gives him an identity."[28]

Archetypes and Myths Bipolar. Archetypes, however, are bipolar. They can be salvific or demonic. Discernment is needed to
interpret them. I find nothing demonic in NDEs. The effects of
the experience satisfy the criteria one looks for in judging the
validity and fruitfulness of mystical experience, at least in its
broadest sense: a sense of peace and joy, a change of horizon
toward the spiritual, a lasting reformation of one's life, and a
greater sense of charity and of the need for growth.

But might not NDEs encourage people to commit suicide? Some authors express this fear. Moody, especially, has discussed this point. Those who have had the near-death experience, and especially persons who have attempted suicide, report an absolute conviction afterward that this is not the way the "light" wished them to face problems. Ring mentions that psychologist John McDonagh gives Moody's *Life After Life* to his patients with suicidal tendencies.

Another negative point about near-death experiences has been brought forth by certain evangelical writers. The "light" or "presence" seems so benign, even humorous, in the face of the faults of so many, that the experience seems contrary to Scripture. Certain points must be brought out in the face of this objection. There is judgment in these experiences, but it is *self-judgment*, a position which many theologians find in no way contrary to Scripture. Second, if one looks carefully, NDEs combine the benignity of "God" with the presence in other dimensions of great distress. This suggests the effect of self-judgment. I say this with the qualification that, according to my position, the visions tell us nothing that is literal about hell or its duration.

The position I have presented here may be invalidated by future research. But tentatively, at least, it seems very plausible that near-death experiences are symbolical, transpersonal, archetypal experiences. At least, this position is somewhat testable by research like that of Grof. For example, one could investigate whether a person who had *very negative* experiences in a NDE was suffering from neurotic guilt feelings built on a superego distortion rather than from a genuine conscience in the theological sense. If so, the set and setting would seem to be the catalyst and the experience of the afterlife would not seem to be a genuine one.

I wish to conclude by emphasizing one point. Most of the authors involved in NDE studies, whether they hold extinction, symbolism, a genuine transition or no position, agree on this one point. The near-death experience is, generally speaking, a very rich, rewarding, and satisfying experience which in a sense crowns one's life with a broad mystical experience. Michael Grosso, who has written on ego loss in both meditation and near-death experiences, says that this ego-loss is "not loss but letting go of control of thought processes." Ego death, he writes, concerns a release from an addiction to what Garfield calls the "logico-deductive method" or, put otherwise, a low tolerance for "ambiguity, logical paradox and paralogical process." "Death marks the boundary the theological-deductive method is experientially incapable of crossing."[29]

For many people living today, death will begin as an *experience,* a mysterious experience of unfathomable realms of consciousness that we are merely beginning to investigate. Many experiences will be joyful, but a few may begin in distress. For many others, we do not know what experiences await them. Only a reasoning faith helps us to glimpse "through a glass darkly" the outlines of what *follows* the near-death experience.

Is the position presented here a "denial of death"? A distinction must be made about this phrase, "the denial of death," which is so commonly used. Two separate meanings are imperceptibly intertwined in the modern usage of this phrase. *The first meaning:* to observe death as a spectator and blithely deny the dreadful suffering, pain, and grief by seeing it as "just a stage." This acts as a defense reaction against personally feeling the brutality of death.[30] Dr. Charles Garfield, who has studied NDEs and who has witnessed many deaths, points out that, despite NDEs, many patients still die in great agony, debilitated by chemotherapy and toxins, and breathing with great difficulty. But, he says, a *caring* environment is an important factor in "maximizing the likelihood of a positive altered state of dying."[31] The nurse or relative who brings to the bedside of a dying patient a loving care, despite great fatigue or personal sacrifice, in order to facilitate a near-death experience is not denying death. *The second meaning:* to deny that death is the end of all. If those who bring such empathy and care to the dying patient also believe that life goes on beyond death, are they "denying death"? This second sense of denying death is often blended imperceptibly with the first sense in which the pain of death is dismissed as just a stage. But the use of "the denial of death" in this second sense is an *a priori* begging of the very issue being investigated.

Notes

1. *Life After Life: The Investigation of a Phenomenon—Survival of Bodily Death.* Atlanta, Mockingbird Books, 1975.

2. Atlanta, Bantam/Mockingbird Books, 1977.

3. *Deathbed Observations by Physicians and Nurses.* New York: Parapsychology Foundation, 1961.

4. Introduction by Elisabeth Kübler-Ross, M.D. New York, Avon Books, 1977.

5. "Life After Death? Yes, Beyond the Shadow of a Doubt, Says the Eminent Dr. Kübler-Ross," *People,* Nov. 24, 1975, p. 66.

6. In the United States the messengers were either relatives or religious figures. In India quite a few of the dying saw "Yamdoots," the messengers of Yama, the god of death, in Indian folklore. The authors see these figures as different only in name and interpretation from the Western religious figures. *At the Hour of Death,* p. 41.

7. "Near-Death Experiences: Their Interpretation and Significance," in *Between Life and Death,* Kastenbaum, ed., New York, Springer, 1982, pp. 73–88; "Depersonalization in the Face of Life-Threatening Danger: An Interpretation," *Omega,* 1976, 7, pp. 103–114; "The Experience of Dying," *Psychiatry,* 1972, 35, pp. 174–184.

8. New York, Nelson, 1978.

9. *Beyond Death's Door,* pp. 118–119.

10. New York, Coward, McCann and Geoghegan, 1980. See also "Further Studies of the Near-Death Experience," *Theta,* Spring 1979, 7, 2, pp. 1–3; and "Religiousness and Near-Death Experience," *Theta,* Summer 1980, 8, 3, pp. 3ff.

11. Ring takes issue with Rawlings on the ideas of "selective recall" of events and "repression" of the more negative visions, and doubts his claim that as many as one-half of the cases had hellish experiences. He notes that Osis had only one such case, and that Moody and Sabom, who also had interviewed patients immediately after cardiac arrest, record no "hellish" experience. (But Moody in his second book, *Reflections on Life After Life,* pp. 28ff., describes a realm of depressed, bewildered spirits.) Ring says also that in LSD induced states, there is no selective recall or repression. And finally, patients seem to separate these negative experiences from the core experience. They are seen to be hallucinatory visions and *qualitatively* different from the core experience. But Ring admits the issue here is still open.

12. New York, Harper and Row, 1982. See also, "Physicians Evaluate the Near-Death Experience," co-authored with Sarah Kreutziger, *Theta*, 1978, 6, 4, pp. 1–6.

13. For a summary of the views of the Gabbard team as well as those of Greyson, see D. Scott Rogo, "Parapsychology at the APA," *Parapsychology Review*, Nov.–Dec., 1981, 12, 6, pp. 6–9; for Garfield's ideas, see "The Dying Patient's Concern with 'Life After Death'," in *Between Life and Death*, R. Kastenbaum, ed., New York, Springer 1979, pp. 45–60. Also see Paola Giovetti, "Near-Death and Deathbed Experiences: An Italian Surrvey," *Theta*, Spring 1982, 10, 1, pp. 10–13; and George Gallup, Jr., *Adventures in Immortality*, New York, McGraw-Hill, 1982. Notice that Garfield has also discovered "hellish" experiences.

14. "The Psychology of Life After Death," *American Psychologist*, 1980, 35, 10, pp. 911–931; "Accounting for 'Afterlife' Experiences," *Psychology Today*, Jan. 1981, pp. 65–75; also see the exchange with John Gibbs and Ian Stevenson, *American Psychologiist*, Nov. 1981, pp. 1457–1462. The first two articles are unusually sarcastic and filled with careless generalization for an article in a scholarly journal.

15. Siegel is a specialist in hallucinations. Cf. *Hallucinations: Behavior, Experience and Therapy*, R.K. Siegel and J. West, eds., New York, Wiley, 1975, pp. 111–161.

16. *The UFO Handbook*, A. Hendry, ed., New York, Doubleday, 1979, pp. 154ff.

17. In *Hallucinations*, Siegel emphasizes that while seventy-two percent of the people studied shared images, and the "form constants," which I have mentioned, were a feature, "no consistent patterns or directions of movement were seen" (p. 111). He mentions image changes, e.g., a dolphin changes into a diver, and that the red color appears often as well as cartoon-like characters. Carl Sagan in *Broca's Brain* has a similar position.

18. "Psychedelics and the Experience of Death," in *Life After Death*, A. Toynbee and A. Koestler, eds., New York, McGraw Hill, 1976, pp. 182–202.

19. See *Realms of the Human Unconscious*, New York, Viking, 1975, pp. 158–171; *The Human Encounter with Death*, New York, Dutton, 1977, pp. 41–62. For books appearing since Siegel's articles, see *LSD Psychotherapy*, Pomona, Cal., Hunter House, 1980, pp. 79–89; and Stanislav and Christina Grof, *Beyond Death*, London, Thames and Hudson, 1980, pp. 26–30.

20. *Beyond Death*, p. 31.

21. *The Human Encounter with Death*, p. 110.

22. New York, Delta, 1966, esp. pp. 144–150. Cf. also L. Grinspoor and J. Bakalar, *Psychedelic Drugs Re-Considered,* New York, Basic Books, 1979, pp. 95ff.

23. P. 180.

24. G.S. Kirk, *Myth. Its Meaning and Function in Ancient and Other Cultures,* Berkeley, U. of California Press, 1970, p. 270.

25. New York, Random House, 1961, p. 302. Jung said that many never drink the cup of life to the lees. These, when they are old, keep looking back. "It is particularly fatal to such people to look back. For them a prospect and a goal in the future holds out the promise of a life beyond, which enables a mortal man to live the second half of life with as much purpose and aim as the first." "Everything psychic is pregnant with the future." C.G. Jung, *Psychological Reflections,* J. Jacobi and R.F.C. Hull, eds., Princeton, N.J., Princeton U. Press, 1970, pp. 327, 331.

26. M. Kelsey, "Jung as Philosopher and Theologian," in *The Well-Tended Tree,* H. Kirsch, ed., New York, Putnam's Sons, 1971, p. 195. The pragmatic coloring echoes William James with whom Jung corresponded.

27. *The Image of an Oracle,* New York, Helix, 1974, p. 359.

28. *The New York Times,* Nov. 25, 1968, p. 25. Carl Rogers says he has a new openness toward death since his now deceased wife had a NDE and after he read Moody's book. *A Way of Being,* New York, Houghton-Mifflin, 1980, p. 88.

29. M. Grosso, "The Mirror of Transformation," *Theta,* 1978, 6, 1, p. 7. See also his excellent article, "Toward an Explanation of Near-Death Phenomena," *J. Amer. Society for Psychical Research,* Jan. 1981, pp. 37–60. Some of his positions are close to my own, but I read his article only after completing this essay.

30. G. Kuykendall, "Care For the Dying: A Kübler-Ross Critique," *Theology Today,* April 1981, pp. 37–49, in an excellent article warns about this danger. The main point of the article is that Kübler-Ross's stages are more *a priori* and hortatory than empirically based.

31. "The Dying Patient's Concern With 'Life After Death'," in *Between Life and Death,* R. Kastenbaum, ed., New York, Springer, 1979, pp. 45–60.

Readings

Consult the footnotes to the preceding article.

XVII.
The New Story: World Community

Thomas Berry, C.P.

(Excerpt from "Contemporary Spirituality: The Journey of the Human Community," *Cross Currents,* Vol. XXIV, Summer-Fall 1974, 172–183.)

Editor's Note

In Chapter I, we began to investigate our individual story. We endeavored to probe that story with intelligent and critical subjectivity. Ego development was studied. Psyche and cosmos, we saw, are related. Finally we arrived at the collective unconscious of Jung and the transpersonal states of Maslow and Grof. We see that the self is more than the ego. We now turn to the notion of the new age of world community. The ideas presented offer background material for the excerpt which follows.

Some thinkers believe that the human journey has led from the tribal, naive and participatory stage of early man who had a non-differentiated sense of self, to the individualist stage with its accent on the ego. The high point of this stage in the West was the Enlightenment. These thinkers believe that we are now moving out of this second stage into a third which will combine the values of the two previous stages. It will be a stage of holistic consciousness (Cousins, 28).

Ego. Some writers speak as if the ego is the cause of all our problems today. I would qualify this by using the phrase "the isolated ego." A collage of various books on consciousness today offers the following kind of picture.

"All sacred traditions begin from the idea of an ordered, intelligent universe, where the idea of hierarchy is central and where each level is related to others in reciprocal dependence. . . . Though (psychology) might recognize and show some serious interest in some of

234

the experiences previously called religious or mystical, man is still perceived as being at the center of things: his ordinary desires, ambitions, hopes and plans, whether selfish or altruistic, are taken at face value and used as a basis for action, for planning utopias and eupsychias. There is no concept of a second purpose to which man can give himself, and, because of this, no real questioning whether the first could be illusory. Ordinary psychology then becomes *another elaboration of the delusion itself,* providing more blindfolds, another ring through the nose, more 'hope' to keep us turning the treadmill" (Needleman, 215).

"The . . . premise of egocentricity states [is] that identity and worth are established by winning recognition and approval of other people. This assumption, which stresses the indispensability of the other, is properly an overall outlook that is called *ego*centric, because in all cases the individual uses other people to achieve something for *himself.* [But consciousness] is not so much an entity with qualities as it is a *medium* for the reflection of qualities. . . . Consciousness is thus never identical with what it identifies with" (Wellwood, 76).

Medard Boss mentions an Indian philosopher who came to Europe to improve his knowledge of European psychotherapeutic methods. But he was made more unhappy by learning Western methods. "Whereas formerly he had accepted the vicissitudes of life, like illness in the family, with great calmness, now every trifle made him nervous, restless and pessimistic. Now he thought he had always to do this or that at once and he made everything worse with haste. Obviously, from his training in Western psychotherapy, he had learned to see himself as a 'psyche.' . . . Now he had to make his way through the bustle and tumult and an external world, based on nothing but a fundamentally unknowable, anonymous, id-like unconscious" (Wellwood, 184).

"Of course the ego has its positive aspects. It certainly existed in the West from about 800 B.C. to 1600 A.D. without massive alienation as its corollary, but it is hard to avoid the conclusion that in its modern form the ego is the product and expression of *pathology.*" Western industrial societies turn out rigid ego-structures with a vengeance (Berman, 170, 164).

The Holistic Paradigm. David Bohm, a physicist-philosopher, has presented a model of the cosmos which he calls "the holocosmic paradigm." He says modern physics has no philosophical foundation for its own findings. "Hence it avoids facing the issue altogether, confining itself to pragmatic goals," to the prediction and control which Bohm charges have all but pre-empted the endeavor of physics.

Such a limited approach is unacceptable to Bohm, who terms "incomplete" any theory of the cosmos that fails to take consciousness into account. Furthermore, the more modern physics approaches the twenty-first century, the closer it seems to get to the cosmology of the remote past (Valle, 123).

A fundamental feature of Bohm's cosmology "is the claim that reality is *one,* an unbroken, undivided wholeness which is the background for everything in the universe, underlying both matter and consciousness, providing the raw material for all manifest entities." This non-manifest matrix Bohm terms the *enfolded* or *implicate* order. It manifests itself in time in various states of matter-energy (Valle, 124; Zukav, 308).

Karl Pribram, a brain psychologist, presents a similar model which he calls "holographic." This model uses the hologram, the result of a process of lensless photography in which the resultant picture is three dimensional, has perspective, can be looked at from all sides, and when a piece of it is broken off, that piece contains the whole picture, though in a less clear state (Valle, 132; Anderson, 119).

Both Bohm and Pribram hold, like some of the Church Fathers, that the entire universe is in some way contained in the individual, not in his ego, but in the transpersonal domain. Our ego, with its three-dimensional mind, squanders much energy to maintain the self-deception and illusion of autonomous stability. There is an ultimate "empiricism" which leads to the experiential certitude that the ultimate source of nature in the universe is an energy of love. But the experimenter himself must know he is in the experiment. He cannot observe the whole and leave himself out.

Berman puts it this way, "Although the denial of participation lies at the heart of modern science, the Cartesian paradigm as followed in actual practice is riddled with participating consciousness." "The deliberate inclusion of participation in our present epistemology would create a new epistemology, the outlines of which are just now becoming visible" (136).

"No longer is it a question of knower observing the known across the gulf of knowing that separates them. That model of consciousness has failed us during the centuries in which we have stubbornly clung to it." Bohm says it must be replaced by "the austere paradigm of a unified field of being, a self-conscious universe realizing itself to be integrally whole and interconnected" (Valle, 134).

Some of the ideas here presented offer a background for the following excerpt. The author, Thomas Berry, C.P., is professor emeritus at Fordham University and the director of the Riverdale Center for Religious Research. The theme is the modern story as the journey to a new global stage.

* * *

As we think our way through the difficulties of this late twentieth century we find ourselves pondering the human meaning of the future. Sometimes the future appears as a yawning abyss about to swallow us up as our present energy sources begin to fail, as pollution darkens the skies and poisons the seas, as tensions between nations and within nations intensify, as military methods grow more destructive, as the multitudes of mankind double in numbers and men swarm toward the great urban centers. There crime and violence increase constantly; arsonists begin setting our cities to the torch. These urban centers and their corresponding difficulties will multiply. In the year 2000 there will be some three hundred cities in the world of over a million people. Earlier in this century there were only a dozen such cities on the planet. So we could continue on with this description of our world in endless detail until we were all driven into a state of paralyzing depression. While such is not my intention, it is my intention to fix our minds on the realities before us with some sense of the magnitude of the human task we face.

This human task concerns every member of the human community in whatever occupation, on whatever continent, of whatever ethnic group, at whatever age. It is a task from which no one is absolved and in which no one is ultimately more concerned than anyone else. Here we meet as absolute equals to face our ultimate tasks as human beings within a human order. We have a question of life and death before us, the question, however, not merely of physical survival but of survival in a human mode of being, of survival and development into the true splendor of intelligent, affectionate, imaginative persons living in ecstatic enjoyment of the universe about us, in profound interior communion with each other, and with some significant capacities to express ourselves in our arts and sciences, in our music and dance. It is a question of interior

PSYCHE AND SPIRIT

richness within our own personalities, of shared understanding and sympathy in our homes and in our families. Beyond this is our extended security and inter-communion with others in an embrace of mind and heart that reaches out to the local community, to the nation, to the larger world of man, to an affectionate concern for all living and non-living beings of earth, and on out to the most distant stars in the heavens. A break, a single destructive antagonism anywhere in the fabric of being is a tear in the heart of every being.

This description of human grandeur may seem a slight exaggeration, a romantic view of human possibilities. To this I answer that this is the basis on which the human venture has been sustained from its earliest beginning until the present. Our difficulty is that we are just emerging from the technological trance into which the human mind has been placed by the scientific-technological modes of thinking that have dominated human existence for the past two centuries. During this period the human mind has been placed within the narrowest confines it has experienced since consciousness emerged from its paleolithic phase. Even the most primitive tribes have a vision of the universe, of man's place and functioning within the universe, a vision that extends to celestial regions of space and to interior depths of the human that far exceed the parameters of the human within the manipulative world of technological man as we have known him in recent centuries.

It is not surprising, then, that when a more expansive vision of the human breaks upon us at this time it should come as a shock, as something unreal, insubstantial, and unattainable. Yet this is precisely what is happening through the instrumentality of science itself. The exclusively analytical manipulative phase of science is over. A counter-movement toward comprehensive integration and interior subjective processes is taking place within a new humanistic vision of the entire universe. Man with all his imaginative and emotional capacities is now seen not as an olympian observer extrinsic to an objective world, but as a functional expression of that very world itself. Man is that being in whom the earth becomes conscious of itself. The deeper subject is the world, the earth, or the earth process. In his own deepest subjectivity man is the earth, as the earth in its consciousness phase is man.

So the most intensive experience of the scientist, the experience that has fascinated the scientist in the deepest realms of his unconscious being, is a mythic, mystical, magical vision that is only now coming to conscious awareness in the mind of the scientist himself. It can hardly be repeated often enough that the dynamics back of the scientist is non-scientific just as the dynamics of the technological endeavor is non-technological. In both instances there is a far-reaching transforming vision that is sought that is not far from the spiritual vision sought by the ancient tribal cultures as well as by the great traditional civilizations of the past. Only such a visionary quest could possibly have sustained the efforts made these past two centuries in both science and technology. Nor could anything less than such a trance state have so blinded scientists and technologists to the devastating impasse into which they have been leading the human venture. Not until Rachel Carson in the early 1960's shocked the world with her presentation of the disasters impending in the immediate future was there any thorough alarm at the situation facing us. Ever since then we have been asking each other: What has happened? Where are we? What can be done? When in 1972 the Club of Rome came out with its *Limits of Growth* a new anxiety gripped us. Since then scientists and technologists have set themselves to the task of devising neo-scientific ways of understanding the universe, and neo-technologies for dealing with the needs of mankind in the future.

That much has been done by scientists and technologists is clear. Their work is indispensable. Yet the very condition of their ultimate success depends on their understanding of the world into which they would lead us. Scientists and technologists, as well as economists, may simply be extending the trivialization of human life in the recent past on into the future. If this is done we can expect continued diminishing of the taste for life, a dying down of the energies needed for the stupendous task of building the global community of the future, and a turn toward what Sigmund Freud designated as a "will to

death." The scientific process has, however, recently begun to
penetrate more deeply into those primordial energies out of
which the galactic systems, the earth, and the life forms of earth
have emerged and upon which the future ultimately depends.
These energies, which are the primary subject of study in all
the sciences, have from the beginning a twofold aspect, a
physical and a psychic aspect. The supreme achievement of
science has been to establish a complete narrative of the innu-
merable physical transformations through which these primordial energies have passed to arrive at the human mode. Less
attention has been given to the numinous psychic transformations which are even more significant than the physical transformations. This sequence of change, especially since the
shaping of the earth began, has been marked by ever increasing
psychic intensity, a deepening subjectivity, which has never
faltered over any great period of time.

In his early tribal period man lived in a world dominated
by psychic power symbols whereby he guided his life toward
communion with his total human and trans-human environment. He felt himself sustained by a total cosmic presence that
went beyond the surface reality of the surrounding natural
world. His sense of an all-pervasive, numinous, or sacred power gave to his life a deep security and enabled him over a long
period of time to establish himself within a consciousness realm
of high spiritual, human, social and artistic development. This
was the period when the gods were born in human consciousness as expressions of those profound spiritual orientations
that emerged from the earth process into man's unconscious
depths, then as symbols into his conscious mind, and finally
into visible expression. All that man has done since then has
taken this same course. The gods have been changed, the
visible expression has been altered, but the ultimate source of
power still remains hidden in the dynamics of the earth and in
the obscure archetypal determinations of the unconscious
depths of man.

These primordial determinations were further developed
in the second age of mankind—the age of the great traditional
civilizations of the Eurasian and American worlds, the age of
Confucian China, of Hindu India, of Buddhist Asia, of the

Ancient Near East, of Islam, of Medieval Europe, of the Toltec, Mayan, Aztec, Pueblo and Inca civilizations of Central and South America. The human structure of life in all these civilizations had many similarities—their sense of the divine, their ritual forms, their social hierarchies, their basic technologies, their agriculture economy, their temple architecture and sculpture. The great volume of man's civilizational accomplishments came in this period, especially in development of the spiritual disciplines whereby human life was shaped in the image of the divine.

But then in the Western world a third great age of human development began. A new sense of human capacity for understanding and controlling the dynamics of the earth came into being. While the efforts of all former civilizations had been to enable man to find his exalted place within the seasonal sequence of the earth's natural rhythms and to establish a spatial center where an intersection of the divine, the natural, and the human planes of reality could take place, the new effort beginning in the sixteenth and seventeenth century work of Francis Bacon, Galileo Galilei, and Isaac Newton sought to understand the physical forces at work in the universe and the manner in which man could avail himself of these energies to serve his own well-being. By the mid-eighteenth century the invention of new technologies had begun whereby man could manipulate his environment to his own advantage. At this time also an "objective world" was born, clearly distinct from man and available to man not as a means of divine communion but as a vast realm of natural resources for human exploitation and consumption. These scientific attitudes and technological inventions became the modern substitutes for the mystical vision of divine truth and the sympathetic evocation of natural and spiritual forces by ritual and prayerful invocation.

Yet, though differing in its method, the historical drive of Western man toward a millennium of earthly beatitude remained the same. The Day of the Lord of the earlier biblical books and the later apocalyptic vision of a coming earthly paradise remained the same. But the means had changed. No longer divine grace but human effort was the instrument for this paradisal realization. The scientists and inventors, the

bankers and commercial magnates were now the saints who
would reign. This, then, was the drive in the third great age of
mankind, the Technological Age, which succeeded the tribal
age and the age of the traditional civilizations. It was an energy
revolution not only in terms of the physical energies now
available to man but in terms of the psychic energies which
came to new modes of expression. Never before had man
experienced such a turbulent age of change, such a variety of
activity, such a movement to alter the world to introduce man
into an earthly redeemed state, and, finally, to give men power
formerly attributed only to the natural or to the divine.

This achievement was associated with a sense of political
and social transformation that would release man from age-old
tyrannies. The very structure of existence was being altered. In
this mold America was founded, achieved independence, and
then advanced throughout the nineteenth century to a position
of world dominance in the early twentieth century. America
took seriously the words of Thomas Payne written in 1775 in
his pamphlet *Common Sense*. There he says, "We have it in our
power to begin the world over again. A situation similar to the
present, hath not appeared since the days of Noah until now.
The birthday of a new world is at hand. . . ." Earlier the pil-
grims had seen this country as the new City on a Hill to which
all mankind could look for guidance into a glorious future.
Throughout the founding years, even until the twentieth century, peoples crossed the Atlantic with a vivid sense that they
were crossing the Red Sea from the slavery of Egypt to the
freedom and abundance of the Promised Land.

Such expectation of a political and social transformation
went with a new exhilaration in man's new powers for technological dominance and industrial exploitation of the earth. This
led to a savage assault upon earth such as was inconceivable in
prior times. The experiences of sacred communion with the
earth had disappeared. Such intimacy was considered a poetic
conceit by a people who prided themselves on their absolute
realism, their aversion to all forms of myth, magic, mysticism,
and superstition. Little did these men know that they themselves had a mythic, magical, mystical and superstitious attitude
toward the earth. Their very realism was as pure a superstition

as was ever professed by man, their devotion to science was a
new mysticism, their technology was a magic way to paradise,
and their entire life attitude was as unreal a mythic vision of
existence as was ever known.

As with all such mythic commitments the awakening process can be slow and painful and filled with exaggerated reactions. Our present awakening from this enchantment with
technology has been particularly painful. We have altered the
earth and human life in many irrevocable ways. Some of these
have been creative and helpful. Many have been destructive
beyond imagination. Here we could repeat the brief description of our present world that I mentioned in the beginning of
this discussion, but there is really no need to do so.

So we must pass on to the next age that is dawning before
us, the fourth age of man, the Ecological Age. I use the term
"ecological" in its primary meaning as the relation of an organism to its environment but also in its metaphorical sense as the
inter-communion of all living and non-living systems of the
universe. This vision of an integral world system into which we
are emerging is of primary importance if mankind is to have the
psychic power to undergo the mental and emotional, the individual and social, the economic and political, the ethical, religious and aesthetic transformations that are being demanded
of us. We must not mistake the order of magnitude in this
challenge that we face. It is not simply adaptation to a reduced
supply of fuels, or to some modification in our system of social
or economic controls, nor is it a slight change in our educational system. What is happening is something of far greater magnitude than all these. It is a radical change in our mode of
consciousness. Our challenge is to create a new language, even
a new sense of what it is to be human. It is to transcend
national limitations to achieve a sense of the human community. It is to alter many of our basic values. A new sense of the directions that human existence should take is involved.

What is happening has been unthinkable in ages gone by.
Man is now in control of forces that once controlled him, or,
more precisely, the earth process that formerly administered
the earth and guided its affairs directly is now accomplishing
this task in and through man as its conscious agent. Once a

creature of earthly providence man himself is now the expression of this earthly providence. Man has the power of life and death not only over human life but over the earth itself in its higher forms of life. For the first time he can intervene directly in the genetic process. For the first time he can destroy the ozone layer that encircles the earth and let the cosmic radiation bring about distortions in the life process. For the first time man can destroy the complex patterns of life in the seas and make our rivers uninhabitable by any form of life. Some areas of river pollution are so bad now that not even bacteria can live in them. So we could go on with our description of man's power over the very topography of the planet.

This change in the relation of man to the earth process can be considered as a change equaled only by the transition from non-life to life, or as the change from life to consciousness, or as a change such as that experienced when the first neolithic civilizations came into being some eight thousand years ago. Perhaps nothing since then, not even the great civilizational structures themselves, produced change on such a significant scale. Such change cannot be managed by partial accommodations or even major adjustments within the civilizational contexts of the past any more than the problems that led to quantum physics could be dealt with by any adjustment within the context of the Newtonian universe.

Humanly as well as physically we are now in a world order that can be dealt with only by a transformed mode of consciousness. This we can see in the political order, for instance, when we consider the United Nations and the problems it is trying to deal with. These problems can no longer be dealt with simply on the level of sovereign nations engaging each other in discussions where each nation sees itself as its own ultimate frame of reference as to what is desirable or undesirable. On this basis the nations can only continue their plundering of the earth in quest of needed natural resources or in quest of national security. That the total human community depends on the forests of Brazil for oxygen or that the entire planet is affected by the pollution of the seas makes little difference if individual nations feel that polluting the seas or destroying the forests is to their own benefit, for however short a time.

Thus no sense of earth responsibility can be expected until the human community is able to act in some unified way to establish a functional relation with the earth process which itself does not recognize national boundaries. The sea and air and sky and sunlight, the living forms of earth, establish a single functional planetary system, a system so unified that biologists tell us that the closest analogy to the biosphere of earth is that of a single cell. Man must learn that he is a functional part of this single cell, that he lives or dies as this single cell lives and dies. The nations must learn a primary allegiance to this larger life system. It will do little good for any nation to seek its own well-being by destroying the very conditions for planetary survival. This larger vision is no longer utopian. It directly concerns the hardest, most absolute reality there is—the reality of the water we drink, the air we breathe, the food we eat. The United Nations and its constituent members have begun to realize this. Thus the Conferences on environment, on technology, on habitation, on water, on all those basic elements of life that must now attain human protection and just distribution for the welfare of the total human community. Planetary welfare is now the welfare of each nation and of each individual.

Much of our trouble during these past two centuries has been caused by our analytical microphase modes of thought. We centered ourselves on the individual, on the nation, on personal aggrandizement, on a competitive way of life, on self-assertion, on money values, on our so-called realism, on scientific evidence, on what we called the facts of the particular situation. We paid little attention to the larger, more comprehensive visions of reality. This was for the poets, the romanticists, the religious believers, the moral idealists. Now we begin to recognize that what is good in its microphase reality can be deadly in its macrophase development. Much of human folly is a consequence of neglecting this single bit of wisdom. For instance, an automobile or a few hundred automobiles with good roads may be a great blessing to man. Yet when the number increases into the millions, the hundreds of millions, possibly into the billions, the automobile becomes a demonic reality capable of destroying the higher forms of life of the entire planet. So with all human processes, undisciplined expansion and self-inflation only lead to destruction. The primacy of the Great Cell must be maintained if any subordinate life system is to survive. So with economics and politics; any single activity must find its place within the larger pattern or it will die and perhaps bring down the larger life system itself. This change of scale is one of the most significant aspects in the change of consciousness that I am suggesting.

But here I would like to shift the discussion just a little in order to clarify further the basic structure of this fourth age, the Ecological Age, into which we are presently moving. It is an opposed though complementary age that succeeds the Technological Age. But in a deeper sense this new age takes us back to certain basic aspects of the universe which have been evident to the human mind from its earliest period but which have been further refined, observed, and scientifically stated in more recent centuries. These governing principles of the universe have controlled the entire evolutionary process from the moment of its explosive origin some fourteen billion years ago, to the shaping of the earth, the emergence of life, of consciousness, and so through the four ages of human history that I have mentioned. These principles that have been known in all past ages by immediate intuitive processes are now understood by scientific reasoning although their implications have not yet been acted upon in any effective way. The new age, however, the Ecological Age, must not only understand but activate these principles in a universal context if the human venture is to continue. These principles on which the universe functions are three: differentiation, subjectivity and communion.

Differentiation is the most primordial fact of the universe observable by man. In the fiery violence of some billions of degrees of heat the primordial energy dispersed itself through vast regions of space not as some homogenous smudge or jelly-like substance but as differentiated atomic and subatomic particles which were distributed through a certain maze of elements. These were further shaped into galactic systems with their individual starry oceans of fire. Everywhere we find this differentiating process taking place. In our own solar system, within the sequence of planets, we find the planet earth taking shape

as the most highly differentiated reality that we know about in
the entire universe. Life on the planet earth finds expression in
an overwhelming variety of manifestations. So too when man
appears he immediately gives to human existence multiple
modes of expression, which themselves change through the
centuries.

In this variety of expression a second primary principle
finds expression, the principle of increased subjectivity. From
the shaping of the first hydrogen atom to the formation of the
human brain, interior psychic unity has consistently increased
along with a greater complexification of being. Much more
needs to be said about this deepening interior or psychic
identity in the structure of reality. Yet we must move on to a
third principle of the cosmic-earth process, that of communion
of each reality of the universe with every other reality in the
universe. Here our scientific evidence confirms, with a magnificent overview, the ancient awareness of man that we live in a
universe, a single if multiform energy event. The unity of the entire
complex of galactic systems is among the most basic experiences of contemporary physics. Although this unity of the
entire world order was perceived by primitive peoples, affirmed
by the great civilizations, explained in creation myths the world
over, outlined by Plato in his *Timaeus* and given extensive
presentation by Newton in his *Principia,* nowhere was the full
genetic relatedness of the universe presented with such clarity
as by the scientists of the twentieth century. To Isaac Newton
we are especially indebted for our understanding of the gravita-
tional attraction of every physical reality to every other physical
reality in the universe, an attraction that finds its ultimate
fulfillment in the affective attractions that exist throughout the
human community. To Darwin we are indebted for our understanding of the genetic unity of the entire web of living beings.
To Einstein and his theories of relativity we are indebted for a
new awareness of how to think the dynamics of relatedness in
the universe.

This emerging fourth Age of Mankind, the Ecological Age,
finds its major support and meaning in the differentiation,
subjectivity and communion experiences of the earth. These in
turn find in the Ecological Age their highest mode of fulfill-

ment. This new age fosters an ever increasing diversification throughout the universe. Each reality at whatever level, whether in the geological or environmental structure of the planet, in the living systems spread over the earth, or in the human communities with all their varieties of expression, each finds its place in this comprehensive complex which affirms diversity as its primary commitment just as it was the primary manifestation of reality at the first moment of the emerging world.

The Ecological Age fosters as its second principle the deeper subjectivity, the sacred presence within each reality of the universe. There is an awe and reverence due to the stars in the heavens, the sun and all heavenly bodies, to the seas and the continents, to all living forms of trees and flowers, to all the forms of life in the sea, the animals of the forests and the birds of the air. To destroy a living species is to silence forever a divine voice. The primary need of man for the various forms of the planet is a psychic rather than a physical need. The Ecological Age seeks to establish and maintain this subjective identity, this authenticity at the heart of every being. If this is so of the pre-human phases of life, it is much more true of the human expression of life.

The third principle of the Ecological Age is the principle of inter-communion of each reality with every other reality of the universe. This aspect of the Ecological Age is of special importance. It is a final test of man's capacity to express what is the deepest reality in the universe, its capacity for mutual indwelling of all members of the universal order of being. As one scientist said in the nineteenth century, as Bergson repeated, and Teilhard reaffirmed, the volume of each atom is the volume of the universe, for each reality is precisely there where its influence is felt. The ancients knew this by an immediate subjective awareness. We have come to know this by objective analysis. The consequence is the same. Nothing is affected without affecting everything. This is the very nature of every ecosystem, from the smallest area of life to the galactic systems themselves.

Only such an Ecological Age can produce the understanding and the corresponding commitment required to stop the world of exploitation, of manipulation, of illusory money values, of mutual human abuse, of destructive violence so intense that it threatens to put the torch not only to the human city but to the planet itself. We have now acquired the power to turn the earth itself into a vast conflagration. But while we stop one world situation we must create another. Thus the need to awaken the energies needed to create the new world, to evoke a universal communion of all living and non-living systems of the universe. So far, however, this new world-order has not had its adequate presentation. Yet when it comes we will see that it will take the form of the Ecological Age. This age can provide the historical dynamism formerly associated with the Marxist classless society, the age of plenty envisaged by the capitalist nations, and the millennial age of peace envisaged in the Apocalypse of John. At the present, however, we are in that phase of transition that can be described as the groping phase. We are like the musician who faintly hears a melody in his mind but not clearly enough to play it through, or like a poet whose vision is too formless to put into precise words. This is the inner agony we experience especially when we consider that the music, the poem, the drama we are creating is the very reality of the universe.

It would be easier for us if we would remember that the earth itself as the primary energy is finding its way both to interior conscious expression in man and to outer fulfillment in the universe. We can solve nothing by dreaming up some ephemeral structure of reality or by giving the direction of the earth over to our bureaucratic institutions. We must simply respond to the urgencies imposed on us by an interior energy that holds the stars within the galactic clusters, that shaped the planet under our feet, that has guided life through its bewildering variety of expression, and that has found even higher expression in the exotic tribes and nations, languages, literatures, arts and music, social forms, religious rituals and spiritual disciplines over the surface of the planet. There is reason to believe that those mysterious forces that have guided earthly events thus far have not suddenly collapsed under the great volume of human affairs in this late twentieth century.

What is clear is that the earth is mandating that the human community assume a responsibility never assigned to any previous generation. We are involved in a process somewhat akin to initiation processes which have been known and practiced by man from earliest times. Mankind is passing out of its stage of childhood into its adult stage of life. The human community must now assume adult responsibilities. As the maternal bonds are broken on one level to be re-established on another level in initiation ceremonies, so the human community is being separated from the dominance of Mother Earth on one level to establish a new and more mature relationship on another level. In the prior period the earth acted independently as the complete controlling principle; only limited control over existence was assigned to man. Now the Earth insists that man accept greater responsibility, a responsibility commensurate with the greater knowledge communicated to him.

This responsibility has so far been more than man could use wisely, just as the new powers of a young adult are powers that he seldom uses without an intervening period of confusion, of embarrassment, of juvenile mistakes. As the child eventually learns a mature mode of conduct, discipline, and responsibility with his limited order, so now men as individuals and as a planetary community will, we may hope, learn their earth responsibilities. Already people shopping for daily household needs know something about the relation of aerosol spray cans to the cosmic radiation. The driver of a car knows now of the poisons injected into the atmosphere. This knowledge is leading to actions that reflect a sense of higher responsibility.

Our problem is, of course, the problem of the human community at all its levels, at the individual, family and city levels, then at the national and pan-human level, until finally we come to the integral context of the total earth process. Here I would observe that human administration of the universe is far too great a task for any controlled process on the part of man just as the movement of the arm to pick up and drink a cup of tea would be hardly possible if we were required to consciously manipulate each movement of the eye, the nervous system, the muscular contractions, the oxygen and blood flow. Yet we do the act spontaneously, simply, immediately, with extensive awareness and control of the act. There is deliberation but also spontaneity. As with our earth in all its processes, so with the human community, there are inner spontaneous all-pervasive forces that are present which are gradually responding to this integral functioning of the total system. What we need, what we are ultimately groping toward, is the sensitivity required to understand and respond to the psychic energies, deep in the very structure of reality itself.

As the child in transition to maturity is groping toward a disciplined understanding and response to the emerging forces within his own being, so now our knowledge and our control is not absolute knowledge or absolute control. It is a cooperative understanding and response to forces that will bring about a proper unfolding of the earth process if we do not ourselves obstruct or distort these forces that seek their proper expression.

I suggest that this is the ultimate lesson of physics, biology, and all the sciences, as it is the ultimate wisdom of the shamanic personality of tribal peoples, and the fundamental teaching of the great civilizations. If this has been obscured by the adolescent aspect of our earlier scientific and technological development, it is now becoming clear to mankind on an extensive scale. If responded to properly with our new knowledge and new competencies these forces will find expression in the spontaneities of the new Ecological Age. To assist in bringing this about is the present task of the new science, the new ethics, the new education, the new man.

Readings

Robert M. Anderson, Jr., "A Holographic Model of Transpersonal Consciousness," *Journal of Transpersonal Psychology*, 9, 2, 1977, 119–128.

Morris Berman, *The Reenchantment of the World*. Ithaca: Cornell University Press, 1981. Many insights about consciousness change.

Thomas Berry, C.P., "The New Story," Riverdale Religious Research Center Papers, Riverdale, N.Y. 10471.

Fritjof Capra, *The Turning Point. Science, Society and the Rising Culture*. N.Y.: Simon and Schuster, 1982.

Ewert Cousins, "Teilhard and Global Spirituality," *Anima,* Fall 1981.

Charles Hampden-Turner, *Maps of the Mind.* London: Beazley, 1981. Graphic maps with commentary.

Peter Koestenbaum, *The New Image of the Person.* N.Y.: Greenwood, 1978. Philosophical study of the ego and the self.

George Leonard, *The Silent Pulse. A Search for the Perfect Rhythm That Exists in Each of Us.* N.Y.: Dutton, 1978.

Jacob Needleman and Dennis Lewis, *On the Way to Self-Knowledge.* N.Y.: Knopf, 1976. Psychotherapy and the sacred.

Richard Ornstein, *The Psychology of Consciousness.* N.Y.: Penguin, 1975. Includes discussion of the two sides of the brain.

Kenneth Pelletier, *Consciousness: East and West.* N.Y.: Harper and Row, 1976. Good summary of ASCs.

Kenneth S. Pope, Jerome L. Singer, *The Stream of Consciousness.* N.Y.: Plenum, 1978. First part excellent.

Michael Talbot, *Mysticism and the New Physics.* N.Y.: Bantam, 1981.

Charles Tart, ed., *Transpersonal Psychologies.* N.Y.: Harper and Row, 1975. Esp. articles by Tart, and by McNamara on mysticism.

Richard S. Valle and Rolf Eckartsberg, *The Metaphors of Consciousness.* N.Y.: Plenum, 1981. One of the most competent studies.

Roger N. Walsh, M.D. and Frances Vaughan, eds., *Beyond Ego. Transpersonal Dimensions in Psychology.* Los Angeles: Tarch, 1980. Excellent anthology.

John Wellwood, Jr., ed., *The Meeting of the Ways. Explorations in East/West Psychology.* N.Y.: Schocken, 1979.

Gary Zukav, *The Dancing of the Wu Li Masters. An Overview of the New Physics.* N.Y.: Bantam, 1979. Physics and mysticism. Somewhat insensitive to alternate views, some unsupportable interpretations. (Cf. *Zygon,* Dec. 1980, 412.)